Happy Birthday.

# LIVING WITH THE CENTURY

Chancellor of the University of Glasgow

# LIVING WITH THE CENTURY

---

ALEC CAIRNCROSS

*i*ynx

Published by
*i*ynx
Countess of Moray's
Fife KY3 0SY

ISBN 0 9535413 0 4

**British Library Cataloguing in Publication Data**

A catalogue record for this book is available from
the British Library

Typeset by Trinity Typesetting
Printed in Great Britain by Redwood Books, Bath

*Dedication*

To
Mary
1919–1998
a wife beyond compare
and to
Frances and Elizabeth
daughters to match

Sir Alec Cairncross
died on 21st October 1998
after this book had been prepared for the press.

Sir Alec had survived by less than four months
the loss of his wife, Mary Cairncross, to whom
he had been married for fifty-five years.

Many years before, he had inscribed a book
which he gave to her with a quotation from a
poem by Peter Abelard:

*Nec ad vitam anima
Satis sit dimidia**

This book stands as a memorial to that
shared and fruitful life.

*For, but with half a soul, what can life do?

# Contents

# Illustrations

# Acknowledgements

I wrote a draft of my autobiography up to 1961 many years ago and added an account of the later years more recently. In preparing the draft for publication, I have had the invaluable help of my daughter, Frances, who has been tireless in suggesting improvements, and editing the entire text with great thoroughness. I also had an interesting suggestion from Mrs Bridget Martyn for a rearrangement of the sequence of the material, which I found tempting but in the end did not adopt.

Glasgow University gave me generous financial support with the project. I was offered help spontaneously with finding a publisher by Professor Jagdish Bhagwati of Columbia University. In the meantime, however, I made contact with my old friend, Dr Douglas Grant, who had published *The Scottish Journal of Political Economy* when I edited it in the 1950s; and, to my great pleasure, he kindly agreed to assist in the publication of this volume.

Lord Jenkins, under whom I served during his first year as Chancellor of the Exchequer, kindly agreed to write the Foreword.

# Foreword

Alec Cairncross's *Who's Who* entry gives his recreation as "writing". The happy matching of this taste with the fact that this succinct but not slight volume of autobiography brings his total of published books (two or three of them with collaborators) to 27, goes far to explain why, of all the very clever men that I have known, he always strikes me as possessing the most equable temperament and perhaps (for who can tell about others?) having enjoyed the happiest and most fulfilling of lives. Certainly this combination has made him one of the most sought-after of advisors, both domestically and internationally.

To have available a man of his intellectual quality without axes to grind or grievances to avenge is indeed a rare bonus, and one which has been well exploited by the Whitehall machine (he was first economic advisor to the government and then head of its Economic Service from 1961–69), by O.E.C.D. and by the World Bank. He next became head of an Oxford college for a decade and then subsequently a member of innumerable committees. But no responsibilities have ever suppressed his desire to write and to record, with an honesty which is sometimes devastating although always without malice, what actually went on.

Alec Cairncross could I suppose be described as a West of Scotland 'lad o' pairts'. He was born in 1911 in Lesmahagow in the upper Clyde valley, one of eight children of a not particularly prosperous ironmonger. He made his way *via* Hamilton Academy to Glasgow University and then to Trinity College, Cambridge. But great though has been his respect for Trinity, the 'greatest college in Christendom', and later for Oxford, Glasgow has always been his *alma mater*. He was an undergraduate and lecturer there, then a professor for ten years, and finally the

Chancellor of the University for a quarter of century. And the reason why 'lad o' pairts' is not exactly an appropriate description is that someone in this category is normally always seeking outside opportunities ('the high road to England', etc.) whereas Cairncross has mostly been trying to get back to Glasgow while only too frequently being called away to higher service.

With his great range of previous reminiscent writing (for example *A Country to Play With*, about his German experiences at the end of the war, and his *The Wilson Years, 1964–69)* it might have been feared that his autobiography would have a certain *rechauffé* quality about it. This is not at all so. I bounded through it, and found, for instance, that his chapter on Germany was one of the most compelling. A longer perspective more than cancels out his having previously written about the subject and the period. I strongly commend this account of a quietly remarkable life.

Alec Cairncross shows that you do not have to be flamboyant to achieve great influence, and that you do not have to be malicious in order to be interesting.

Roy Jenkins
13.7.98

# *Living with the Century*

The twentieth century has been the century of the economist. When it began, professional economists were a rare species. Today, they seem ubiquitous. Through a century in which the influence of government has been extended to an unprecedented degree, economics has emerged as the unifying discipline that connects most aspects of policy. It has developed both as an academic subject and as a tool of government in a way that would have seemed unimaginable when I was born in 1911.

In 1890, when the Royal Economic Society was formed, university teachers of the subject in Britain numbered no more than 20; and 40 years later the staff in Political Economy at Adam's Smith's old University of Glasgow consisted of a Professor and two lecturers with two others covering social economics and economic history. It is doubtful whether the British government ever knowingly employed a professional economist in that capacity before the Second World War, except to serve on a committee. Although some of the most distinguished economists, including Keynes and Hawtrey, had served in government before the War, the post of Economic Adviser in those days was held for many years by someone who was *not* a professional economist.

Today, the number of economists and the public understanding of economics have grown beyond recognition. Far more are now employed both in government and in the City than ever before. There are 400 economists in government service and a further 200 in the Bank of England. In international agencies such as the IMF and the World Bank there are far more.

In the private sector, too, employment of economists has expanded a long way. And in academic life as well: where Cambridge conferred one PhD a year before the War, now they confer 15 to 20.

My life has also been the story of this change. I became an economist almost by accident. Having grown up in a small Scottish village, the child of a local ironmonger, I had intended to embark on a career as a chartered accountant, a secure and rewarding form of employment as it seemed to me at the age of 17. I was studying at Glasgow University for a university degree that would allow me to qualify as an accountant after an apprenticeship of three instead of five years, when I yielded to the attractions of the discipline I was studying — Political Economy — and gave up all thought of accountancy.

The fact that I was drawn to this new discipline was partly a reflection of the pressures exerted by the times in which I lived. My undergraduate years between 1928 and 1932 coincided with a period of rising unemployment when it became clear to me that economics, by providing a panoramic view of the business world, was indispensable to the framing and answering of many of the major questions in the life of the country: unemployment, devaluation, and fluctuating exchange rates, budget deficits, debt conversion and so on. In the mining village to the south of Glasgow where I had grown up, these questions were fundamental to the future of the community. How could alternative employment be found for the miners and what could be done in the meantime to provide them with a livelihood? The social consequences of high unemployment in poverty, ill health and low morale were all too apparent. The tensions of the General Strike in 1926 and the deepening of the depression a few years later brought home to me the urgency of these seemingly intractable problems and the importance of economics as a discipline for resolving them.

After I had taken my first degree, I spent three years working on my doctorate in Cambridge, at that time in the early 1930s the leading centre in the world in the study of economics. The subject was undergoing major changes, in which John Maynard Keynes, author of the "General Theory", took a prominent part. Keynes was one of my teachers, and so I had a firsthand view of the way economics was changing. At least three separate revolutions in theory were in progress. To all of them, Cambridge economists were prominent contributors.

First and most important was Keynes's development of macroeconomics: his explanation of what governed the level of economic activity as employment expanded or contracted with capital investment and the level of demand. It is true that there were elements in Keynes's thinking that were not entirely new. But he was putting forward ideas of the greatest importance about the scourge of the interwar years — unemployment

Next there were the ideas that were emerging — not exclusively in Cambridge —about the competitive process. Instead of a sharp antithesis between competition and monopoly, economists were developing theories of imperfect competition that explained why a limited group of competitors were likely to maintain higher prices than would rule under what was called 'perfect competition' as, say, in the market for sugar or wheat.

A third revolution that began in the 1930s was the introduction of national accounting. By estimating the national income and output, it was easier to see what would be the impact of any change of policy on income generation and expenditure. Armed with national accounts, the government began to draw up budgets that took more systematic account of their likely effects on the economy and to make short term forecasts of changes in the level of activity.

These various revolutions laid the foundations for economics as a central tool of practical policy. They were also accompanied by an improvement in the data that could be used to judge whether a policy worked. They made economics a way of anatomising the economy, identifying underlying changes and assessing the economic consequences of government policy.

The experience of watching these fundamental revolutions in economics shaped what followed for me. My life has had two strands: the academic and the practical. Just as economics is an academic discipline aimed principally at resolving policy dilemmas, so I have moved back and forward between academic life and government.

I have had a constantly absorbing life as an economist, each episode in which I took part contributing to my further education in the subject. Just as I was fortunate to study economics at a time of great academic ferment, so I was fortunate to begin my career just as the Second World War opened the doors of Whitehall to economists. During the War, about 50 professional economists served in the various departments of government. For the first time in Britain, economists were at the heart of government: a small group was recruited to the War Cabinet Offices as top-level economic advisers, and I had the good luck to be invited to join them in January 1940. The group advised on the most urgent problems in organising for war and ensuring that available resources were used to the full and for the most important purposes. The experience, like my subsequent spells in Whitehall, allowed me to supplement my knowledge of how the economy functioned with an understanding of the ways of government: a matter of particular importance to an economist if one regards the whole purpose of the subject as not just to explain how the economy works but also to devise policies to make it work better.

Economists were not only routinely involved for the first time in shaping policy at this high level: they also played a part in more practical areas of policy. Thus, after 18 months in the War Cabinet Offices, I came to feel the need for a more active role and moved to the Board of Trade, trying to build up a 'blitz reserve' of requisitioned premises which usually found immediate use instead of being set aside for emergencies. From there I moved to join another group of economists in the recently formed Ministry of Aircraft Production and spent the next four years planning the production of aircraft components.

The experience taught me much about one of the areas where the services of economists have been frequently in demand: preparing government plans. My own recollection of planning at MAP before economists took it over was of muddle qualified by doses of organisation, rarely completely successful. Under Beaverbrook planning had been regarded almost as a form of sabotage, unsuited to a rapidly changing situation. But in the absence of planning there was usually more muddle. Besides, constant shocks, combined with technical difficulties, frequently made improvisation necessary and, indeed, unavoidable. For example, when I joined the Ministry I was told that there were 300 Wellingtons (a two-engine bomber) on the beach at Blackpool without propellors, so that for every two additional propellors I could add to the output, the Royal Airforce would acquire an additional aircraft.

Experiences like mine were common during the War. They allowed economists to show the value of their "technique of thinking" in a context with which they were previously unfamiliar. They were taught to think of their subject as "the logic of choice", viewing decisions in terms of alternatives foregone and seeking to lay bare the true options. Such an approach was particularly appropriate when there was a clear limit to available resources, so that if they were used for one purpose, they were automatically unavailable for another that might be of greater value. This treatment of cost as opportunities foregone was in strong contrast to the popular conception of cost in terms of outgoings.

Throughout my career I have been drawn to government as by a magnet: to assist in the framing of public policy has always seemed to me to be a natural employment for an economist. When the War ended, I had intended to work in the private sector, as a journalist on *The Economist*. But I found myself dividing my time between journalism and serving on the Wool Working Party, one of 17 committees set up by Stafford Cripps (then President of the Board of Trade) to consider the organisation of industries that were not to be nationalised and how competing firms might give joint effect to considerations of public policy — problems to which government had given little systematic thought. I ended by writing most of the Report; and when the Board of Trade asked me in October 1946 to come back as Economic Adviser I felt that if staying at *The Economist* meant giving most of my time to the government and leaving it to *The Economist* to pay me, I had better move back to the public sector and unite service and pay.

I worked in the Board for three years, first under Cripps, and later under Harold Wilson. My time allowed me to see from the inside the events leading up to the 1949 devaluation of the pound. In this, there was a certain irony, since my next period as a civil servant, beginning when I returned to Whitehall in June 1961 as chief economic adviser to a Conservative government, later involved me once again in a devaluation under a Labour government, this time led by Harold Wilson. My years between 1964 and 1969 as Head of the newly established Government Economic Service meant that I was closely involved with the 1967 devaluation of sterling.

Both my periods in Whitehall were marked by reluctance on the part of Ministers to face an inescapable choice. In the 1940s, they set their faces against raising the price of dollars as a means of overcoming a dollar scarcity. Cripps in particular was strongly against devaluation, arguing that exchange rates were a matter to be settled, not by market forces, but by administrative decision. In 1967 Harold Wilson held views very similar to those of Cripps, and his Chancellor of the Exchequer, James Callaghan, had moral scruples about changing the value of the pound. In the event, it was market forces that prevailed in both cases, rather than the pressure of government economists. Economic events, it appeared, had far more power to determine the actions of governments than economic advice.

In international as in national policy, the main role of economists is to look ahead and expose the real choices that politicians face. My first experience of involvement in international affairs was when I was sent to act as a kind of Treasury expert in the negotiations between economists from Britain, the United States, France and the Soviet Union in Berlin in the winter of 1945–46 on German reparations. I took on the job, remembering how Keynes had wrestled in 1919 with proposals to reconstruct Europe by making Germany pay impossible sums in reparations, and fearing a repetition of the same sequence of events, with yet another world war at the end of them. Since it had already been argued at Potsdam, in a post-war conference on Germany between America, Britain and the Soviet Union at the end of July 1945, that Germany should be left enough equipment to make it possible to sustain an average European standard of living, there was at least some possibility of a reasonable agreement. But the Potsdam formula was open to widely differing interpretations, as became apparent when a decision was taken in January 1946 to allow Germany to use no more than 5.6m tons of steel a year — far below what seemed to me indispensable. I argued with my American, French and Soviet colleagues day after day throughout the winter of 1945-46. Eventually the Americans, who had initially backed the steel agreement, changed their negotiating position in May 1946 and refused to allow any reparations to be taken from the zone of Germany that they controlled. In that decision, the British later joined them.

After the War, I spent two more periods abroad. At the end of 1949 Cripps persuaded me to go to Paris as Economic Adviser to OEEC, the organisation which later became the OECD. I spent a full year there. In the summer of 1950 I witnessed the beginnings of the Schumann Plan (which brought France and Germany together in a joint organisation of their coal and steel industries) and the foundation of the European Payments Union (a kind of currency clearing union between the 17 members of the OEEC which took the place of dozens of bilateral payments agreements). Later I joined Per Jacobsson, who was then Economic Adviser to the Bank for International Settlements in Basle and in 1956 became Managing Director of the International Monetary Fund, in framing proposals to put to the EPU for dealing with the acute balance of payments crisis from which Germany was suffering in the autumn of 1950.

My third spell abroad came in the mid 1950s when I advised the World Bank on ways of improving economic management in developing countries and subsequently spent 18 months in Washington launching the Economic Development Institute, as a means of educating senior officials from developing countries on how to handle economic problems.

Since the second world war, a growing number of international institutions have been created with powers over different aspects of economic activity. Argument is at least as likely on what these institutions propose to do as on the policies of national governments. The IMF, the World Bank, the European Union. OECD and many other bodies have wide powers establishing them at the centre of international economic policy; and the chances are that they will be increasingly active participants in the management of the international economy. If one intends to devote one's life to the study of economic problems and the policies for dealing with them, it is as well to have some first-hand acquaintance with the kind of international agencies charged with devising and administering economic policies. Equally these agents are dependent on advice from economists on the ways in which national economies interact with each other. If countries are to co-operate successfully they need to have a clear understanding of these complex interactions and so, too, do the international agencies that seek to co-ordinate their activities.

My periods in government and in international institutions were interspersed with periods in academic life. That had the great advantage of allowing me to avoid a sense of obsolescence and to replenish my familiarity with current theory. Economic problems change, although the old problems tend to recur; the received academic wisdom also changes, although again, views that have fallen from favour sometimes regain popularity.

Before the war I had served for four academic years as a lecturer on the staff of the University of Glasgow, and had written most of what was to be the first modern economics textbook. In 1951 I returned to Glasgow to take up a chair. There, I built up a research department, concentrating on urban and labour problems and bringing the staff together on an anatomy of the Scottish economy. I conducted seminars for the honours students and joined the Professor of Accountancy in management courses for local businessmen. My next spell in academic life came much later, as the Master of an Oxford College at the end of my time in the Treasury. By that time I was more interested in public affairs than in theoretical niceties and more interested in the role of historical change in economic problems.

My time in academic life in the 1950s was also a period of much travelling. I went, for instance, to the Moscow Economic Conference in 1952, an unusual event that provided foreign economists with a rare glimpse of the Russian economy at that stage. I travelled to offer advice in Yugoslavia in 1957; to attend an economic conference in Turkey the following year; and to take part in a discussion of economic planning in, of all places, Addis Ababa, at the end of 1959. I gave lectures in various parts of Europe: I spoke on monetary policy in the Wicksell Lectures in Stockholm; and gave lectures in French in Nancy and in English in Bologna. In the spring of 1959 I was asked to attend the Konigswinter Conference, an annual post-war event intended to bring together opinion-formers in Germany and Britain, and so was able to revisit Berlin.

Academic economists tend to find that they are in heavy demand from committees. I have been no exception. For instance, at the beginning of 1957 I found myself on two utterly different government committees, the first on anthrax, and the second the Radcliffe committee on the Working of the Monetary System.

While Head of a College at Oxford, I served on one committee after another: the brewing industry, Northern Ireland, the Channel Tunnel, police pay. The role of the economist on such bodies tends to be to keep an eye on the broader aspects of the problems they raise, and advise on the influence of economic forces at work.

Economists also have social duties. I served successively as President of the British Association, of the Royal Economic Society and of the Scottish Economic Society. In 1972 I was elected Chancellor of the University of Glasgow — an appointment for life. I edited the books of friends and then from 1980 onwards took to writing them myself, publishing them either on my own individually or in collaboration with a colleague. I took an interest in a number of aspects of international affairs: first in policies for the European Community in association with Professor Giersch and others and then in developments in China, visiting the country five times over a period of 15 years and contributing to a scheme to bring a select group of officials and academics to Oxford and educate them in modern economics.

Keynes once remarked that 'Economics is an easy subject at which few excel'. One reason for this is that economics deals with a changing world in which the picture is inevitably obscure. The level of employment and the flow of income do not remain the same from year to year or even from month to month. The simple fact of economic growth is ample testimony to the uncertainties and discontinuities associated with economic change in all its forms: for example new ideas, new forms of organisation, new practices — to say nothing of strikes, wars, slumps and change of government. We can foresee only so much of the future and even then without certainty. It is dangerous therefore to be very precise in one's thinking as an economist and try to bind the future with mathematical formulae. As Per Jacobsson, the Managing Director of the IMF, used to say: 'One must always be ready for the unexpected.'

Economics is a subject that has to call on other disciplines: on philosophy in its use of fundamental concepts; on mathematics where magnitudes are involved; on history in exploring social and economic change; on technology in dealing with developments in technique that are commonly the key agency in economic progress. It has a wider perspective than other social sciences and those well versed in it have a broader view of social change. Not only are they constantly examining what could usefully be done at the political level but they have a grasp of economic and social interactions that fits them particularly to act as co-ordinators. If I look back to what I was called upon to do in government it frequently involved some form of co-ordination: in the War Cabinet Offices, the Board of Trade and the Ministry of Aircraft Production specific problems had to be viewed as part of a much wider problem impinging on still other problems, and it was largely to ensure that due regard would be paid to possible interactions that economists were brought in.

It is unlikely that the problems of the next century will bear any close resemblance to those of the last. Throughout the present century, governments have continued to enlarge their role and have spent more and more of the national income. But the chances are that, in the next, the role of individual governments will shrink, as international bodies of all kinds come to exercise more power. In Europe, the concept of a common currency is producing pressure to ensure closer co-ordination between the economic policies of governments.

At the same time, the world is in some ways becoming more like the period that I described in my PhD thesis, which dealt with capital flows in the final years of the nineteenth century. Once again, vast flows of international capital have strengthened the links between one country and another, and the scope of international competition has steadily widened. As was true a century ago, what happens at an international level grows in importance relative to what happens within national economies. The task of economists in the next century is likely to be to find ways to manage a truly international economy through appropriate agencies, under safeguards that protect the freedoms that have been developed in the struggles of this century.

## 2

## *A Scottish Upbringing 1911–20*

When I was born in 1911, Glasgow was in the final years of an extraordinary three-quarters of a century of prosperity. Thanks to ample supplies of coal, much of it in Lanarkshire, the region to the south-west of the city where I grew up, and to the fact that the River Clyde flowed west, providing an Atlantic port, Glasgow had become the northern hub of Britain's Victorian growth. It had, of course, pockets of dire poverty. But in the main, it was an elegant, wealthy city where commerce prospered on the back of heavy engineering.

Yet by the time I finished school, in 1928, this era of prosperity had ended. Glasgow and the region around it had begun to feel the effects of the Depression, of the long miners' strike of 1926 and of the industrial decline which was to run through the rest of the century. For an economist, and especially for an economist with an interest in the influence of economic history on the life of the country, it was an ideal environment in which to grow up.

Scottish education was then in its heyday. Young Scots took the view, so common in poorer countries, that education offered the most accessible ladder to success. And the education they were offered was superior to that available to the mass of people south of the border (or in Ireland). By the time I went to university, Scotland had twice as many graduates per head of population as England, and far more graduate teachers. Even in my schooldays, many of my teachers were graduates — something that would not have been true at that time in comparable English schools.

When I think back to my beginnings, I am conscious of being of Scottish stock for as far back as I can go. On my father's side there are Scotts, Wilsons, McCartneys and Kirklands, and on my mother's side Wisharts, Andersons and Camerons. None of these were town dwellers; they all lived in villages in the west of Scotland within reach of Glasgow but far enough away in the days before the motor car to mark off village life and make journeys to town an unusual event for most people.

My father was an ironmonger in the Lanarkshire village of Lesmahagow all his life. When I was a boy, the life of the village rested on farming on the one hand and coal-mining on the other. The mines lay to the south-west round Coalburn and were driven under the moors and into the hills bordering on Ayrshire. Many of the miners lived in Lesmahagow, cycling to and from Coalburn. From our upstairs window I could watch miners returning covered with coal dust and preparing to wash it off before their evening meal. As for the farmers, they might for all I knew, be well off, but that was not how it looked to me as a boy when I was asked to join the men after the harvesting in their meal of cold porridge, or when a farmer's wife explained to me how when she was younger they baked no bread but fed throughout the winter on oatcakes, all made in the autumn and stored in a full "meal kist".

In a village like Lesmahagow life was very rural. The railway to Glasgow was almost our only link with the world outside. Motor cars and buses were rarely seen until the 1920s and the aeroplane was unknown. It was still, in rural Lanarkshire, the age of the horse, or rather the Clydesdale, for this was the ubiquitous breed that drew the milk van and the plough, brought in the hay on special flat carts and pulled the beer wagons up the hilly streets of Glasgow.

My father's father, Andrew, had arrived in Lesmahagow in 1864. Andrew was the tenth and youngest child of Alexander, who had been born in 1777 and was a gardener at Douglas Castle, six miles to the south just off the main road to Carlisle. In the 1840s Andrew took employment with Messrs Arthur and Company, a well-known Glasgow warehouse and rose to be the chief buyer at a salary of £600 per annum. In 1864, when he was nearly 40 years of age, he left Arthur's to marry Margaret McCartney, the daughter of a merchant in Lesmahagow. As Thomas McCartney had no surviving sons, he naturally turned to Andrew for help in his business in the main street of the village.

It was this draper's shop and general store that evolved into an ironmonger's and afforded a livelihood to two generations of Cairncrosses. My father, born in 1865, was the eldest of the six children of the marriage.

Thomas McCartney, Margaret's father and my great-grandfather, was a nephew of "Purley Wilson", a Chartist from nearby Strathaven, who was hanged by the authorities for leading a demonstration some years after the Napoleonic Wars. Thomas became a man of some property but it availed his grandchildren little because at the age of 83 he married for a second time. His bride, who had been his housekeeper, was strongly disapproved of by my grandmother, Margaret, so much so that she refused to let my father attend his grandfather's second wedding. Thomas survived for six months only, long enough to bequeath all his property to his new wife, who left the village as soon as she had taken possession of her inheritance, neglecting only to possess herself of the house; and even this proved eventually to be a liability since, by the time my father died, it had become little more than a slum.

As was customary in Scotland in the case of the eldest son, my father was given his paternal grandfather's name of Alexander. The name has been frequently used in the family and was borne at the end of the 17th century by that Archbishop Cairncross who was Chancellor of the University of Glasgow at the accession of James II and VII and turned out of office when the King was trying to assert his authority before the revolution of 1688. I, in turn, was given exactly the same name as my father, including his maternal grandmother's maiden name of Kirkland. This may have been because of the proximity of our birthdays: I was born, as I sometimes put it, the day before my father. His birthday was on the 12th and mine on the 11th February. Only, as he was born in 1865 and I in 1911 there were 46 years between us.

When I arrived, I was the seventh child with only my youngest brother John still to come. I was presumably unplanned — or perhaps more than usually unplanned — for my sister Annie was just over 13 months ahead of me. There were four boys and four girls, all born within the space of 12 years. The oldest, Andrew, was my senior by ten years. He was sufficiently like me to be mistaken for me in later years and when told, as happened in the War, "You look ten years older, Cairncross" was ready with the reply, "I *am* ten years older." All of us survived into adult life, the first to go being the third child of the family, William, who died in May 1940 of wounds received at Dunkirk.

I saw no great difference between our family and others in the village, although scholastically we might be rather cleverer. We all attended the village school where my mother had taught. Most of us did well: my eldest sister Elsie and I were dux medallists — the top academic honour in a Scottish school — both there and at Hamilton Academy to which we moved for our last three years of schooling.

In adult life, five of us took university degrees and three of us, Andrew, myself and John, all held university chairs at one time or another. Andrew, in his spare time as a secondary school teacher took his D Litt at Glasgow University with a thesis on Matthew Arnold and also became a Shakespeare scholar. Elsie, after graduation, became an elementary school teacher like her mother and by prudent investment had accumulated a portfolio of £500,000 by the time she died in 1990. Margaret, the fourth in the family after Bill, had a similar career and at one time had some literary ambitions. Next came Helen who contracted disseminated sclerosis and died a few years after Bill. She had married a scientist who later became an FRS but the marriage broke down and she came back with her only child, a boy, to the family home. Annie, my "twin", trained as a professional cook, worked for many years in a children's hospital in Liverpool, and married in war-time, a year or so after me.

My youngest brother, John[1], was intellectually the most distinguished of the family. A graduate of the Sorbonne and of Cambridge, he came first in both the Home Civil Service and Foreign Office examinations in 1936 — a unique achievement. Although he later achieved notoriety of a different kind, he became one of the leading authorities on the French dramatists of the 17th century, particularly Molière.

I have no doubt that my father, who was highly intelligent, would have liked to go to university. His younger brother, Tom, not only took a degree and became a Church of Scotland Minister but wrote poetry, essays and novels. But, as the eldest son, my father was expected to go straight into the family business. I never knew him engage in serious study or play games (other than bowls and patience). He enjoyed what leisure he had,

---

[1] See the Appendix for a further discussion of John and my recollections of him.

smoked a pipe in the evenings and read a great deal of fiction from the local library. He was good-tempered, considerate and of a calm disposition, popular with the farmers who were his main customers and a well-known figure in the village.

But he was never one to talk much and I can recall only one letter — and that very brief, written on the back of an account — that I ever received from him. He liked us to be silent at meals and himself said little. The only rebuke from him I can recall consisted of the occasional exclamation, "Mun, you're a fair gomeril" — "dunderhead" would be the English equivalent. When he was present at meals he said grace — at some speed and invariably in the words: "Heavenly Father bless these mercies, pardon our sins for Christ's sake Amen!" It was a useful way of procuring silence before my mother started to serve but it often caused conversation to languish thereafter. Or at least, for whatever reason, meals were not very chatty, the males being constitutionally uncommunicative and my father given to suppressing any exchanges with a "That's enough now."

My mother, Elizabeth Wishart, was nine years younger than him and was married on 5 April 1900 when she was 25 (I can remember the date of the wedding because a horse called April the Fifth won the Derby in my youth and I wasn't enough of a gambler to back it). She, too, was the oldest in her family, having three sisters and a brother. There had at one time been money in the family. My grandmother's grandfather was a bleacher and was ruined overnight by the bursting of a dam near Neilston. Both my mother and her sister Janet, however, were able to train as teachers at the Normal School in Glasgow and my mother took up her first and only appointment in Lesmahagow in 1896 in her 22nd year.

I have two versions of my parents' first meeting. My eldest sister Elsie told me that the story she had (presumably from my mother) was that my father was standing, as he often did, outside the front door of the shop in the main street when the horse-drawn brake came down from Brocketsbrae — the railway terminus a mile and a half away — and when my mother stepped out he fell for her at once. But my father told my wife shortly after our marriage, "We met at a mutual improvement evening and it's been mutual improvement ever since."

Certainly, as in so many Scots homes, education played a central part in the family. My grandfather's family included two children educated for a professional career, one a minister and the other an engineer; five of my father's family were graduates; and all five of my children have university degrees. In addition, the dominant tendency was to become a teacher. My mother, aunts and two older sisters were schoolteachers and so was my oldest brother until he retired and became a university professor in Texas. Teaching has been the traditional social ladder in Scotland, particularly for girls. In the 1930s an analysis of Glasgow graduates by a student of mine, Adam Collier, showed that children of manual workers tended to become teachers but that teaching, unlike other professions, was not self-recruiting: children of teachers chose other professions.

Part of our education came in the form of church attendance, which was more or less compulsory. Every Sunday we set out at 10.50 am and took our seats in the backmost pew. My father, equipped with a "poke" of imperial mints which he sucked along with the sermon, counted the attendance and reported the score at lunch. I took some interest in the sermons, chiefly from the point of view of technique. Reviewing the argument and the objections to it was not a bad training of the mind.

No one inquired into my religious beliefs. As a child — between say five and eight — I was intensely religious. Heaven was a reality to be played for and that meant keeping commandments, "being good" and doing as you were told. So I went through at an early age phases of religious experience not unlike those of the lower orders in earlier centuries, following a subservient moral code in the expectation of future but unknown benefits.

While any religious beliefs gradually faded away in my middle teens when, like most young men, I found a wide gap between what was logically demonstrable and what I was asked to believe. I continued to be fascinated by the varieties of religious experience — but as phenomena to be explained rather than shared in. I studied metaphysics and gave it up as futile. Under the influence of Aldous Huxley and others I turned my attention to neo-Platonism, pantheism, mysticism and, in due course, thought transference and parapsychology. But I took an increasingly detached view of these, unwilling to dismiss as unreal what many people claimed to have experienced if it could be shown to be real. My interest had turned from religion to what would now be called the sociology of religion.

My Parents and their family - Autumn 1913. First row: Helen, Annie, John (in mother's arms), Alec (in sailor suit). Behind: Margaret, Andrew, father, Elsie, Bill.

## Village life

Largely because of its educational system and the advantage taken of the opportunities it afforded, Scotland had a much less rigid class structure than England. In my own case I have never been conscious of class barriers of the kind that are said to exist in England. I counted among my immediate ancestors a master slater, a shopkeeper, a buyer for a large warehouse and an estate gardener. Most of my schoolmates were coal miners' or farmers' children. So if I accept the label, lower middle class, as an indication of my social origins, it has to be remembered that this involved contact within and outside the family with a wide variety of occupations and very different social backgrounds. It is true that there were at some distance from the village, physically and psychologically, a number of "big" houses but I hardly ever saw the occupants or thought about them, any more than I thought about the Minister's son who went to Eton and became in due course a professor of Greek and Vice Principal of Hull University.

It is also true that there was a kind of proletariat with which I mixed at school and in the Boys' Brigade and from which I drew an occasional friend, particularly if they continued their education. Some of them came from the council houses built between the wars, in an area on the Glasgow side of the village. But these contacts virtually ceased when I went to Glasgow University at the age of 17. To a boy who lived in the village community and hardly ever left the village even for a day, the reality was never class as such but manners and interests. There were those who were tough and given to fighting and bullying, just as, among the parents, there were those who drank heavily and led disorderly lives. Then there were those of less aggressive habits who enjoyed a game and had interesting hobbies or unfamiliar skills.

There was never any real physical injury and more menace (from which one could run away) than mugging in after-school encounters. The only incident I can still recall was one that took place when I was six or seven: a new school cap of which I was proud was snatched from my head and thrown among some trees and never found again. In comparison with life at a Prep or Public School, which echoes so unpleasantly in English literature over the past hundred years (but in the literature of no other country) my school days seem in retrospect to have been remarkably free of incident.

Nor did the outside world intrude much. I was three when war broke out in 1914 and remember very little about it. I must have been taught to read early because I seem to recall bringing back the evening newspaper in 1916 with the headline "Battle of the Somme" without any inkling of the thousands of men who had died in the battle. On the day of the Armistice we were all paraded in the school playground and given a holiday. There was no radio, television or record player and for all practical purposes I saw no newspapers. So my knowledge of what was going on was negligible and my understanding of what war meant was even less.

Far more present to me was the ubiquitous fever van. There was a time in the mid-19th century when 40 per cent of the deaths in Britain were of children under five. Even when I was born in 1911, well over one child in ten died under one year of age, compared with one in 150 in the 1990s. What impressed itself on my young mind was the risk of death from scarlet fever. Every child in the village seemed to catch a fever in one of other of the frequent epidemics and the sight of a van outside the house of a victim was a familiar one. We were lucky: no member of the family caught scarlet fever as a child.

On the whole we must have been a healthy family, for apart from the usual children's ailments I can recall no major illnesses. My parents never seemed to be ill, no-one was ever in hospital, and we rarely saw a doctor (or, for that matter, a dentist). But I recall vividly the pain of chilblains every winter and the agony of having them dressed on hand and foot. In the years after 1916 when my schooling began, the winters seemed far more severe than any I have known since. And we all had the measles, six of us at the same time in 1913. I have a dim memory (or rather, a memory of a memory) of being caught when I had measles — presumably in 1913 — standing between the window and the blind when the blind had been drawn to prevent the bright sunlight from affecting my eyes. On another occasion my eldest sister continued at school when two of her brothers had measles and she was even given a prize for perfect attendance!

Our meals began with breakfast, usually at 8am so as to allow my father to get to the shop by 9am. There was always porridge and, latterly at least, a cooked meal of ham and eggs or fish. Lunch (which we called dinner) was at noon and occasionally my father would bring with him, always unannounced, a traveller who had called at the shop. We had tea at 4pm, or when we got back from school, and this developed into high tea, which meant that the usual cakes and scones were preceded by eggs or some other dish. Green vegetables and fruit were largely absent from our diet; as in many other parts of Scotland, there was no greengrocer in the village. Dinner was never served in my boyhood, but once we grew up we had coffee and biscuits or some other form of supper before bedtime.

It is the pleasures of those days that linger longest in the memory: the Sunday School picnics when horse-drawn brakes took us miles away into some country field and left us to enjoy races or games until we had another ride back to the Church hall, where we were presented with a large "parley" or parkin never seen on any other occasions; the paper chases and picnics with my mother and some of the older children by a stone dyke higher up the hillside; the peacocks displaying and the red squirrels scampering about in the wood opposite our house; holding the cows' tails in the byre when we climbed to the nearest farmhouse for milk; raiding the pantry for sultanas or a few grains of crystallised sugar.

A little later in the early 1920s there were family outings on summer afternoons "up the hill" to a disused Belvedere by the side of a wood where we could gather an endless variety of wild flowers, pick blaeberries, conduct sham warfare or play hide and seek among the heather.

I loved to watch the harvesting and ride on the flat carts that were "inning" the corn stacks. This was made easier because some of my closest friends as a child were the children of neighbouring farmers. My schoolfellows when I was somewhat older used to earn a little pocket money picking strawberries, sometimes in fields planted by a mining family to supplement their income. This I would not have been allowed to do. But although, unlike modern children, we were never given regular pocket money, I don't recall that I chafed greatly at this prohibition.

I have no regrets that I was brought up in a village at some distance from any large city. We were within easy reach of open country and surrounded by farms. Time did not press on us, since there was little or no homework; nor did it hang on us with so much of interest to do. There was no lack of companionship: among my schoolmates were several of outstanding ability.

I don't recall that I found life boring as a boy. Yet I had few of the toys or sources of amusement which young people now take for granted. I can recall no visits to the local "picture-house" to which most of the children went on Saturday afternoons, often with an empty jam-jar in lieu of entrance money. (A friend whose father once owned a cinema explained to me that for many working class families a visit to the cinema was the cheapest way of keeping warm.) The only music I heard was in Church (i.e.hymns), or from a pipe band or when my sisters played the piano. Once in a while a travelling menagerie visited the village or I might be taken to see Hengler's Circus in Glasgow, with a spectacular water act as the climax. But to go to a theatre was a major event.

One relied then far more on one's legs and thought nothing of walks that now seem extraordinary. I remember walking in a day from home to the top of Tinto and back — a distance of over 20 miles. Similarly I cycled long distances (or what now seem to me long distances) on an old gearless bicycle, for example to Nithsdale, through the Dalveen Pass by Durisdeer and back by the Mennock Pass. Every Sunday afternoon for years I would go for a long walk with two other boys.

Walking still came naturally to me when, in my first year at Glasgow (in the spring of 1929) I accompanied my eldest brother Andrew to Paris. He had completed a doctoral thesis on Matthew Arnold and was travelling to discuss with a M. Louis Bonnerot, the leading French writer on Arnold's career, whether the Marguerite of Arnold's verse was real (as Bonnerot thought) or imaginary (as Andrew suspected). I recall my first sense of being in a foreign country as I woke up in the train at Sheffield to the sound of *English* voices. Once in France, the feeling intensified at the quayside as the waiting train hooted impatiently. During our visit we set out to walk from Paris to Chartres and on our first day got as far as Trappes. Next morning we saw our first ox-cart in the street outside our hotel (where only fast cars can now be seen) and spent a long hot day walking by the high road (instead of the valley of the Eure) to Chartres which we reached in the evening dog-tired. We left early next morning by train without setting eyes on the Cathedral we had come to visit. Later we rejoined the Bonnerots in Amiens where we *did* see the Cathedral and I was given a fascinating introduction to the iconography of Norman cathedrals by our hosts.

However, until I went to University in 1928 I had never been far from my home in Lesmahagow. From time to time I was taken to see my grandmother and cousins in Neilston. This meant two train journeys: one to Glasgow and one from there to Neilston. Several times at New Year my father took me to a football match, to see Queen's Park play Corinthians at Hampden Park. Occasionally I was taken to Arthur and Company to be measured for a new suit. But otherwise, except in the holidays, or when I travelled to school in Hamilton, I lived wholly in the village, hardly ever read a newspaper and had only begun to listen to the radio when I made a one-valve set for myself in about 1928 or 1929. The world outside Lesmahagow and certainly outside the west of Scotland was known to me almost exclusively from books.

Just when I first travelled by bus I can't be sure, but I expect it was about 1921 in the bus that took the Boys' Brigade to camp by the river Clyde at Abington, a little to the south. In 1925-28 we travelled daily to school in Hamilton by a fast Lancia motor coach with a collapsible hood. The only motor car I ever rode in before the 1930s was my Uncle Harry's Jowett and I had no occasion to drive myself until 1933 when I bought a second-hand Jowett in Cambridge for £20. (No driving test was needed).

Some years after the war, when we began to go for an annual family holiday to Rothesay in the Isle of Bute, we did spend some time away from the village. It was quite an upheaval to make the move and it involved quite a feat of organisation, since so much in the way of sheets, towels, clothes and other requirements had to be carefully packed and forwarded to the holiday address. Fortunately the task was made easier by the system of passenger luggage in advance under which the railway would collect, transport and deliver at modest cost the trunk (or, in our case, wicker hamper) in which everything was packed. Once in Rothesay my father invariably headed for the bowling green while my mother would go with some of her children to the sandy beach at Ettrick Bay in one of the trams that Glasgow had discarded but which were found adequate to carry passengers from one side of Bute to the other.

Of all the happy memories of my life in Lesmahagow, the best are of my time with the Boys Brigade, an organisation rather like the Scouts. I joined the local Boys Brigade at the age of 10 or 11 and rose to be a lieutenant. We met in the local Church Hall on Friday evenings throughout the winter, under a succession of captains of whom the most striking was undoubtedly George Buchanan, the eldest son of a local railwayman and a natural leader of men. He had a great influence on me: he combined authority, modesty and humour with a certain moral inflexibility that commanded respect. We were made aware that the Boys Brigade was not just a boys' club but had a religious basis to it.

Most of the evening went in Swedish exercises and games; in the spring and summer we took advantage of the good weather to play football. In the early years we also drilled with dummy rifles, but by the mid-1920s these were withdrawn. From time to time we had a church parade, marching behind our pipe band of which I once or twice took command. On the first occasion I remember giving the order as we mustered after church, "By the left, quick march" almost as soon as the boys had formed in line, and was taken aback by the curious noises from the bagpipes as the band tried desperately to blow up their bags in the few seconds they had been allowed.

The great occasion of the year, however, was the annual camp. We began by camping at Abington, a dozen miles or so away in the valley of the Upper Clyde. As time went on we covered a progressively bigger distance, camping at North Berwick, Strachur (Loch Fyne) and in Kintyre. We used bell tents and rotated fatigue duties, including cooking, over the week to ten days of the holiday. Once we spent a week in Kintyre. There we had a particularly enjoyable camp. It started unpromisingly at a bracken-covered part of the coast at Grogport. When I emerged from my tent in the early morning, I was astonished to see how dirty my hands were. Looking more closely I saw that they were covered with midges so thickly as to obscure the flesh. We struck camp precipitately and moved further along the coast to a sandier and midge-free site at Carradale.

There, small boys could fish from the pier with herring as bait and catch huge saith, bigger than themselves. Older boys could persuade the fishermen to take them out with them in their boats on a night's fishing. We could all bathe in safety on a perfect shelving beach and look out over the glorious Firth of Clyde at the gannets wheeling and diving all day long. If I could pick one week to recapture the pleasures of my youth, that would be it.

## Early schooling

In the days before the 1870 Education Act, there had been no state school in the village and my father went to a kind of Dame's school at a penny a day. A primary school was built across the river in Turfholm where the poorest families lived and it was there that my schooling began in 1916 in the middle of the first world war. The children of miners and farmers formed the majority of my class at school, with a few children of shopkeepers, artisans, teachers, a chimney sweep and others mixed in.

Of my six pre-secondary years at school, half were at Turfholm and half in the school at the other end of the village near the railway station at which my mother had taught. My teachers were all women, none of them graduates but good at their job. What they taught me in the first three years, apart from reading and writing, I can't now remember. I do recall that we used slates and slate pencils, never paper. I remember, too, the strips of locust bean that I bought occasionally for a halfpenny as a sweet and, much more vividly, the shame of being strapped for an offence I had not committed. The strap or tawse was a long strip of leather, still used in Scottish schools in the 1970s or later, even on children of six or seven. The unfortunate victim was asked to hold out his right hand and the strap was brought down on his palm - hence the expression "given a palmy". I recall being called out on one occasion, charged mistakenly with scattering the shells of monkey nuts under my desk, and given several of the best. These things did not increase a child's appetite for school.

When I was seven or eight I entered the class of Miss MacKay who was a contemporary of my mother's and came from Inverness or further north (she died somewhere on the Cromarty Firth at the age of 90 or more). There were 72 of us in the class and the proceedings were highly organised. When we had to file out Miss MacKay rapped out the orders. "Class stand. Class move to the right by number: 1,2. Class, forward march." I came to understand then something of what lay behind the Victorian tradition: particularly the discipline that sheer size of family or class imposes.

It was an attractive aspect of the teaching that one was constantly moving up or down in class. One day I would be sent to the bottom for bad behaviour: another, when I came back from some minor illness, I would find myself sent to the top, presumably as a sympathetic gesture.

What we were taught I can hardly imagine. There were long hours spent in learning to write when I could already write. We copied page after page of copper plate in an effort to acquire legibility, but my handwriting stayed obstinately ragged until somebody revealed to me the secret of making my letters bold and round, especially *round.* Then for some brief years I wrote a simple characterless, rather childish hand of immaculate rotundity.

Long afterwards it became clear to me that the indefatigable pursuit of a legible script through copying models resulted from the hopelessness of teaching more important things to so large a class. I remember looking at lists written by schoolchildren of the titles of books and newspapers available in their homes. The long lists written by children of educated parents were of doubtful legibility; but the few lines written by children from the Glasgow slums were beautifully clear and pleasing in their legibility and deadly in their implications for education priorities.

In the next class under Miss Thornton I came across the first subject that kindled my imagination: history, often history of battles long ago. I particularly remember the first real history book I read — a textbook on great figures in European history, starting with Charlemagne. We also started to learn geography in her class, and the experience was one I will not readily forget. We sang. We sang the names of the longest rivers and the highest mountains. We sang the names of the countries where the rivers flowed and of the counties in Scotland where high mountains were to be found. Not once, but over and over again. "Schiehallion in Perthshire. Schiehallion in Perthshire. Schiehallion in Perthshire." Sing three hosannas and you never forget. In other subjects it was much the same. You followed the teacher's pointer as it moved along the blackboard to words and phrases the class repeated like an incantation.

My last year in primary school was in the "Qually" or qualifying class. This was the last year of very large classes before the door to secondary education — in the Higher Grade as it was called — was closed at 11-plus to those unable to obtain a qualifying certificate. Those entering the Higher Grade were joined by children from the surrounding villages where there was no Higher Grade. The rest moved on to what was then called the "Advanced Division". Some children, however, were allowed to leave from the Qually, presumably at the minimum age of 12 since attendance was compulsory up to that age until the 1918 Act and in 1921–22 (when I was in the "Qually") full effect had not yet been given to the raising of the school leaving age to 14 in the 1918 Act.

As we moved higher up the school, things changed as intellectual challenges appeared. Instead of the mumbo-jumbo of arithmetic, we started algebra and geometry. We began to read English literature and real poetry. We made little contact with science but were taken for country walks to help us begin studying botany. Our English master, Robin Macintyre, not only taught us to act scenes from Shakespeare and prepared us to take part in drama festivals, but as spring moved towards summer, he took us out to survey the golf course with chain, plane table and theodolite, showed us how to sight with a prismatic compass, and demonstrated the value of trigonometry (which I have sometimes doubted) in converting our observations into a sketch plan.

He also encouraged us to produce scenes from Shakespeare. We had no costumes or scenery and confined ourselves to single scenes from plays like *The Tempest*, and *The Merchant of Venice*. The emphasis was on verse speaking and gesture, since the school room did not allow much movement. But we rehearsed thoroughly and competed (often successfully) against other schools at the Annual Drama Festival in Lanark. Macintyre also made us learn passages from the Book of Job by heart — for which he has my everlasting gratitude — and with his fine resonant voice kindled in us something of his own love of poetry.

Then there were foreign languages, Latin and French, about which I felt some ambivalence. I don't think I saw any positive value in Latin until I came to read Tacitus after five years study of the language: nobody expected you to talk in Latin and I had an impression that you learned a foreign language in order to converse in it. On the other hand, the way in which the French were said to pronounce their language was so absurd that to speak

French was a sure way of making a fool of yourself. So my enthusiasm for foreign languages was somewhat restrained. Nevertheless I enjoyed the discovery that there were other ways of expressing the same idea or sentiment and came increasingly to relish the study of languages in the way an actor takes to the study of a new part.

Our French teacher, Miss Williamson, was another contemporary of my mother's and at least as formidable as Miss MacKay. As we moved into our last year at Lesmahagow (I was then 13 or 14) she decided to use the last two periods on Friday afternoon to teach the boys in the class to darn while the girls went off to the gymnasium. There was even a prize for the best darner but it was one prize I did not win.

In my class in the Higher Grade was a future Cabinet minister, Tom Fraser, and a future Chief Constable of Edinburgh, John Inch (later Sir John). In 1924–25 Tom Fraser was rather shy, quiet spoken, friendly and unassertive. He came to Lesmahagow Higher Grade school from Blackwood, for the first three years of secondary school, and left to become a coal miner. When I next heard of him he was a lay preacher, then in 1945 he was returned as a Labour Member of Parliament and in the Labour Government of 1964 he was for a time Minister of Transport.

While Tom Fraser was not a very conspicuous member of the class, nor one who ever showed the gifts one associates with a political career, John Inch was a big cheerful, determined fellow, who entered the police force after graduation. He made one of the best puns of my school days. We had a new physical training instructress, a young lady of considerable sex appeal, who was overheard by the class to explain that she weighed 8 1/2 stones, "stripped for gym". "Lucky Jim!" came a voice from the back of the class, almost certainly John Inch's.

Although I used to win prizes in every class, I never had cause to regard myself as brighter than my school fellows. The margin was usually a narrow one, and I observed that my closest rivals at each stage in my career, sometimes boys sometimes girls, tended to leave school early and drop out of the scholastic race, a fact that was sufficient to dispose of any tendency to look on those who stayed on to University as some kind of intellectual elite.

But a far more powerful corrective to vainglory was that I was such a duffer at carpentry or art or sport or any employment involving the use of hand and eye. To do well in class seemed little to boast of when other boys (and girls) excelled outside the classroom: they had more daring, more strength, quicker repartee, a firmer grasp of the practical arts. I managed to work my way into the school football team, only to be dropped for good after my first appearance. "The Cairncrosses can't draw," was the compelling judgment of our Art master, Mr Huck, yet another of my mother's contemporaries.

Outside school it was the same. If we went "guddling" for fish I never came within sight of catching one. If we went bird nesting it would be the other boys who spotted the nests. Yet I tended to assume that what others could do I could learn to do too if I tried. I took it for granted that I would have no difficulty in riding a bicycle until in my teens I was invited to do so. Nevertheless I did manage in the end to acquire some of these skills and learned to use my hands *after* I left school in many different ways: for example, making bookcases for myself, french-polishing under instruction from my oldest brother, and assembling simple radio sets. My lack of manual dexterity and deficiency in kinaesthetic sense did not trouble me unduly. But it did drive home the lesson that we all have our various talents and that one should cultivate what one has, not sigh for what one has not.

## Hamilton Academy 1925–28

Higher Grade schools covered only the first three years of secondary education: for the following three years before University entry it was necessary to go to Hamilton Academy, 13 miles away. This absorbed children from other schools at 14-plus in the same way as Lesmahagow Higher Grade did at 11-plus. The academy went back to the days of John Knox and the universal free education he helped to introduce. It was founded in the year of the Armada and had high educational standards. Indeed, it was one of a group of first-class secondary schools in the Glasgow area, several of which have been destroyed by post-war educational ideology, when, as with so many old Grammar Schools, it was turned into a Comprehensive after the second world war: i.e., made to take children whose abilities would not previously have won them admission.

When I was a boy, though, Hamilton Academy could count on up to ten of the first 100 places in the examination for bursary (or scholarship) places at Glasgow University. The University published the names and schools of the first 100 candidates and there was keen competition for the top places. Some people left the Academy after two years, having taken their Higher leaving Certificate. Others came back for a third year, often with the intention of sitting the bursary examination in the following June.

The teaching was excellent, particularly in English, Latin and Mathematics. In Scotland it was usual at this stage to balance arts and science: the course I took combined English, French and Latin with Mathematics, Physics and Chemistry. I enjoyed the English class under Duncan Herriot, then under Mr Annand, an easygoing, pawky teacher who extended our knowledge of English literature a great deal. We read with him through Tamburlaine, Samson Agonistes and a collection of longer poems in a volume entitled *The English Parnassus.*

What we were taught in class was, of course, supplemented by what we read at home. I had begun to read voraciously from about the age of 11. Not newspapers, because we took only an evening paper that contained little. Not magazines because there were few in the house. Not at first modern novelists and dramatists. But books — at first, Kingsley, Defoe, Merriman, Swift — the usual mixture. I don't recall reading novels until I was 13 or 14. I developed a passion for Hardy when I was about 16 and accumulated his collected works as school prizes. Later it was Galsworthy, Scott, Dickens, Thackeray and Jane Austen. But I don't think I ever strayed much off the beaten track. I knew nothing of George Meredith, or George Moore, very little of Wells or Shaw or Arnold Bennett or, for that matter, D.H.Lawrence. Even at University I remained largely unfamiliar with all of these except Shaw. Aldous Huxley had far more influence on me: he gave me my only access, at that stage in my life, to what the literary intelligentsia in Britain were saying at that time.

In Latin one of our two teachers, Charlie Durno, was stone-deaf and had to rely on lip-reading. As may be imagined, this gave rise to frequent interjections and exchanges between his pupils which he could not easily detect but to which he was alerted by the resulting signs of merriment on the faces of class. It made him chronically suspicious without ever catching anyone, not even

Tom Hamilton, a boy who could make fun of him looking him in the face without detection since he could talk without moving his lips. In spite of such baiting Charlie remained a collected and able teacher, popular with his pupils. The Latin we were taught did not, until very late, open any doors in my imagination. Virgil, Livy and the rest were a set of passages for translation. They went with the grammar as riders went with mathematical theorems. The idea that Virgil wrote poetry comparable with, say, Milton's hardly crossed my mind. It was not until we came to Tacitus that I saw the power of another language to convey what could not be conveyed in English.

The same applied to French. Apart from De Maupassant no French prose writer made a particular hit with me — partly, I expect, because we read nothing by the great masters of French drama (not a single play by Moliere, Racine or Corneille) or by the kind of prose writer who now appeals most to me: Montaigne, Montesquieu, de Tocqueville. Yet I carried away a particular relish for the French language and used to spend hours studying French turns of phrase and idioms in the dictionary.

Mathematics had a particular appeal; but in retrospect I regret that I spent so much time on trigonometry, conic sections, modern geometry etc which were of no subsequent value to me, but was given no instruction in calculus which I had to pick up on my own with great pain and sweat, partly because I had philosophic doubts about the underlying logic.

In chemistry I was the only pupil in my final year and was allowed to conduct experiments with very limited supervision. One day I turned the stopcock on my burette by mistake, spilling bromine into the sink, and thus creating a poisonous gas. In spite of my embarrassment I could not help admiring the presence of mind of the chemistry master, Mr Middleton, a small man with a military moustache and a somewhat military manner. He threw open all the windows, mobilised the class sharing the laboratory with me and marched them out into the corridor in the space of seconds.

I sat the Bursary examination at 16 in my second year, having already sat my Highers, and took 19th place (my younger brother John, in similar circumstances, came 5th). I was offered a bursary worth £40 a year which was about as much as the first bursar was likely to get. So there was no strong reason for delay on financial grounds and no impediment on grounds of age — in the 1930s I had a boy of 15 in the first year class in Political Economy. But I decided to spend a third year at Hamilton chiefly (if I thought about the matter at all) because I wanted the distinction of being first bursar.

In the end I came second in the 1928 Bursary Examination and won two scholarships, one worth £40 and the other £30. With these scholarships and a contribution from the Carnegie Trust which paid my annual fees of 15 guineas a year, I did not at any time have to ask my parents for financial support while I was at Glasgow. Indeed, there has never been a time in my life at which I received a regular monetary payment from my parents, not even by way of pocket money.

It did not seem to me self-evident that I should go to university. My limited observation of careers suggested to me that I ought to become a chartered accountant. I might not know enough to foresee that the business world would become the accountant's oyster, but I understood that accountancy was a safe, reputable and lucrative profession, and that seemed to me to settle the matter. Here as in other directions I made up my own mind and was advised neither by teachers nor parents. It was only when I discovered that an apprenticeship of five years could be shortened to three if one had a University degree that I reconciled myself to four years' study at Glasgow. I also had a certain reluctance to refrain from using the scholarships I had won.

When I look back on my education, I recognise a particular debt to the succession of English masters who taught me — a debt beyond any I owe to teachers of other subjects. They awoke in me a regard for style; a recognition of the variety of ways in which a thought can be given utterance and the power of words to convey far more than their bare meaning; a passion for lucidity and simplicity and at the same time, vividness of expression. The awakening was slow and largely unconscious so that my teachers may well have remained ignorant of the changes they had set on foot. But it left me with an understanding of the importance of conveying ideas clearly. In economics, where literary skills now seem so rare, style and clarity are especially important.

I realise too that I was fortunate to grow up in the 1920s, in a period that was relatively peaceful and uneventful in comparison with the turbulent years of depression that followed. Even the

General Strike in 1926, however revolutionary it might seem, led
to no violence of which I was aware, although I recollect seeing
crowds of idle workmen at Bridgeton Cross and other intersections
on journeys into Glasgow by bus. What had more serious effects
in the village was the long-continued miners' strike, reducing
many of the miners' families to extreme poverty. These economic
and social strains formed the background to my years at university,
when I was to make the discovery of economics, the discipline
that I came to see as their most hopeful remedy. To those years
we now turn.

## 3

## *Learning the Craft: Glasgow University*

My university years were spent against the background of the deepening of the world slump from 1929 onwards into the worst economic recession of modern times. Unemployment had been severe in Scotland all through the 1920s, particularly in the mining areas, and now reached a scale which made it the major preoccupation of the entire country. It was a matter of accident that I chose to study economics at Glasgow; but by 1931 the world seemed to me to be so constructed that economics was the only subject worth serious study. To engage in research in Cambridge, the leading centre in the world, between the publication of the "Treatise on Money" in 1930 and "The General Theory of Employment, Interest and Money" in 1936 was in a way "very heaven", especially as few others did research in economics in the United Kingdom at that time.

My student years coincided, too, with the political excitement generated by the depression, by the growth of fascism with its Blackshirt supporters in the south of England, and by the simultaneous lurch towards Communism among the young Oxbridge intelligentsia. Burgess and MacLean were at Cambridge just after my time, but I knew Kim Philby well, although he gave me no indication of Communist leanings. The Spanish Civil War was in progress before I left Cambridge and several of my contemporaries took part. Two at least were killed: a young New Zealander called MacLaren and David Haden Guest, a deeply committed Marxist who had been an announcer on Moscow radio.

A further important influence was the radio. I found radio talks a useful source of instruction — rather like having an extra

John and Alec Cairncross at front door in Helenslea,
Lesmahagow, 1922.

set of lectures — and *The Listener*, a weekly magazine that reprinted and discussed many of them, was the one paper I took regularly in the early 1930s. It covered a wide range of subjects in a way that was both readable and intellectually satisfying.

At both universities I began with a certain feeling of inferiority. Especially at Cambridge, the clever young men around me seemed to have a far wider experience of life, to ooze a sophistication of which I was incapable, and to have non-academic gifts which it had not previously occurred to me to envy. At Glasgow, too, some of my fellow students had clearly come from well-to-do families and had had broader opportunities than I had had.

I had the good fortune to be in a rather outstanding year. It included Charles Wilson who took a double first in Modern Languages and then in Economics and Politics and went on to be Vice Chancellor, first of the University of Leicester and then of his own University of Glasgow. Just ahead of me were a number of men who made their mark as public servants, such as Stewart Bates who later became head of the Canadian Central Mortgage and Housing Corporation; Bill Strath, who became Permanent Secretary of the Ministry of Supply and effectively the first Managing Director of the Atomic Energy Authority; and Matthew Stevenson, whom I was to meet again in the Treasury and who became Permanent Secretary first of the Ministry of Fuel and Power and then of Health. Here, as at Cambridge, discussion and argument with members of my class was an indispensable ingredient in my education in economics.

Social life for Glasgow university students was bounded, then as now, by the fact that most of us continued to live at home. I lived at home all through my first and part of my second year, travelling to Glasgow by an early bus and returning in the late afternoon. This took up at least three hours of the day and made it difficult to find time to study or make adequate use of libraries. In my second year I arranged "digs" near the university with Ian Smith, a mathematics student in the year ahead of me. My younger brother John joined us the following year.

I made some tentative but unsuccessful attempts to write for the university magazine. By my fourth year I was one of a small group who launched a new university magazine, "The Critic". We took ourselves very seriously and excluded the kind of flippant

comment favoured by the Glasgow University Magazine (or
GUM, as it was known). For example, I contributed an article
arguing for an end to reparations. As all those who contributed
to it graduated and left at the end of the academic year, the
magazine expired after its first issue. At one point, it looked like
involving us in financial loss until Hector McNeil, a fellow
student who later became minister of state in the Foreign Office
as Ernest Bevin's protégé, persuaded the publisher to be content
with the takings from advertising. McNeil was financially astute
in other ways: he augmented his student income by gambling at
dog races, having first carefully studied the past performance of
the animals*.

So far as student societies were concerned, my interests were
mainly in the Dialectic Society and the International Club,
which held an Easter conference annually near Pitlochry. Glasgow
has always had an outstanding record in training debaters, but I
formed no part of it; when I did make a short speech, it was
reported succinctly in the University magazine as "Mr Cairncross
interrupted".

The East-West Conference of the International Club, on the
other hand, was one of the few occasions when students —
mainly from developing countries — could discuss, in a relaxed
and friendly atmosphere, problems of interest to them in the
development of their countries, members of staff joining in the
discussion. I also joined the union but I did not stand for office.
At that time the Union was housed in the John MacIntyre
building, a much older and less grand affair than the two Unions
completed later. Even though there were only 4,000 students
then, compared with 16,000 now, the building tended to
become very crowded when some prominent and popular speaker
such as J B Priestley appeared. But we didn't find it seriously
inadequate, even though there was not a single bar (we couldn't
afford anything but tea). Today, three are considered necessary.

* At the time, the bookies did not know what odds to quote, because dog racing
was quite new. Hector made a practice of looking up the record of each dog during
a visit to the Mitchell Library, and so was able to assess their chances on the basis of
past performance. When he started to win regularly, he found a tribe of other young
men attaching themselves to him. But, he said, after they had backed the first two or
three dogs he had put his money on and lost, they were discouraged and gave up
accepting his choice of dog to back. Meanwhile he, by persevering, nearly always ended
the evening a net winner. Of course, in time the bookies learned their lesson and
quoted odds that made the game no longer worth while.

In my third year I stood for the Students' Representative Council and was elected by a substantial majority, much to my surprise. As a result, I acted in my final year as Transport Convenor for Glasgow University's Charities Day. This was a big affair: the takings were often well over £20,000, or over £600,000 in terms of present-day money. My task was to arrange with Glasgow firms to let us have the use of their lorries for the Saturday when the parade took place. The lorries were then decorated as floats by groups of students, in fancy dress to match the theme of their float. All this was done early on Saturday morning in University Avenue and when the signal was given, the floats moved slowly off with ample infantry support towards the City Chambers a mile or so away. There they filed past the Lord Provost and other notabilities who took their stance in front of the City Chambers in George Square.

Unfortunately I was not informed at what hour the Lord Provost expected us, nor in what way I should communicate with him. No doubt my natural impatience made me give the signal a little too early. So the procession swept forward unannounced, and by the time I got to George Square it had already passed a vacant saluting base. Nothing daunted, I reassembled the floats and sent them into action once again, only to find that by this time the Lord Provost had grown tired of waiting and departed, so that the procession passed a second time before an empty stand.

There were times in my post-graduate days when the question was put to me: "Have you ever organised anything?" It was put, for example, by the Provost and Fellows of Queen's College Oxford when I appeared before them as a candidate for a Fellowship in 1936. Perhaps rather disingenuously I was able to reply, "Yes, I have been Transport Convenor on Charities Day in Glasgow". But I was never asked whether I had *disorganised* anything.

The first-year classes in Glasgow were enormous, rowdy and very mixed in ability. In my first year I took English, History and Political Economy, and in each case the classroom was full. The first-year class in English was one of 700, taught in three separate groups and in some other subjects, such as Logic and Moral Philosophy, not much smaller. We invariably opened with song. "Ye Mariners of England", "Napoleon had an Army", and

"MacNamara's Band" were among the favourites, and no lecturer could hope to proceed until the singing had ceased. Professor Macneile Dixon, a popular lecturer with a manner at once lofty and urbane, would raise his monocle at the end of each verse and allow it to drop into his hand as the class swept into yet another stanza.

In History Professor Medley, who was completing his thirtieth year in the chair, puzzled me a good deal by writing on the board at the beginning of each lecture a long list of books which I took to be his bibliography, but which I gradually perceived was intended as a reading list. I feel sure that nobody ever read through the books listed and doubt whether anybody even consulted them. We relied heavily on our lecture notes and the only thing that made students actually read was the necessity of writing a class essay twice, or in some classes, thrice, a year.

In Political Economy we had Professor W.R.Scott, under whom I subsequently served as a lecturer for four years. The class was held at 2pm, which put a premature end to many games of chess I started after lunch, and ensured for the lecturer a rather comatose audience. Scott was a man of great erudition and was frequently away on some Government committee. But I found his lectures unbearably dull and used to take down what he said verbatim because I felt sure that in later years I would not otherwise be able to credit hearing sentences so long and so obscure from one so learned. Even so, there were times when I gave up. The Professor, seeing me pause and lay down my pen, would then benevolently repeat his last phrase in the belief that I had not caught what he said.

The practice in Glasgow — and it is one of which I entirely approve — was for most of the lecturing to the first-year class to be undertaken by the Professor while his staff of lecturers took a bigger part in the more advanced classes. But the mixture varied. In Political Economy the Professor, in principle, aimed to take all the classes all the time, and the lecturers were let loose to lecture only in his absence or, at most, on a special subject for an hour a week. On the other hand in English we had at least four different lecturers in the first year. The standard of scholarship was high and with only one or two exceptions anybody who lectured me on any of the subjects I took subsequently occupied a chair in that subject. Ironically, the few who did not were often the most helpful lecturers.

Instruction was almost entirely by lecture and all or most of the lectures were intended to be taken down more or less verbatim. Sometimes the lecturer dictated a passage and then elaborated and illustrated what he had dictated. Sometimes he spoke at dictation speed. But there were also some who lectured in the ordinary way and left the student to register his own summary for future use.

When it became my turn to lecture some years later, I found myself with the task of conveying to young students of accountancy (many of them, however, older than myself) the elements of economics in 40 lectures over ten weeks. The lectures started at 5.15pm when the accountants had already done a full day's work and were correspondingly lethargic. I therefore prepared a one-page summary of what I proposed to say and distributed it at a charge of a penny a lecture, warning my audience that what I had distributed absolved them from taking notes since it was likely to be a more accurate digest than any they could prepare themselves. I knew that most of them would read no text book and that their understanding of economics was based exclusively on what they heard in 40 hours of lecturing. The marvel was that they learned anything at all and, to tell the truth, most of them learned very little, especially about the economic theory of cost.

It is easy to make a case against lecturing in comparison with more labour-intensive methods of instruction and for that matter in comparison with self-instruction by reading and writing. As has often been pointed out, nothing is so effective in making one learn something as having to lecture on it, or still more having to write a text book on it. Listening to other people's lectures is a poor substitute but it has some potential advantages. It is the cheapest way of exciting an interest and arousing the mind in a way reading never really does; and it obliges the student to give sustained attention to a complex argument for an hour at a time, which sitting with an open book rarely does. Apart from all this, it familiarises the student with the appearance and some of the habits of distinguished scholars and provides him with a different perspective of what study involves and produces.

The factor of cost is perhaps the most easily overlooked in teaching methods. Whatever else may be urged against reliance on lecturing, it enabled thousands to complete a university degree at Glasgow at an average annual cash outlay in fees of 17 guineas when fees were not, as they became, a relatively small element in university revenue, but sufficient to cover well over half the total cost.

But there is also some truth in the view that bad lectures are the root of assiduous study. In my first year I learned little or nothing from W.R.Scott, except the necessity of finding out for myself (whereas in Moral Philosophy I found A. A. Bowman to be so overwhelmingly articulate that I concluded that further study would add nothing of importance). The names of Maynard Keynes and his Cambridge contemporary, Dennis Robertson, who were transforming the whole subject of economics, or indeed the name of any contemporary economist, never cropped up in any of Scott's lectures. Instead, week after week, we were immersed in the finer points of the theory of value as seen by a moral philosopher or in the bibliographical problems of "The Wealth of Nations" and the events in the life of its author before its publication.

So I had to read by myself such works of the current literature as Keynes's "Treatise on Money" (a two-volume birthday present from my sister Elsie) and Robertson's "Banking Policy and the Price Level". Fortunately there were few journals with which one had to keep pace. I also benefited from discussion and argument with other members of my class. I particularly remember engaging in lengthy discussions on Richard Kahn's famous article in the 1931 *Economic Journal* on the multiplier with Jim Chapman, who was to have a successful career in business with Colman, a food company, before dying in the 1960s in a mountaineering accident. As he was writing an undergraduate thesis on unemployment and public works, this helped the two of us to unravel the modern theory of employment as it stood before the appearance of "The General Theory".

I gained most, however, from the preparation of a lengthy thesis on "Capital Transfer and the Terms of Trade". This was prompted by my reading of "International Trade" by F.W. Taussig, a Harvard economist, and by the controversy over the payment of German reparations between Keynes and Bertil Ohlin, of Stockholm University in 1928-29. Writing the thesis forced me to read most of the standard works on international trade theory and even to learn enough German to follow the articles by Fritz Machlup and Gottfried Haberler, Austrian economists whose work was then starting to appear in German periodicals. This was the origin of my interest in international capital flows at a time when such matters were considered highly technical and the idea that a phrase such as "the terms of trade" might make a newspaper headline would have seemed totally absurd.

The thesis was to be important to me in more ways than one. It brought me into correspondence with Dennis Robertson, who was at that time a Fellow of Trinity College, Cambridge, and stimulated me later to take issue with Roy Harrod, a prominent Oxford economist, on some aspects of his "International Economics." It also provided me with material to submit to Trinity College, Cambridge, when I applied for a Research Studentship there.

The idea of continuing my studies at Cambridge came to me in my final year. I had gradually abandoned my intention to take up accountancy and was uncertain what to do after graduation. But I thought it still possible that I might win enough scholarships to go for at least a year to Cambridge, which was then the Mecca of Economics, and I wrote to King's and to Trinity for information. I chose these colleges because Keynes was at the first and Robertson at the second. Both colleges told me they offered scholarships, but the Trinity one was much the larger: £300 a year for three years, or the present-day equivalent of about £9,000. I determined to enter for it without much expectation of success. Nobody from Glasgow had ever gone on to study economics at Cambridge, and the only Glasgow scholarship that would have offered sufficient financial support, the Snell Exhibition, was not open that year to economists and was in any event for study at Oxford, not Cambridge.

With my thesis I submitted to Cambridge a long essay on the Idealist Theory of Sovereignty, which was essentially an attack on Bernard Bosanquet, a distinguished moral philosopher, who endowed the activities of the state automatically with virtues. I argued rather that each activity of the state had to be separately justified. At that time honours examinations took place in September, so that the last concentrated effort of revision went on through the summer. I sat in the garden at Lesmahagow trying to make sense of my notes and fill in the gaps in my reading. For a week I camped with Jim Chapman while we debated issues in applied economics that might feature as questions in the examination papers. Then one morning a telegram arrived to say that I had been awarded the Trinity Research Studentship. No condition as to the class of my degree or anything else was attached. I was astonished, gratified and wildly excited.

The final examination was an exhausting and protracted affair. There was a long interval between some of the papers (there were seven in all), and the examination extended over a period of more than a fortnight. So although I quite enjoyed the early papers, apart from the fear of getting cramp while writing so much at speed, I found myself very tired when the last paper was finally over. I have often wished that I could read those papers again. In at least one of them, I developed a quite original line of argument on international trade theory, but I have no recollection now what it was. By the time the results were announced — four firsts, of which I had one — I was already in Cambridge.

# 4

## *Learning the Craft: Cambridge and Keynes*

When I arrived in the autumn of 1932, Cambridge was almost my first experience of a foreign country. It was an inland city of the plains with wide horizons and no hills this side of Gog and Magog to interrupt the east wind blowing from the Urals. It was almost untouched by industry and the splendour of its quadrangles spoke of wealth, antiquity and learning. No greater contrast to Glasgow, that Victorian beehive, slummy, Philistine and warm, could be imagined. The university dominated the town where in Glasgow it was almost a thing apart. It was residential and international in a way Glasgow had not been: nearly three-quarters of Glasgow's students lived at home, and there had been hardly a foreigner in the whole of the Arts Faculty (although other faculties had quite a sprinkling of students from Africa and Asia).

Above all, the undergraduates were English, and predominantly well-to-do English. They dressed like upper-class Englishmen even when they wore the customary sports jacket and grey flannels; their speech was upper-class English even in its slang; their physique, their complexion, their looks were quite unlike what one found in typical Glasgow students. I summed them up as Normans and started a sonnet:

Gods in whose image I have not been fashioned —
Full-chested gods, handsome and debonair
With voices measured, cool and unimpassioned
Sophisticated gods oozing with savoir-faire.

But this was only a first depressed reaction, as I recognised by scribbling alongside this quatrain:

"Have you ever been lonely? Have you ever been blue?"

I was amused to find how radical these young aristocrats were, how ready to toy with Communism, how confident that they knew the mind of the average worker; whereas the predominantly lower middle class students of Glasgow were intensely conservative, or at best liberal, and certainly did not idealise a working class that they knew at first hand. It was also revealing to see how much political sympathies rested on temperament and taste rather than on reasoned arguments, still less on any programme of action (except for the seizure of power) or analysis of the measures that might improve the functioning of the system as a whole.

At Glasgow I had been a liberal (though never a member of the party or even of the student association, because I could see that the Liberals, thanks to Keynes, had at least some idea as to the *mechanism* of social and economic change, and how government could use its power to manage the economy if so minded. The Labour party seemed to me to be visionary and quite unprepared for the tasks of social and economic management; and the events of 1931 had confirmed me in this belief. To my mind, the choice was between Liberalism of the kind that both parties in due course adopted in one form or another) and Communism. Had I been thinking of a political career I might well have opted for Communism from sheer self-interest; and I could well understand the appeal of this form of religion for those who regarded themselves as pre-destined high-priests. But to an economist it offered little unless capitalism collapsed or the danger of a fascist dictatorship made it necessary to choose between almost equally unattractive alternatives.

The years around 1935 were without equal in the number of distinguished economists who graduated from Cambridge. Among those who completed their degrees between 1934 and 1936 were Richard Stone, who was to become a Nobel-prizewinner; Brian Reddaway, who later more or less ran clothing rationing during the war; and Bryan Hopkin, who would later be chief economic adviser to the government.

Research students, of whom I was one, were few. But many able foreigners were attracted to Cambridge to study economics under Keynes and the other distinguished economists who were members of the Faculty. Most of them, even if they had a degree, came as undergraduates. There was a large contingent of Canadians, including Bob Bryce, who went on to become a power in the Canadian government as deputy minister of finance; Lorie Tarshis, who taught for many years at Stanford before returning to the University of Toronto; and Harry Wolfson, who was to become economic adviser to Ben Gurion in Israel, and came as a research student, as did Walter Salant, who later became a member of the Brookings Institution in Washington D.C. V.K.R.V.Rao, or Alphabet Rao as someone later christened him, became successively Minister first of Transport and later of Education in India and founded not only the Delhi School of Economics but *two* institutes of economic growth in his home country. Rao came to stay with me in Lesmahagow one vacation, giving that village its first startled sight of an Indian face.

The friendships I formed at Cambridge have been a major influence in my life. I mixed with fellow Scots in the Four Airts (a Scottish word meaning "points of the compass") Club for graduates of the four Scottish universities, attending St Andrew's Nights and Burns Dinners which were addressed by some Scottish Master of a college or a distinguished Scottish don. On one occasion Hugh Carmichael, who later ran Dounreay nuclear power station, clambered on to the table after the dinner and recited the whole of Tam O'Shanter with gusto.

Most of my Cambridge friends came from abroad. Five of my closest friends, then and for the rest of our lives, were Wolfson, Bryce, Salant, Rao — and Hans Singer, who arrived from Istanbul as a research student shortly after I did and eventually became perhaps the best known economist in the less developed countries. Matthew Arnold says somewhere that intellectual associations are the most lasting and so I have found. It is often the friends one makes at University that continue longest.

When we arrived, Cambridge had no living PhD in economics, not even among the Fellows. There had been one, G.T. Jones, who produced a study (later a book) on "Increasing Returns to Scale", but he was dead, run over, so it was said, by a bus in Germany. None of the dons had a PhD. Only one other Cambridge student took a PhD in economics before I took mine: Ronald Walker, an Australian who became economic adviser to the Tasmanian government and then an ambassador in later life. When Walker was awarded the degree in the spring of 1933, the research students clubbed together to celebrate this token of better things by holding a dinner for him. Not more than half a dozen PhDs in the subject had been awarded by the outbreak of war in 1939, including one to Hans Singer and one to V.K.R.V.Rao.

The list of those teaching economics at Cambridge in the years I was there is a pantheon of the founders of the discipline. Keynes was lecturing each Michaelmas (autumn) term from the proofs of his "General Theory" and Dennis Robertson, Richard Kahn, Joan Robinson, Colin Clark, Gerald Shove and Professor A.C. Pigou were all on the syllabus. Dennis Robertson, in spite of his sharp wit and the trouble he took to make sure that what he said was up-to-date, gave us lectures on money that were full of detail and rather prosaic. Richard Kahn was lecturing on the short period (the opposite of the long-term, on which so much of 19th century economics had concentrated) and showed a self-confidence not altogether in keeping with his diffident efforts to find out our reaction as we walked back with him afterwards. Joan Robinson was beautifully articulate and logical in spite of increasingly evident pregnancy. Shove and Pigou were, in different ways, the best lecturers of the lot: lucid and anxious to ensure that their audience understood what they were saying. Colin Clark was undoubtedly the worst: he faced the blackboard and talked inaudibly to it.

Gerald Shove, who was such a perfectionist that he could rarely be induced to publish, was a rather solemn lecturer, but he provided us with amusement through the numbers of waistcoats he wore. Every now and again he would tug one down, concealing the others for a few minutes. But the outer layers would then creep up and one waistcoat after another would come into view — although we were never sure of the full score. His wife, Fredegond, whom we never saw, was a poet and a daughter of F.L.Maitland, the distinguished Victorian legal historian. She kept cats in such number that Shove was said to stay out of their way in embarrassment.

Shove's technique was to turn half of each lecture into a resumé of what he had said in his last lecture, and the other half into an exposition that would in its turn be summed up in the next. So progress was slow. But as he was recasting the whole of micro-economics this was no disadvantage. What he had to say about the play of competition was, in its way, just as profound as what Keynes had to say about full employment. It seemed to me to take in most of what mattered in Mrs Robinson's revolutionary views on the workings of competition, without getting lost in geometry. He never wrote a book, but his work might still command attention if it were published now. The exposition of these matters in my textbook, most of it written in 1938–39, owes much to Austin Robinson but, less obviously, at least as much to Gerald Shove.

Of the younger dons, two were particularly helpful to me. One was Duncan Burn, an industrial economist who wrote copiously and later became industrial correspondent on *The Times*. He appeared to be something of an outsider: he was not attached to any college and lived some way out of Cambridge in the Gog hills. He and his wife helped me to come to terms with Cambridge without being bowled over by the latest development in economic theory and to learn to couple theory with observation. Long after I left Cambridge, I found him an invaluable guide to the state of British industry, and drew extensively on his knowledge in the 1960s after I entered the Treasury.

In some ways, though, it was Colin Clark who gave me most help. I had embarked, like him, on trying to marry economics and statistics before econometrics existed and was trying to fashion, from imperfect material, evidence on the way the economic system worked. The imperfect material had to be eked out by plausible theories which in turn had to be reconciled with the statistical data. That required a certain amount of boldness and an acceptance of Keynesian ideas as a framework. Colin was bolder than I — sometimes, I thought, too bold — but I had a wider knowledge of the literature, especially in international economics. So he was just the man to give me the necessary encouragement.

I think I adopted him as my supervisor, but am not certain whether this was ever formally confirmed. At first I was assigned to Pigou and summoned to see him half way through my first term. The summons was conveyed on an illegible postcard which, fortunately, had "King's College, Cambridge" printed on it. This helped me to interpret the hieroglyphics at the end of the scribble as A.C.P., Pigou's signature. It appeared to be an invitation to come at 4pm to his rooms, but whether on a Tuesday or Thursday I could not decide and never discovered, since I took the precaution of calling on the first day possible. Pigou expressed no surprise, nor did I risk reproof by unnecessary inquiry.

Of that interview and the one that followed in Hilary (spring) term, two things remain in my mind. At the first he asked whether I had a good memory, and went on, "I have a memory like a sieve. Yesterday, for example, I spent my morning correcting the proofs of my new book ["The Theory of Unemployment", a highly mathematical treatment] and when I had finished I went out for a walk. When I tried to find the proofs after lunch, I couldn't find them anywhere. I didn't want the bother of correcting another set because they were full of mathematical symbols and not easy to get right so I racked my brains to think where I had put them. Then it occurred to me that I had thrown something in the waste-paper basket. When I looked, it was empty. But this meant that it had been cleared, so I made further inquiries. In the end I had to insist on the midden being raked, and sure enough, they found the proofs."

On the next occasion when he returned to me a copy of my undergraduate thesis, which I had revised extensively over Christmas, I was curious to see whether he would comment on a chapter critical of his own views on the transfer problem. He made no comments on any part of the thesis, but contented himself with recommending me to develop a theory of my own to serve, as he put it, as a vice. "It's easy", he pointed out, "to criticise the views of other people, but you should have a view of your own. You need a vice", he said, causing me to gape: "a vice to take a grip of the relevant material. You should concentrate on making a vice for that purpose."

It was advice which I did not follow. But reflecting on the controversial issue whether an outflow of capital turned the terms of trade against the country exporting the capital I came in the end to a theory in terms of what would now be called "expenditure-switching" and developed a new concept which I called "the elasticity of transfer", measuring the ease with which resources could be transferred from meeting domestic demand to improving the balance of payments. I found that some of my ideas had been anticipated by Roland Wilson, an Australian; but I concluded that most of those who had written on the transfer problem had asked the wrong question, since they excluded from consideration whether a capital flow in one direction might not initiate a flow in the opposite direction, greatly reducing the net transfer of capital; and I suspect that this remains true of those who have written since the 1930s.

What I did conclude was that high theory was not my forte; and this was also Dennis Robertson's judgment when I came to take leave of him in 1935. "You should write a book on the building industry," he said. "But avoid theory: that isn't your line." I should like to have followed the first part of his advice. But there were many other more important things to do. I resented the second part all the more because I knew that it was well-founded.

## Keynes

I was already a Keynesian when I came to Cambridge, although not without reservations, since I thought him unsound on the transfer problem (the question whether, if you transfer capital from one country to another, you shift the terms of trade against the first country). In my first week, Dennis Robertson invited me to tea, and I found myself talking to C.R.Fay, an economic historian, Gerald Shove and other economists when Keynes entered and I listened, overawed, to the subsequent discussion. Much of it dealt with pig-rearing in Russia and the problems of artificial insemination in breeding — not a subject on which I felt able to contribute. Fay tried to make me feel at ease by asking after his friend W.R.Scott, my professor at Glasgow. I made some replies that must have sounded a little churlish. The main outcome of the occasion for me was an invitation to attend the first meeting of the "Keynes Club".

It was Keynes's practice at that time to come down from London for the weekend, carry out his duties as Bursar of King's College on Saturday, lecture at noon on Mondays in Michaelmas Term, hold meetings of his "Club" on Monday evenings and return to London on Tuesday morning. The meetings of the club were held in his room in King's College at 8.30 pm and were attended by dons and selected students. A paper was read to the club that might be by an undergraduate, one of the Cambridge dons, a distinguished visitor or, on rare occasions, by Keynes himself. The undergraduates were usually the young flyers, although there were some who must have been included on grounds of promise rather than scholastic achievement. How the dons were selected or invited, I do not know. No ladies were present except that Mrs Tappan Holland, a Fellow of Girton and a lecturer in economics, once read a paper. Pigou never appeared. Sometimes Keynes brought visitors: it was at a meeting of the club that I first set eyes on R.H.Tawney, the economic historian, who sat silent throughout, and gave no sense of the fire that burns in his writings.

The organisation of the club was in the hands of Richard Kahn, and he it was who, once we had assembled, came round with a bunch of slips from which each undergraduate had to draw one and, if it contained a number, speak, however briefly, from the hearth at the conclusion of the paper. It was in a very real sense baptism by fire. One had to stand, back to the blazing fire, facing the circle of dons and undergraduates with Keynes in an armchair on one's right. He would sit slumped with legs stretched well out, much as he appears in David Low's well known cartoon of him, except that he put each hand up the sleeve of the other arm.

The six undergraduate speakers were followed by any dons who chose to take part. I recall little of what they contributed, except Dennis Robertson's description in 1933 of the world depression as a "sloom followed by a bump." Keynes himself usually said little, if anything, until he came to wind up. But now and again he would intervene. Once, when somebody describing the dilemmas of American policy remarked that Rexford G.Tugwell (a member of Roosevelt's Brains Trust) was on a razor's edge, Keynes interjected like a flash, "Then there will soon be two Tugwells."

I gave, in different years, two papers, both on investment, to the club. Keynes commented, I remember, that all my calculations were done in terms of gross investment, rather than net: he had noticed that this was something that everybody who worked on capital theory tended to do. Keynes read a cut version of his memoir on Malthus, one of a number of essays on economists that he wrote. Gerald Shove read a paper on methodology which, as with nearly all his work, he was reluctant to publish. Among

Alec Cairncross by the Cam, Trinity College, Cambridge,
Spring 1934.

others whom we heard were two Australian economists returning from the Ottawa Conference in 1933, which heralded the introduction of extensive import duties in the British Commonwealth; and Ronald Walker, who demonstrated that wage cuts were no solution to the unemployment problem. Hubert Henderson, author of "Supply and Demand", the most successful textbook on economics at the time, gave a paper attacking public works as a cure for unemployment. Henderson, an old colleague of Keynes, was to become his chief critic.

Keynes's summing up was always the high point of the evening. It invariably contributed some new reflection but also conveyed a sense of measured judgment that made us feel very immature. A few of the things he said remain in my memory. He was emphatic, for example, that the future lay in a mixed economy, not one in which the State either played a very limited part or sought to take sole charge as in a Communist regime. At the same time, he thought it a pity that Germany had not "gone Bolshie" after the first world war, since this would have been a more interesting test of what Communism could do than the experience of Soviet Russia. Of the two great communists of the 19th century, it was Engels who commanded his admiration. Engels, he maintained, had given Marx his ammunition and had the more original mind.

After 1933 the attendance of dons seemed to decline and there was a time in 1935 when Keynes was away and meetings were held in Dennis Robertson's rooms in Trinity College. One of these meetings was on wheat and, as the discussion of wheat prices became increasingly zany, I felt compelled to draw attention to the paradox that "only the consumers want to pay high prices for wheat".

Some other glimpses of Keynes stay in my mind. I remember his account of his method of working when he entertained Bryan Hopkin and myself to lunch, early in 1935. "I don't really start", he said, "till I get my proofs back from the printer. Then I can begin writing in earnest." There was talk of Bagehot, partly because he had asked me if I could tell him where to find the Victorian saying (which I had quoted): "John Bull can stand many things but he can't stand two per cent." When I commented on Bagehot's sagacity, Keynes said, "It was native to him. He had a feel for the way things work."

I also remember Hans Singer's description of Keynes coming down to breakfast chortling over the answer he proposed to send to those who kept thrusting their books on him. "Mr Keynes thanks Mr X for sending him his book and will lose no time in reading it."

Keynes's lectures were attended by about 100 students from all over the world, many of them prominent later in public life. In those years he was busy on "The General Theory", and although I heard him in three successive years, I had no feeling that he was repeating himself. He was an excellent lecturer, speaking conversationally and with lucidity, and interspersing his arguments with forays into history and philosophy. One such foray dealt with originality in economics, prompted by some reference to David Ricardo and W.Stanley Jevons. New ideas, he said, never had the precision that later critics assigned to them when they came to define their terms. They were apt to be like balls of wool, fluffy and with no sharp edges, and the relations between concepts were equally woolly when first perceived. Intellectual rigour of the Ricardian type was apt to get in the way of original thinking.

The presence of Keynes at Cambridge attracted a number of figures from elsewhere. Some of them came to address the Marshall Society. Often the speakers were not themselves professional economists but business men or holders of public office. I heard Gordon Selfridge with some disrespect because there seemed to be no intellectual content to his talk and a great deal about what he owed to his mother. Later, we had Major C.H.Douglas, the originator of Social Credit (a doctrine asserting that there was a chronic shortage of purchasing power). He was pursued round a circle of argument by Abba Lerner, then a student at the L.S.E, who happened to be in the audience, ending up, to our amusement, with the original proposition from which Douglas had been dislodged at the beginning of the argument.

Other visitors came to the Sunday morning seminar which the graduate students set up for themselves. Some L.S.E. economists joined us, Abba Lerner among them; they were intensely interested in what Keynes was thinking. These joint Sunday morning seminars were to continue at least until the second world war. With the L.S.E. students we launched the *Review of Economic Studies*, which still exists, in spite of Joan Robinson's derisive reference to it as "the children's newspaper.

The most colourful visitor to our seminars was Louis B. Zapoleon, an American who had been a member of the US Tariff Commission with rimless pince-nez, a large square face, a large square body, jet-black hair and a lisp. He was roughly double the age of the research students whom he took up with, and full of stories about his irresistible attraction for the opposite sex. He had played Alekhine, then the world champion, at chess, and when I once ventured to take him on with the advantage of a rook, he mated me in just over ten moves.

He came to Cambridge — nobody seemed to know why — and King's College was kind enough to give him the use of their guest room. Zapoleon took this hospitality for granted, and when he was obliged by the college to vacate the room after a day or two, he could think of no other explanation but Keynes's unease at the proximity of a possible rival. Rival he certainly was not: his contribution to discussion at our seminars invariably took him into illustrations from his experience on the U.S.Tariff Commission, many of them preceded by the injunction: "Let us take the case of the lowly cocoa bean."

Long before my dissertation was submitted I had to think what to do next. But there was no need to think very hard. In the spring of 1935 I received a request from J.W.Nisbet, one of the two lecturers in economics at Glasgow, asking me to help out for a term by replacing the other lecturer there, Alec Macfie, while he was having an operation. Shortly after my return to Cambridge I had another letter from Nisbet. It told me that he had been appointed to a lecturership at St Andrews and that he had been commissioned to ask whether I would be willing to take his place in Glasgow. This meant starting as a full lecturer — a very rare thing at any time — at a salary of £440 a year, and appointment simultaneously to a lectureship at the West of Scotland Agricultural College worth a further £150 a year. Thus before I had my PhD I was due to start academic life with a total salary of nearly £600 a year: an income that was equal to about four times the wage of an average manual worker at that time and that for a single man spelled greater affluence than any income I have earned since.

Meanwhile my dissertation was less advanced than I had hoped. I had given little thought to its shape and taken far too few notes of my reading. Instead I had concentrated on the writing of the theoretical part, which was never published, and on the preparation of key statistical series. There was, therefore, a great deal of writing still to be done and this took me well into August 1935, with lecturing at Glasgow due to start early in October.

The theme of my dissertation, " British Home and Foreign Investment 1870–1913", had been in my mind since 1933 and was the subject of a paper to the Keynes Club. I submitted it in five parts, of which the fifth had already appeared in *The Review of Economic Studies* as "Did Foreign Investment Pay?" The first part was on the theoretical aspects of capital investment (including an appendix on the capital transfer controversy); the second was on the capital market; and the third contained the nub of the matter: an analysis of the behaviour of home and foreign investment before the first world war and their interactions with one another.

The starting point of all this was a point that has struck me again and again: that if an economist says that A causes B, he ought always to ask, what if it is the other way round and B causes A (or conceivably that A and B are both caused by something else)? The common impression that higher investment is what makes for higher income is far less true, for example, than the alternative proposition that higher income makes for higher investment. In the same way, when Taussig devoted so much time to demonstrating that capital outflows turned the terms of trade against an investing country, I concluded that his evidence might just as well establish the converse: that a country like the United Kingdom might be more prone to export capital when the terms of trade moved against it. This was perhaps just as much an over-simplification as Taussig's; but at least it served as a hypothesis that provided a perspective on the past.

The dissertation was duly submitted, and my examiners, Claude Guillebaud, a nephew of Alfred Marshall, and Roy Harrod (the external examiner from Oxford), made a favourable report. It satisfied them but it did not satisfy me, and I made up my mind to give it a thorough overhaul before publication. But it was 1953 before the central parts of it were published, hurriedly revised in the middle of other duties. For the moment, Glasgow beckoned, and I began my career as a lecturer.

## 5

## *The Birth of a Textbook: Glasgow 1935–39*

The doctorate thesis which I completed and submitted in August 1935 was effectively the product of two years' work, since I did little research for it in my first year at Cambridge. Once I started lecturing at Glasgow, I had no time to prepare it for publication. What I did not foresee was that it would go into cold storage until 1951, when I at last returned to academic life after the War and was able to find a publisher to bring it out in 1953 as "Home and Foreign Investment: 1870–1913".

My time at Glasgow was to result in, among other things, the publication of another book of quite a different sort. I found "digs" in Glasgow near the University and got down at once to preparing my lectures for the winter. At that time the other staff in Political Economy consisted of Professor Scott, then aged 65; and Alec Macfie (who was 12 years my senior). There were three classes at different levels, and the professor taught all of them. The lecturers took over only when he was away — as he often was, at short notice. In addition, Macfie and I shared responsibility for a class in economics for accountants which met down town at 5.15 four evenings a week. I held a further appointment at the West of Scotland Agriculture College where I taught a little farming history and gave a course in agricultural economics.

As it happened, Macfie had repeated spells of illness[1] deriving from his war service, which prevented him from taking the accountants on any of the nine lecture courses that I gave between October 1935 and the end of 1939. So I had a heavy

---

[1] He suffered from stomach ulcers, had one perforation after another until finally he had to have his stomach removed entirely — an operation duly reported in the medical journals as he was the first in this country to undergo it.

load, and it was quite a tight fit. I might find myself lecturing at the University on Gilmorehill at 2pm to the Ordinary (first-year) class, catching a bus to bring me to Blythwood Square for a lecture at 3pm to the agricultural students and ending up in St Vincent Street in time to lecture to students of accountancy at 5.15pm. I can remember one week when I delivered 17 one-hour lectures in all.

On top of that was the work of correcting and marking, which fell entirely to the lecturers. There was an Ordinary Class of about 150 who wrote two class essays and two class examination papers in term time (and, of course, a university-degree examination). The essays could be very lengthy: some ran to 80 pages of foolscap, and none were typed. It was not enough merely to put a mark at the end. Comments were expected and a short verdict to go with the mark. I can remember also engaging in a little research before returning one essay with quotation marks at the beginning and end in lieu of criticism.

In terms of physical strain, the low point was usually in March, before the Easter vacation. The Glasgow winter, with its wind and rain and long, dark nights, could be trying — it rained pretty well every day throughout my first term in 1935 — and one could usually reckon on at least one dose of flu before the spring. In my second or third year I fell a victim to Bell's Palsy, which freezes one side of the face and makes it necessary to talk out of one side of one's mouth. I first suspected something was wrong just before I was due to lecture on purchasing-power parity, and by the time I had made repeated attempts to articulate that phrase I was convinced of the need for medical attention.

The Ordinary class, while enjoyable to teach, did not offer the same scope as the classes for which I had full responsibility. The practice afforded me by the class of accountants was particularly valuable. I found myself with the task of conveying to young students of accountancy (many of them, however, older than myself) the elements of economics in forty lectures over ten weeks. By the time the lectures began, the accountants had already done a full day's work and were correspondingly lethargic. When I went in to give my first lecture I was ready to give up in fright and wondered how one could possibly find enough to say to fill the hour. I had written some notes which I dictated and then developed, and found that the hour was not as long as I had feared.

As time went on, I soon found that I had far more to say than the time allowed. I gave up dictation, and instead handed out a mimeographed one-page summary of what I proposed to say and distributed it at a charge of a penny a lecture to cover costs. This had an added advantage. Instead of taking notes which (to judge from examination papers) were a travesty of what I said, the young accountants could have an accurate record to consult in their more wide-awake moments. They might then catch the drift of an argument that had escaped them. In any event they would be free to concentrate entirely on the lecture instead of trying, in a somewhat comatose state at the end of a busy day, to combine listening and summarising. I knew that most of them would read no text book and that their understanding of economics was based exclusively on what they heard in 40 hours of lecturing. The marvel was that they learned anything at all and, to tell the truth, most of them learned very little, especially about the economic theory of cost. I, however, learned much from teaching them, and from the first-hand experience on which the accountants could draw in answering examination questions. Indeed, I used some of their illustrations of a point in industrial economics when I came to write my textbook.

I have never in later years come in contact with any of the hundreds of Glasgow accountants whom I taught except on one occasion in the House of Lords. I found myself opposite a noble lord who happened to mention that he had taken his training in accountancy in Glasgow and, later, that he had been born in Hong Kong. I knew at once that he was a son of Field Marshal Lord Milne: I had published a study of the social origins of Glasgow accountants and recalled that only one had any association with Hong Kong. I was also sure that he had won a prize and this he confirmed. But he was so vague as to who taught him economics that I did not disclose to him my part in his education.

At the University the classes in economics included many who later won distinction. The first year class was often taken by students in some other subject who might be contemplating a career in the civil service or the church or in business. Several became professors; some were killed in the war. The honours class experienced a kind of four-year cycle with a bumper crop in 1932, 1936 and 1940. I look back on these years with some bewilderment, since there is no obvious explanation: not even the strong tendency for good students to interact and provide opportunities and incentives for one another to work harder.

Apart from teaching, I took part in a number of extra-academic activities during these years before the War, of which the most important was my chairmanship of a Conciliation Panel of the Co-operative Union. The Union was the management side of the retail and wholesale Co-operative movement in their negotiations with their staff; if negotiations could not resolve a matter, it was submitted to the Conciliation Panel for a binding decision.

The Panel included some impressive and forceful characters, such as Baillie Elgar, a Glasgow councillor who placed great emphasis on fairness. There must have been times when he found me rather green: it was my first experience both of conciliation and of chairmanship and I found I had much to learn. For instance, I discovered the complexity of wage structures: change one wage, and there was an impact on many others. The issues of principle were of great interest to me as an economist: for example, the principle of fairness, so hard for economists to interpret in concrete terms, plays a huge part in wage settlements. The differences of opinion that the panel had to resolve brought home to me forcibly the complexities of the labour market and of industrial relations even within the co-operative movement.

### Grand Tour: America, summer 1936

I had agreed with my Canadian friend from Cambridge, Bob Bryce, to join him at Harvard in the summer of 1936 and accompany him on the tour of the United States which, as a Commonwealth Fellow, he was required to make at the end of his first year. At the end of May, I sailed on the Corinthia for Boston and New York.

It was a great adventure to make a long sea voyage, and I can still vividly recall the excitement of seeing land again after ten days as we came into Boston harbour. To travel by air seems in comparison so banal, so incapable of producing that mounting expectation and gradual surrender to the foreignness of things. As the horizon became defined and the coast separated itself from it, we could see fields, then roads, then vehicles on the roads and finally, with the same access of curiosity as Columbus must have felt, human beings.

My curiosity was indulged soon after I landed by a taxi-driver who revealed many of the habits I expected to find in Americans. As we drove through Boston he proved to be a veritable handbook of official statistics, telling us the width of the road, the height of the buildings, the cost of gilding a dome here or erecting a skyscraper there. I had never encountered anything like it.

Bob Bryce had made all preparations for our trip, including the purchase of a large V8 Ford car, a tent and other camping equipment. But as he still had work to do at Harvard, we did not set off at once. This was just as well, because I did not have a driving licence, and it was generally held that Massachusetts licences were given only after very stiff driving tests. In the meantime, on a weekend visit to Vermont, I had no sooner taken over the driving from Bob than I dented the front fender by running on to a verge and hitting a rock. This made it apparent, particularly to Bob's sister who was in the back of the car, that no passenger who valued his life would ever let me drive him. It was no use my protesting that I had never driven anything with a quarter of the power of the Ford. I was obviously in need of driving lessons and these, on my return to Harvard, I proceeded to take.

My instructor took me over the course again and again and I persevered in making every imaginable mistake: stalling, turning left when asked to turn right, taking turns far too wide, etc, etc. At the end of the course the instructor, thankful to have survived, wished me luck in a mournful voice as if it was likely to be the other fellow who would need the luck.

On the day of the test I was on my mettle. Bob, who had agreed to come with me, looked at me with some consternation. "You can't go like that," he said. "You must wear a tie." I protested that driving a car and wearing a tie were separate activities but he insisted on taking me to a nearby store and buying me a red tie which, worn with a blue shirt, looked a little like litmus paper emerging from a bowl of acid. However, it stood me in good stead. For, while I managed by luck to avoid most of my usual mistakes, it was clear that the tester was not impressed by my driving. I explained to him that I was on a visit to the U.S. and that my share of the driving would be confined to the open road. He looked at me hesitantly, took in my tie, remarking, "Yes, you'd better keep to the wide open spaces," and then handed me my driving licence. So when puzzled friends asked later how I contrived to have a Massachusetts licence, I pointed to my tie as a sufficient explanation.

We drove thousands of miles round America: south to New Orleans and across the Mexican border, west to Los Angeles and San Francisco, north to Portland and east to Detroit, finishing at Bob's home in Toronto.

It was for me the equivalent of the 18th century Grand Tour. We visited factories, museums and great works of construction like the Grand Coulee Dam in Oregon. We went from one National Park to another, including Bryce (inevitably, but no relation), Zion and the Grand Canyon. We made a pilgrimage to Bob's boyhood home in Silverton, Colorado. We dined at Antoine's, then the grandest restaurant in New Orleans. We drove over mountain passes in the Rockies and across plains and deserts. And of course we talked: with businessmen, with officials, with casual strangers and old friends. It was an education of the most agreeable kind but an education all the same. I came to look back on it as of at least as much value as anything I had learned at school or university.

It was an election year, and we heard much from the businessmen we met of their hatred for Roosevelt. Had we judged from out contacts around the country, we should have expected Alf Landon, the Republican candidate, to romp home. But of course he did nothing of the kind. The experience came back to me in 1956 when Douglas Jay, President of the Board of Trade in a later Labour government, told me that he found it possible to predict the result of Presidential elections with consistent accuracy so long as he stayed in Britain but found it much harder when he was in America.

It was also the time of WPA (the Works Projects Administration), TVA (the Tennessee Valley Authority) and all kinds of other initials that were born in the slump. There seemed to be great new dams going up all over the country — Fontana, Chickamauga, Boulder, Grand Coulee — and we saw most of them under construction. In Chattanooga, Tennessee, we talked with a trade union organiser about race relations on his site — that being the hot subject of the era. We got him to write down his name when we left. It read:

Cardinal Wolsey
Chickamauga Dam,

Chattanooga,
Tennessee.

As we drove south, we saw cars of every vintage, often with the family belongings piled on top. We gave lifts to a succession of hitchhikers, some of whom I remember vividly: two old people from Eastern Tennessee who spoke an English we hardly understood — probably Elizabethan — and described with a kind of placid relish Saturday nights in the village with the knives out; a girl carrying a baby in her arms and a small suitcase, who was making a journey of over 1,000 miles on her own; and a Mormon missionary who casually assured us that he had seen God.

Many other details of American life intrigued me. Prohibition had gone by 1932 but traces of it lingered on. There were states like Tennessee where one could not even have a beer in the ordinary way, while in other states there were no restrictions of any kind on the sale of liquor. Air-conditioning, which was completely new to me, was already well-established in the south, particularly in hotel coffee-rooms. At the height of summer I found it hard to imagine how it had been possible to maintain the pace of American life without it.

What I learned most from our trip were the different aspects of a large industrial economy. Bob had been furnished with introductions to people all over America, either by friends and relatives or by the Commonwealth Fund, and we took full advantage of these introductions. One day we would be talking to Lauchlin Currie, an adviser at that time at the Federal Reserve Board in Washington, D.C, while he explained to us that it was part of his duty to keep the "cranks" file — a record of people who wrote in with odd ideas on monetary policy; on another day we would be visiting the San Francisco or Chicago Stock Exchange; on yet another, we would be going round the Ford plant at Deerborn.

I had been brought up to believe that, while we in Britain went on using old machinery long after it was obsolete, Americans were ruthless in scrapping it and would use nothing but the latest and best. It was immediately obvious that this was nonsense, and that American equipment was often just as old as ours. I have never seen such ancient motor cars. Figures showed that the average age of American locomotives was much the same as in

Britain. I saw an oil-refining plant that was 20 years old when everyone agreed that this was one of the industries in which obsolescence was very rapid. When we entered Pabst's brewery in Milwaukee, the first thing we saw was a huge condensing machine which we were told had been installed in 1841 — and the management had no thought of replacing it.

At the end of our journey, when we reached Toronto, there was a further industrial tour. Bob and his father travelled north to Kirkland Lake where men of different nationalities were mining gold. We were shown over one of the deep mines and, on our way back, over the International Nickel mine at Sudbury. All this gave me an education in industrial technology and a sense of what life in a large enterprise was like.

### "Introduction to Economics"

In 1938 I started work on an elementary textbook. It was not my idea; I was approached by the Glasgow School of Accountancy. This body conducted correspondence courses in economics, and wanted a more up-to-date textbook to recommend to their students. At that time, there were no really good textbooks available. University students were asked to read "Elements of the Economics of Industry" by Alfred Marshall, which was half a century old and quite unsuited to beginners, or perhaps the two-volume edition of Taussig's "Principles of Economics". To anyone educated in modern economic theory, these and similar works were pre-Keynesian and therefore out of date.

I explained that, while I saw the need for a new textbook, I had to give priority to my research (including revision of my Cambridge dissertation). It was put to me that all that was wanted was the publication of the textbook I had already written — i.e., the summary sheets that I handed out to my accountancy students. This so appalled me that I asked what text was in current use. The volume they showed me was crammed with errors, or unintelligible and almost unreadable. I was so taken aback that such stuff should pass for economics that I changed my mind at once. I agreed to prepare a textbook in return for an assurance that the School of Accountancy would take 2,000 copies a year (an assurance of which nothing more was heard).

I made good progress and was within a chapter or two of finishing by September 1939. At that point I set the book aside for several years. About the end of 1942 or early in 1943 I contrived to find time in the evenings to scribble some extra pages and round the book off. It was published late in 1944.

By then, I had had a difference of opinion with my publisher, Butterworth's. They had been the choice of the School of Accountancy, and I had accepted them under the illusion that they were Thornton Butterworth, the publishers of the Home University Library. As I learned later, my textbook had been seen by the chairman of Butterworth's as the opening move in the transformation of a legal and medical publisher into the McGraw Hill of British publishing. Unfortunately the chairman with these ambitions died in the war, and I was left to deal with a publisher's representative who was new to the job. When I asked him how many copies were being printed, he said: "Two thousand. But I doubt whether it will sell as many. Nobody coming back from the war will want to study economics." I told him that he had got his decimal point wrong, but that if *he* thought sales would not exceed 2,000, no doubt that was what would happen. What was the largest number of copies sold of any book that Butterworth's had ever printed? The answer was that a book on bankruptcy had sold 15,000. I assured him that this would be comfortably exceeded, and he doubled the printing order.

Over the years, the book, published as "Introduction to Economics", went through six editions. It was, in effect, the first modern economics textbook, with the possible exception of a book by F.C.Benham which I thought rather dull and humdrum. Only when Paul Samuelson wrote his textbook, "Economics", was there a more popular competitor.

**The coming of war**
During my years in Glasgow, the outbreak of war never seemed far away. In 1935 I had gone on a walking tour in the Black Forest with a friend to celebrate the completion of my thesis. I had scruples about going to Germany at all under Hitler and by way of penance vowed to refrain from cutting any hair of my head or shaving any bristles from my chin. Nobody in Germany seemed to take it amiss and when I got back I returned to normality. I have often wondered why hair and protest should often be so closely allied.

But as the years passed, the threat increased. Manchuria had been the first demonstration of the impotence of governments confronted by unmistakable aggression. Abyssinia revealed the British government's willingness to connive and conceal — again from weakness — and awakened doubts as to its sympathies and intentions in face of the growing menace of Fascism. The reoccupation of the Rhineland in 1936 finally set the alarm bells ringing for my generation. It was one thing to see a mad demagogue in power in a disarmed Germany; but quite another to see that power grow unchallenged when there were legitimate grounds for intervening that no one seemed anxious to invoke. Not only did we let this breach of the Versailles Treaty pass, but we threw our weight against action by the French. My old Cambridge friend, Hans Singer, whose forecasts of Nazi intentions were to prove remarkably accurate, warned me not only that there would be war, but that Germany would sooner or later attack Russia.

From then on, I felt one of a doomed generation with no trust in my own government or governing class. It could be only a matter of time before we had to stand and fight or yield to the Fascists. In spite of British rearmament, the government had no stomach for a fight and seemed only too ready to accommodate the claims of Hitler.

The Spanish Civil War clinched my doubts. It was all too obviously a rehearsal for a larger operation. No issue of policy stirred my generation so much. It seemed a touchstone of the intentions of the Conservative government; and the feebleness and double-talk and apparent willingness to be deceived that was typical of British policy in the mid-1930s boded ill. The older generation would have liked to have washed their hands of the Spanish conflict instead of treating it, as we younger men did, as simply the first round in a struggle for Europe. Instead of rallying to the support of the Spanish government, Baldwin seemed to take pains to deny them aid. Non-intervention in the circumstances was not only shameful but a charade. The Italians were there in strength and the German air force was obviously using Spain as a proving ground. Their preparedness would be highly dangerous to our military prospects when it came to outright war. It was no thanks to non-intervention that Franco maintained neutrality when war did come. It was a piece of good luck on which it was not possible to reckon in advance.

Yet, although I had no confidence in the Chamberlain government, I looked for a real stand against Hitler in 1938 and was correspondingly shaken to find a first-class disaster represented as a triumph for British policy. The apotheosis of Chamberlain after Munich revealed how little the public understood what was at stake. Whatever the historians now think, the reaction summed up in one of my more melodramatic couplets still seems to me just:

"Uncrucified, you bring us others' sorrow
And shame that former gods were wont to borrow."

If we had to give way to force, it would have been wise not to represent the Munich agreement as anything else.

But the illusions of the 1930s were by no means all on one side. There were those whom the Treaty of Versailles afflicted with a sense of guilt and a readiness to extenuate appeasement, whatever form it took. There were others so carried away by claptrap that they saw no difference between Fascism and Communism and were violently opposed to the use of sanctions, rearmament and indeed any resolute action against the dictators. One had only to use the magic word "class" for the most incredible things to be accepted as fact and the most obvious truths to be heatedly denied. It was a decade of despair and self-deception blinded by lies and dogma — by far the most terrible decade of my life.

While I despaired of my own country, I despaired also of help from elsewhere. In America in 1936 there had been a detached interest in Western Europe as in a country stricken by plague. But there was no sense of involvement, no indication that the USA would lift a finger to help in the event of war. We were to be pitied and lectured; but that the US would come to our rescue a second time was unthinkable.

Similarly, it seemed futile to look to the Soviet Union. We did not know much about what was going on there, but the famine, the trials, the shooting of generals spoke of chaos and disaffection. It was obvious also that the Russians put no trust in the West and were deeply afraid of being left in the lurch. Nevertheless I did think at the time of Munich that we might have counted on them to join the Czechs in resisting Germany by force of arms. Some time later I was assured by my brother John (then in the Foreign Office) that this view was mistaken, and I expect that he was right. (I discuss his involvement in these matters, of which I was of course unaware at the time, in the Appendix.)

The forebodings of those years are now a distant memory. If I had been asked, I would have put my expectations of life pretty low, for I did not expect to survive a war. But in youth, one does not act on rational assessments of probabilities, and I lived my life as if these great clouds on the horizon would pass. However, I appeared from time to time on public platforms either in support of the admission of Jewish refugees or demanding a firm stand by the government. I was particularly horrified when I found my university willing to lend itself to an obvious piece of Nazi propaganda: the celebration of the 550th anniversary of the University of Heidelberg. A letter to the *Glasgow Herald* in protest was returned to me on the grounds of lack of space, but it was clear that it had been set up for publication and omitted because of an editorial intervention.

I also acted as Glasgow (and later Scottish) Secretary of International Student Service — the body now known as World University Service. This meant initially raising money for Chinese students seeking to continue their university studies in the disturbed conditions of pre-war China; then helping two Czech refugee students brought to Glasgow after Munich; and later making arrangements for German and Austrian student refugees directed to the Scottish universities from the English branch of ISS. The two Czechs owed their bursaries to the generosity of a Glasgow lady who was moved by a letter in the *Glasgow Herald* from Oliver Franks, who was Professor of Moral Philosophy at Glasgow at the time. How they were selected by ISS I was never told, but they were not a very happy choice. My efforts to win admission for them to the University did, however, open my eyes to some of the less attractive aspects of the profession of medicine. One was a medical student and the medical faculty refused to admit him. I tackled some of the professors, including E.P.Cathcart, a distinguished physiologist, but with little success. Cathcart seemed astonished that anyone should wish to argue for the admission of a refugee, and assured me condescendingly that when I had a family I would see things differently. Fortunately I got the Czech admission to the Anderson College of Medicine;

Alec with Frances, our first child, 1945.

but I did not forget how a mixture of nationalism and professional exclusiveness can stifle compassion and generosity of spirit.

Nearly all the German student refugees arrived in the autumn of 1938 and one or two had already moved on to the USA by September 1939. Of those who remained, some had too little money to continue their university career and so entered uncomplainingly into industrial employment. The others were distributed between the four Scottish universities. They included two who later became well-known economists, Paul Streeten and Kurt Rothschild. Streeten was originally due to come to Glasgow and Rothschild to go to Aberdeen, but when it turned out that Rothschild was married, I arranged for a switch, since Glasgow was more capable of carrying the cost. For many years, these two were the only ex-student refugees with whom I had any contact. But in the 1990s I met one who had become a professor of chemistry in London and another who had made a reasonable living in industry. Both appeared to have enjoyed a happy and fulfilling life once settled in Britain.

I had another reason to be grateful for my time with ISS. I attended two of its annual conferences, in 1938 at Nice and in 1939 at Grove Lodge, Roehampton, in west London. At the first, German representatives appeared for the first time and walked out when they took a quotation I made from the historian George Unwin to be a slighting reference to Goering (although that thought had not crossed my mind). Some of them sat at the same table as I did and peace was maintained with difficulty through the efforts of Georges Bidault, then a schoolmaster and editor of *L'Aube*, later leader of the French resistance and after the war Prime Minister of France. He had been the principal speaker on the opening day of the conference, taking as his subject the extraordinary topic of "Latin as a European language."

Bidault was not the first or last person I have met who later rose to the top in politics but at the time gave no sign of opting for a political career. Others include Tom Fraser, my old Lesmahagow schoolfellow, of whom I mistakenly thought I had heard the last when he left school to become a coal-miner; Harold Wilson, a colleague in Whitehall in 1940; and Pierre Trudeau, eventually prime minister of Canada, whom I first met in Moscow in 1952 when he was a student at the L.S.E. and a journalist writing for *Le Devoir*. The future greatness of colleagues and friends often goes unsuspected.

While the Nice conference left many memories, above all of the railway journey through Provence (my first sight of the area) in the early hours of a warm summer morning, its influence on me was of little consequence compared with the conference of 1939. For it was there that I met Mary for the first time and knew at once that I had found the answer to the most troubling question of all.

6

*The Economic Section*[1]

My first experience of government service dates from January 1940. Apart from six months on the staff of *The Economist* in 1946 when I thought I had broken away from government and was committed to a career in the private sector as a journalist, I spent the whole of the 1940s in the service of one government department or another.

I was lucky in my first appointment. It brought me into the Cabinet Office at the beginning of 1940 as a member of what became, a year later, "The Economic Section". I found myself one of a small group of professional economists at the centre of government — something altogether without precedent in Britain. As with nearly all the jobs I have done, the appointment was not of my seeking but was pressed on me in a telephone call from Austin Robinson just after Christmas 1939.

In the summer of 1939, although war was imminent, I had no idea what I would be called upon to do. When war broke out, on September 3rd 1939, I had just returned to Glasgow from a meeting of the British Association in Dundee. I had motored there in the middle of the week with some Glasgow friends in the vague hope that Mary might be there, and uncertain whether I would ever have a chance to deliver a paper on "The Finance of New Industry in Scotland" which had occupied me over the preceding months.

The paper (now lost) was delivered on the morning of Friday September 1st when news was just coming in of the invasion of

---

[1] The early days of the Economic Section are described in "An Early Think-Tank: the Origins of the Economic Section" which I contributed to the December 1984 issue of the *Three Banks Review*; and in Chapter 4 of Cairncross and Watts, "The Economic Section 1939–61: A Study of Economic Advising", (Routledge, London 1989).

Poland. It followed one by Harold Wilson on "Exports and the Trade Cycle" which drew mild criticism from Sir Arthur Bowley, a well-known statistician, largely on technical grounds. My own paper was no sooner delivered than the conference broke up. It was the last paper read to Section F for quite a number of years.

As we headed back to Glasgow that afternoon we had little doubt that war would be declared. We knew nothing of the government's hesitations, although my Czech friends kept asking me over the next couple of months why the R.A.F. didn't bomb Poland! As I walked in the blackout through the streets of Glasgow the following evening, I had no realistic notion of what lay ahead. I had been brought up on the doctrine that "the bomber always gets through" and had heard rumours of plans to receive vast numbers of corpses in the Kelvin Hall, Glasgow's large exhibition hall. My mind was full of the imminent danger that the whole of Glasgow might be blotted out, taking it for granted that Glasgow must rank high in the list of bombing targets the Germans had prepared. At the same time I felt, as many others did, a sense of release now that it had come at last to outright war and the shameful compromises of the past were over.

As I listened next morning to Chamberlain's broadcast at 11am, I asked myself what I could do while still carrying on my lecturing duties. I decided to join the Auxiliary Fire Service and did so in the first week. In the ensuing months I learned the difference between male and female couplings, the fireman's lift, and how to tie all kinds of knots. But I only once had practice in the use of a hose and am glad in retrospect that I was never called upon to put out a fire.

There was a long lull in September before term began and it was difficult to take academic research or writing with any seriousness. So I had time on my hands and went occasionally to the country for long walks. In the mood of release that I have described, I even began to learn Swedish and the violin (neither with much success), two things I had long intended and put off for lack of time.

I expected to be recruited to Whitehall sooner or later but as the months went by there was no news. In the meantime I was approached by Niven McNicoll of the Scottish Office with a suggestion that I might take charge of a kind of public opinion survey from Edinburgh to keep an official finger on the pulse of public morale. This would have involved organising reports from all over the country, to be supplied by visitors to pubs and other places, on the public attitude to various matters of interest to the government. It sounded to me like a combination of Mass Observation and a state-subsidised binge. But there was a more professional element involved. McNicoll wanted me also to start an economic information office for the Minister so that if questions arose about, say, shipbuilding capacity, I would be able to furnish the answers.

I had already agreed to start work in Edinburgh in January 1940 when I was rung up from London by Austin Robinson in late December with a pressing invitation to join him and another economist, John Jewkes, in the War Cabinet Offices as an economic assistant. He explained that Lord Stamp, who was advising the government on economic planning, had been empowered to recruit a technical staff of which he and Jewkes were the first to be appointed and that they were united on seeking to persuade me to join them.

Shortly before this a telegram had arrived from Noel Hall, professor of economics at University College, London, offering me a post as Principal in the Ministry of Economic Warfare (at a substantially higher salary). So I now had to decide between three employments, all of them offering scope to a trained economist. It did not take me long to make up my mind. I persuaded McNicoll to release me from my acceptance of the post in Edinburgh, declined the offer from Noel Hall, arranged with the University to be given leave of absence for the duration, and caught a train to London where my younger brother provided me with a bed in his flat in Warwick Square.

When I turned up on January 5th at No.8 Richmond Terrace, neither Austin Robinson nor John Jewkes was on hand. They had gone off to Harrogate to talk to the Air Ministry. It was a day or two before I found out what was going on and began to see what I might usefully do.

## The Economic Section of the War Cabinet Offices: January 1940–June 1941

The entry of economists into government in a full-time, advisory capacity dates from the end of 1939. It would be going too far to say that until then no British government had ever knowingly hired a professional economist. But it would not be very far from the truth. There might be people before 1939 who were given the title of Economic Adviser or even Chief Economic Adviser, but however often they gave vent to strong opinions on economic matters, they had rarely studied much economics. There were also one or two influential civil servants holding administrative appointments who had made contributions to economic theory; but they were unlikely to be used by the government in a professional capacity. What did not exist — and this was the really significant contrast with more recent experience — was a full-time staff at the centre of the government machine consisting mainly of trained economists and concerned exclusively with framing economic advice. The nearest to anything of that kind was the Economic Advisory Council, set up by Ramsay MacDonald when he was prime minister in 1930, which fizzled out after a year or so, leaving behind the Committee on Economic Information that emerged from the entrails and produced a long series of (unpublished) reports in the 1930s.

Since July 1939 Lord Stamp had presided over a small group of government advisers engaged in preparing a Survey of Economic and Financial Planning for the War Effort, called for short "the Stamp Survey". Their task, after the outbreak of war, assumed a new urgency and they felt it necessary to recruit a technical staff, beginning with John Jewkes from Manchester and Austin Robinson from Cambridge. This started life as the Central Economic Information Service (CEIS), blossomed in January 1941 into the Economic Section of the War Cabinet Offices, and 12 years afterwards moved to the Treasury, still labelled the Economic Section. It was this that I joined at the beginning of 1940 and served in until I left to go to the Board of Trade in June 1941.

The Stamp Survey was what would nowadays be called a "think tank". In addition to Lord Stamp, Hubert Henderson and Henry Clay, it included Francis Hemming who was both Secretary and a full member, and Piers Debenham who was Assistant Secretary. They met from time to time to consider papers submitted to them or written by one of their number. It was not at all obvious to me then, and is even more obscure now, how it was intended that the papers they wrote or commented upon were intended to influence the conduct of the war. They did not report to any Minister but could make submissions which, after consideration by a committee of senior officials, might or might not be discussed in Cabinet and lead to decisions to do something. The impression left on me was that the Survey had been set up on the lines of a small Royal Commission, had then been overtaken by the outbreak of war, and was now trying to gear itself up so as to advise on high economic policy at a pace more in keeping with the requirements of war. Looking back, I would regard the collection of papers which they circulated in 1939–40 as one of the best primers I have come across on the fundamental principles of a war economy.

The survey's staff, the CEIS, when I arrived, consisted of Austin Robinson, John Jewkes (who eventually became the first director of the Economic Section), Harry Campion (later head of the Central Statistical Office) and myself assisted by Joan Marley and Mary Stewart, but it grew rapidly as the year went on. The first, and in some ways the most important, addition was Ely Devons, who joined us from Manchester in March at the age of 26 to tackle with Harry Campion the assembly and circulation in a series of statistical digests of the secret statistics collected by government departments and the various war-time controls and official agencies.

Stamp, with whom it all began, was a formidable statistician in his own right, an ex-Director of Economic Intelligence in the Board of Inland Revenue, an ex-President of the British Association, a disciple of Keynes and Chairman of the London Midland and Scottish Railway. He was a big, benevolent, slightly corpulent figure with a round face, thick moustache and a brisk, almost breathless, delivery. He had been offered a place in the Cabinet as Chancellor and declined it. Although my contact with him was limited, he took trouble to be helpful, arranging for me to see his expert in the LMS on railway statistics and interesting himself in any papers I wrote on transport. He died in an air raid the following spring when a bomb fell on his house at Shortlands in Kent.

Some years previously Stamp had been chairman of the Economic Advisory Council. I remember hearing that he succeeded in concealing from the meeting that he had not had time to read the papers by reading them out paragraph by paragraph, calling for comment, which sometimes allowed him to gallop ahead and skip a paragraph or two. I was rarely present at any of the Survey meetings and so do not know how they were conducted, but I suspect that Hubert Henderson made most of the running.

Henderson had been editor of *The Nation* in the 1920s. He was familiar to all young economists as the author of "Supply and Demand", the first in a series called "Cambridge Economic Handbooks". I worked quite closely with him, fascinated by the logical power with which he developed and drove home a line of argument, usually with a minimum infusion of statistics, closing off one by one escape routes from the conclusion towards which the reader was relentlessly propelled. He would go off for the weekend and return with a finished, hand-written manuscript that was singularly free of deletions, insertions and other signs of hesitation.

Henry Clay, the other economist on the Stamp Survey, was the author of one of the few good elementary textbooks then available on economics, and was widely respected as an authority on industrial relations and manpower problems. In 1930 he became the first British economist to be designated Economic Adviser to the Bank of England, a post which he held until he was appinted Warden of Nuffield College, Oxford in 1944.

Francis Hemming was more of a buccaneer than a bureaucrat. He looked on us, I have no doubt, as a gang of pirates who would sally forth under his command to attack some stately permanent secretary or board some ill-managed committee. In the Spanish Civil War he had been Secretary *both* of the Non-Intervention Committee *and* of the Non-Intervention Board and had written letters in one capacity to himself in the other capacity making proposals which he then rejected for reasons propounded in his reply to himself. He married three times and explained to me once in 1940 that "a first marriage is something to be got over as quickly as possible. You need to get on to the second because that's the one that matters." In fact, his second marriage didn't last long and it was only when he married yet again, later in the war, that he arrived at a stable relationship — this time with Peggy Joseph, then a member of the Economic Section.

The Assistant Secretary, Piers Debenham, was in some ways just as unusual a civil servant as Francis Hemming. He was a son of Sir Ernest Debenham, and his family was associated with the department store of that name. He was used to associating with county families; but he was also passionately interested in economics and had done a good deal of dabbling in quantitative economic history on his own account after coming down from Cambridge where he studied under Dennis Robertson. He had been Assistant Secretary of the Economic Advisory Council more or less from its inception, just as Hemming had been Secretary, and was probably as well equipped intellectually to cope with government economic problems as any of the professional economists then arriving in Whitehall. It was Piers who taught me that I must not expect governments to pay attention to important problems — they gave priority to the urgent ones of which there were always plenty. Governments, he maintained, always thought in terms of priority when what really mattered was usually allocation. He also held that what distinguished English society was that the rich didn't fear the poor: this was fundamentally why Fascism had not "caught on".

With the fall of one country after another to the Germans, the work of the Survey faded away while the work of the staff steadily expanded. In the early summer we were joined by Lionel Robbins (who was a professor at the London School of Economics), James Meade (who later won the Nobel Prize in Economics), Evan Durbin (a junior Minister in the Attlee government after the war who was drowned in 1948) and a number of others. There was a strong Manchester contingent including Jewkes, Norman Chester (later Warden of Nuffield College, Oxford), Harry Campion, Stanley Dennison (later Vice Chancellor of the University of Hull) and Ely Devons (the keenest and liveliest mind among us). After we moved into the New Police Building, Richard Stone was added and he and James Meade began their collaboration on national income accounting. We also found a room for William Beveridge and his 24-year-old assistant Harold Wilson.

We were and remained very small in numbers — half a dozen at the beginning of the year, a dozen or so at the end of the year. So we could keep in close touch with one another's work, argue things out, develop a common outlook, maintain our spirits and interest at a high pitch, agitate. Equally, we couldn't afford passengers. Everybody had to be of unquestioned competence;

and everybody had to develop his own special interests, his own contacts and clientele. The oldest of us — Lionel Robbins and Jewkes — were in their late thirties or early forties and several of us, myself included, were in their middle or late twenties.

At an early stage, Jewkes assumed the intellectual leadership, not because he ranked as a theorist with Lionel Robbins or James Meade, but because he had the experience, assurance and administrative *nous* to direct the group. He had a boyish enthusiasm, a salty humour and above all a grasp of the practical and the significant that fitted him for the job of linking economic ideas to policy formation through an administrative machine. It was not as if there was anything very sophisticated or complex in the ideas we brought to bear. As always, it was the marketing, not the production, side of the business that was of the first importance.

One of Jewkes's strengths was his ability to command the respect and collaboration of those who worked for him, and particularly of Ely Devons, who worked closely with Jewkes. It was the genius of Devons that contributed most to what we did. That sharp, attentive mind missed little and made sure that we missed little either.

When I joined the War Cabinet Offices Duncan Burn, whom I had known at Cambridge as one of the most reliable of industrial economists, urged me to keep a diary. I thought it good advice and started, rather tentatively to keep a few notes. But my notes were among the many things in a tea-chest of possessions consigned from Lesmahagow to London in 1943 and lost on the way by the LMS Railway. Not that they contained much that was in any way secret, still less that they would have thrown much light on the workings of the Cabinet Office. The habit of diary-writing was to remain with me for most of my working life.

The War Cabinet Office in which we worked was only loosely connected with the War Cabinet, which of course we never saw. Not only was the building at 8 Richmond Terrace, in which most of the Cabinet Secretariat was housed, on the "wrong" side of Whitehall, but it was never visited by any Cabinet Minister that I can recall. It was an old rabbit-warren of a building, shared with the military side of the War Cabinet Secretariat. Until the outbreak of war it had been a private house, with an imposing exterior, a spacious entrance hall leading to a broad, marble staircase and beautiful dark red mahogany doors throughout. Converted into a suite of offices, rambling and chilly, it was far from ideal. Parts of Richmond Terrace had been used by the government before the war — it was in a vast room at No.2, previously used by Robert Peel, that I first encountered Piers Debenham — and parts remained in private hands until the outbreak of war gave the government an excuse to swoop on the wealthy "interlopers" who lived there.

I was assigned a small ex-bedroom upstairs with an empty fireplace and, from March onwards, shared it with Ely Devons. Austin Robinson shared with John Jewkes a desk that was not much larger than a tea-table so that they could not escape discussing everything together.

We moved out in the autumn of 1940 to the New Police Building, a much grander steel-framed erection next door, now part of the Ministry of Defence and at that time shared with Scotland Yard. In the winter of 1940–41, my colleagues slept happily in the basement when the blitz was at its height, unaware that they were in a highly vulnerable part of the building. Then in March 1941 we moved once again, this time to Great George Street, at the St James's Park end, into rooms formerly occupied by the Board of Trade and now the habitat of the Treasury.

Life in Richmond Terrace was a mixture of farce and tragedy. If we hadn't been able to laugh at bureaucratic foibles we should have found the strain and the frustrations intolerable. Most of all we laughed at the way the BBC handled the bad news. Things went from bad to worse so fast that cool reflection would have reduced us to a settled state of gloom. It didn't even need much reflection, for the Chiefs of Staff themselves put into circulation some pretty dire appreciations of our military prospects. Laughter was an anaesthetic.

There were moments of real tragedy too. At the beginning of June I had a call from my brother John to tell me that Bill (another brother) had died of wounds in Lancashire after evacuation from Dunkirk. It was news that affected me deeply, all the more because we had been on very distant terms for some years and I had heard nothing of him since he joined the Warwickshires. To this day I know nothing of how he came to be wounded and who brought him back. John and I caught a sleeper train to Scotland that night and next morning I woke as we neared Beattock to see a morning of unbearable beauty, with a cloudless deep blue sky above the moors. Before the funeral, the undertaker opened the coffin and for the first time I saw a dead man: the familiar face drained of blood and marked for dissolution.

Later, when the bombs fell, there were others. One morning, late in 1940, I woke under the marble staircase in the hall of 8 Richmond Terrace (where I was on fire guard) to hear the sound of a woman sobbing uncontrollably. She was a cleaner who had just been told of the destruction of her home and family. It was an incident only too common but one that I have never been able to forget. It was about this time too that a bomb on the Treasury killed some of the senior civil servants on duty. On some nights it seemed as if all London was in flames and next morning we were utterly astonished to see no sign of damage as we made our way to the Strand for breakfast.

The early months of 1940 were the peak of the phoney war period when time seemed to be slipping away and the country was only too obviously not fully mobilised. I had carefully read the writings of Arthur Salter, who had been Chairman of the Allied Maritime Transport Executive in World War I. As a result, I decided to concentrate on imports, stock-building, shipping and transport. These seemed to raise some of the central economic problems of a war economy and to provide ample scope for policy-making. It was all too obvious that submarine and air attacks might cut off our imports and bring us to our knees. So I set to work to understand the import programme, to press for the assembly of figures of stocks, to see what could be done to get more ships built, and to make contact with the key figures in the Ministries of Transport and Shipping. In particular I made inquiries about port capacity and the activities of the Shipping Diversion Room which allocated incoming tonnage to ports. The approach to East Coast ports was open to attack by air and submarine so that virtually all imports had to come in through Liverpool, Bristol and Glasgow.

From the beginning our line was that we would need all the ships we could get, that we should set out to build up stocks of imported goods, and that we should be ready with plans to make as much use as possible of whatever ports remained open. We read the unpublished history of munitions production in the first world war and I remember paying particular attention to the account given there of the debate over standard ships and the difficulties experienced in 1916–17 in trying to get the shipyards to move over to standard designs. It had been found more productive to begin with a system of repeat orders for certain types of ship rather than to standardise prematurely.

Rumours reached us from time to time (often through our military colleagues) of the unsatisfactory state of the defences in France but no one suggested that they would crumble in a month. The Norwegian campaign came as the first unpleasant shock and it was obvious that we had been caught unprepared. We began at once a series of papers for the Cabinet, "Economic Consequences of the Loss of...." which moved as the months went by from Scandinavia, to the Low Countries, then France.

But writing papers was not a very useful activity unless they were read and we wondered what notice was taken of them. This became a major question after Churchill took over in May 1940, especially as he had his own advisers, including Roy Harrod and Donald MacDougall. We were the staff of the Stamp Survey, but its work was near to an end. In practice we were largely self-directing and exerted personal influence through friends and contacts in the economic departments. We had to find some way to ensure that ministers paid attention to what we wrote. In May 1940 we christened ourselves (mainly in fun but also to give ourselves some standing) the Economic General Staff and instead of P(E and F) S(40) — i.e., Plans, Economic and Financial, Staff — put EGS(40) as the series number on our various papers. This lasted for some months but I doubt whether we persevered beyond the autumn.

After Churchill took office, we acquired a minister for the first time: the Minister without Portfolio, Arthur Greenwood. But he was rarely to be seen — I don't recall ever seeing him at 8 Richmond Terrace — and neither a very forceful nor a very sober Minister. We soon found it necessary to fall back on our old channels of communication.

We were a small group, fairly closely knit, and thrown much together by living most of the time in the office, frequently overnight. Our information of what was going on and our ideas about what ought to be done were easily pooled. We had few routine duties and formed no part of an administrative hierarchy, so that there was ample time to concentrate on the issues we had selected. Most of us had contacts in other departments, but we were not obliged to attend meetings of departmental or inter-departmental committees. We found it quicker to keep track of official thinking by reading the minutes of such meetings or by lunching with friends.

We learned as time went on that our task was less to hit on wonderful new ideas or to enunciate neglected principles so much as to get hold of the issues in debate within and between departments and lend support to what we thought right by briefing Ministers in good time. We could do this more successfully once we had the ear of the Ministers who had responsibility for resolving these issues. This was easier as time went on, because on the one hand, an increasing number of economists (or of officials who thought in economic terms) achieved positions of influence in more and more departments, and on the other hand responsibility for the co-ordination of economic policy came to be the recognised province of a single minister — the Lord President, Sir John Anderson — to whom the economists at the centre were linked as advisers and for whom they acted as a secretariat. But that did not happen until after I left the Economic Section in May 1941.

Since we were acting as a think-tank, we were free to choose issues of policy on which to work. These were inevitably rather general and interdepartmental but became gradually more specific. They ranged from the issues of imports, stock-building and shipping in which I was principally interested to problems of allocation of materials and rationing of foodstuffs and other consumer goods, the investment programme, and manpower policy. For instance I remember taking part with Harold Wilson in 1940 in a rapid Manpower Survey that involved us in a journey to Glasgow to investigate the degree of labour shortage there. We had no hand in monetary or financial policy and did not develop an interest in price policy until near the end of 1940. The main bias of our thinking was how to contract civilian claims on resources so as to leave enough for the conduct of the war: that is, it was essentially negative and not concerned with the positive organisation of resources for the benefit of the armed forces. It was partly this reflection that disposed some of us to move on in the spring of 1941.

We had plenty of opportunities to submit papers to Cabinet. In the spring of 1940 we had worked on a proposal for a 35m ton import programme at a time when that seemed very pessimistic. After the fall of France we busied ourselves with one for 8m tons, consulting experts on nutrition with a view to minimising imports of food and pushing for the replacement of bulky materials by finished manufactures. This proposal was never adopted, but it convinced us that we could if necessary ride out a submarine campaign with far less imports than had previously been thought indispensable. One aspect of the economies we contemplated was a big reduction in imports of feeding stuffs and a corresponding slaughter of pigs and poultry. We drew on advice from Professor McCance, a physiologist who had been living in the Lake District on home-grown food, with a high milk and vegetables component in his diet. We also took account of experiments at the agricultural research centre at Rothamstead that showed how much the potato crop might respond to far larger applications of phosphate.

But of course we were aware that a switch of the kind proposed would cost dollars that we did not possess. Papers were written on the comparative value of shipping and foreign exchange so as to let us judge how far to push economy in the one at the expense of the other. In the end what settled the matter was the need to cut the import programme with each fresh crisis and we simply ran out of dollars and turned to the US to see us through.

As part of my work on imports, shipping and stockbuilding, I spent, at some stage in 1940, a week or two with the Ministry of Transport. I recall a meeting with Sir John Reith, who had been Director-General of the BBC and was then Minister of Transport, at which I was treated almost with deference. I was not used at this time to dealings with Ministers but Reith seemed to me quite human in spite of his majestic bearing. He was encouraging, intrigued and, I suspect, baffled, as I outlined what I was doing.

I spent much time also with the Ministry of Shipping, talking to Sir William Elderton and P.N. ("Ha-ha") Harvey, two actuaries who were engaged for the second time in their lives in planning the use of shipping tonnage to meet an import programme. They used to offer me snuff before we got down to business and both were courteous and helpful.

In my efforts to assess importing capacity I also went to see Hector Leak, the head of the Statistics Department of the Board of Trade, whom I had met before the war and was to meet frequently when I joined the Board of Trade in 1946. He was a tall thin man with a small head, spectacles, a high stiff wing-collar and a large Adam's apple. He was an administrator turned statistician and I sometimes wondered if he had been chosen to succeed Flux, Fountain and Plummer, his three distinguished predecessors, because his name with its watery associations carried the promise of some continuity. Leak was meticulous to the point of pedantry, mild in manner and so formally dressed that one almost expected to see a quill in his hand.

One result of my visits to the Ministry of Shipping and the Board of Trade was that I established that figures showing the tonnage of shipping arriving with cargo were recorded on a ten-day basis and I arranged for these figures to be supplied and analysed. This gave us a much more up-to-date picture of the trend in the volume of imports than the figures derived from the Trade Returns. So far as I know, these thrice-monthly returns continued to be collected and used throughout the war.

In early June 1940 I made contact also with the new Ministry of Aircraft Production (at that time headed by the wayward Lord Beaverbrook) by calling on Edwin Plowden, who was chief executive of the Ministry in 1944. He was handling imports of various commodities including bauxite, and I put it to him that there might be scope for reducing shipments of bauxite over the next few months. To my astonishment he readily agreed. I had not expected any member of Beaverbrook's department to make concessions without Ministerial approval and I was all the more impressed to find someone with the honesty of mind to do the sensible thing without pressure.

Later in the year — or it may have been early in 1941 — I also spent a week in the Treasury deputising for Dennis Robertson. Dennis was trying to keep track of the balance of payments and found the work rather perplexing. I can't recall that I made any contribution to the resolution of his perplexities, nor that I was brought much into contact with Treasury officials whom I did not already know.

One of my special interests in 1940 was inland transport and the delays in rail transport occasioned by the so-called "exchange points". These were the points of intersection of the four main-line railway systems and as each railway system had engines with different characteristics, goods trains reaching these points had to wait while their engines were changed. This meant the sacrifice of through-train operations and a pile-up of scarce rolling stock of all kinds at points where enemy action might have had serious consequences. I acted as broker between John Simon (an old pupil from Cambridge) in the Mines Department and Harold Fisher, the Undersecretary responsible in the Ministry of Transport who was persuaded to investigate the situation at first hand and take action to reduce the delays.

At the end of 1940 there came a bolt from the blue that separated the economists in the Section from the statisticians. The Central Statistical Office was created out of the small group, consisting of Campion, Devons and Joan Marley, that was preparing statistical digests that we circulated. The rest of us were for the first time christened the Economic Section of the War Cabinet Secretariat. At the time we saw in the split the hand of Professor Lindeman, who was Churchill's special adviser, and suspected an effort to diminish the influence of our group on the principle of divide and conquer. This suspicion rested on a certain rivalry with the Prime Minister's Statistical Section, which included Roy Harrod and Donald MacDougall and was closely linked with the Prof. It may also have owed something to the portentous way in which the news was disclosed to us by Hemming in a meeting from which I remember emerging under the impression that we had just suffered a major setback and amused to find that Dick Stone was so little shaken that he at once resumed in mid-sentence the argument he was developing before the meeting began.

The "official" story was that Churchill had been increasingly put out to find that the figures of shipping tonnage presented to him were sometimes expressed in terms of gross, sometimes net and sometimes of deadweight tons. This had led to constant confusion in Cabinet, and had moved him to set up the C.S.O. in order to avoid arguments over figures, so beginning a separation of economists from statisticians that many in both camps had cause to regret. Initially, however, nothing much changed since we all continued to work side by side. John Jewkes became the first Director of the Economic Section and Hemming the first head of the CSO.

## Wartime London

At this time I was living with others in the CEIS in Bedford College in the middle of Regent's Park. The undergraduates (including Mary) had gone to Cambridge and the College was anxious to make use of its accommodation so as to meet the cost of maintenance. So began a curious regime in which many senior civil servants, including most of my immediate colleagues, took up residence, enjoyed an excellent cuisine in spite of war-time restrictions, and came almost to regard the College as their club. After dinner we would walk in the rose garden and assemble to listen to the news, mocking the veneer of invincible optimism that the BBC unfailingly applied to successive disasters.

The Dutch Cabinet made their appearance among us after one of these disasters and I retain a vivid picture of their Prime Minister, Professor P.S.Gerbrandy — or Cherrybrandy as we found it easier to call him — queuing up for his next course with the rest of us, looking like a small and cheerful walrus.

In June and July we prepared for the worst with some elementary fire drill, but no bombs fell on London. Then the College, for some unknown reason, decided that the students could now come back from Cambridge and that we must consequently vacate the College to allow it to be prepared for their return. We moved out to live in the office in August, and we had hardly moved when the first big raid on London took place, on 7 September. It was immediately obvious that there could be no question of re-establishing the students in London. Not long after, some incendiaries fell on the College and there was a disastrous fire which our amateur fire brigade had no opportunity of putting out.

I found refuge in 1941 in Warwick Square in a flat occupied by Peter Bauer (now Lord Bauer). There had originally been three tenants, including Bill Wade (later Master of Gonville and Caius College Cambridge) and Stanley Dennison (my colleague from the CEIS). But Bill had gone off to America on official duties and Stanley Dennison had also moved out. Peter, whose firm had migrated to Dorking "for the duration" had tried for a time to live in Dorking but preferred to return to London and travel out, as he did throughout the war, regardless of the bombing.

We were looked after by a Mrs Dormidello who, whatever failings we eventually found in her (she proved to be untrustworthy) was a most skilful cook and succeeded in producing wonderful soufflés and other delicacies from unpromising materials. We were lucky to escape any bomb damage and lived very comfortably until, with Bill Wade's return, I had to move on again — to my brother's flat in Notting Hill Gate — in early 1943.

By that time I was engaged to Mary and at the end of May 1943 we were married at her parish church in Ilkley. It was the most important event in my life. I was then 32 and Mary eight years younger. She had been brought up in Ilkley by her parents who had lived in India before the war. She was the youngest of a family of three of whom the eldest, a young surgeon of great promise, had died of Weill's disease after fishing in the Wharfe. Mary's sister Shirley, who served in the Polish Army in 1939, had been born shortly before the First World War and so was more or less a contemporary of mine while Mary was born just after it in January 1919. Since she was training as a Women's Housing Manager in the North and I was a fixture in London, we saw one another only at rare intervals and never for more than a day or two. I don't think we can have passed more than about half a dozen days in each other's company when we were married but it proved enough, as the first 50 years have shown. I am conscious that Mary has changed me both in habit and character and whatever I have been able to accomplish in life is ultimately her accomplishment.

Our first home was in a small flat at the top of 90 Lexham Gardens off the Cromwell Road in Kensington and we lived there for about a year until about a couple of months before Frances was due when we prepared to move to a maisonette at 84 Philbeach Gardens near Earls Court. We spent six weeks cleaning and furnishing it in the summer of 1944 while the V1s fell all around. In August I thought it safe to invite Mary's mother to join us for the last weeks of the pregnancy.

It was a fateful invitation. On the very first evening, 2 August, a large number of V1s were launched on London and one fell next door, killing several people. We slept in the basement in the mistaken belief that it was safer. After my mother-in-law had gone to bed I found that I had left my pyjamas in her room at the back of the house. When Mary offered to go and fetch them I rashly maintained that "Hitler won't choose to bomb us on the very night I have no pyjamas." I was awoken in the early hours by pieces of plaster falling on the bed and one that left a mark on my nose. The room was full of dust and fallen plaster but both of us were unhurt and my main problem was to find a wrap before going to the rescue of my mother-in-law. She too was uninjured but the window had been blown in, her hair was full of splinters of glass, and the heavy iron weights had been propelled from the window frame on to the bed within a foot or two of her head.

I set off rather late for the office and on my return it was arranged that we would sleep in the crypt of the church across the street. That night a record number of V1s fell on London and we seemed to hear all of them. Moreover the thought of all that masonry high above us was far more disturbing than sleeping in a basement ever was. It was not the ideal way to treat a pregnant wife or entertain a mother-in-law on her first visit to London since war began. Next day the two of them set off for Ilkley.

From then on I slept in the office after arranging for the storage of our furniture and locking up in a small basement room all our miscellaneous possessions so that I could still have access to them if required. A few weeks elapsed before I could visit the house again and I then found to my horror that the basement room had been broken open and many of our wedding presents taken. This had undoubtedly been done by ARP workers — even grand pianos sometimes went — who had been removing things that took their fancy one at a time but fortunately had not had time to take a great deal. Nevertheless when I reported the loss to Mary without quite knowing what had been taken it caused her more grief than if everything had gone through enemy action.

In due course the V1 menace disappeared but not before we heard the familiar drone once again. I had gone to Ilkley for Christmas and we were sitting quietly by the fire one evening when Mary, much to my amusement, announced that she could hear a V1 and ran to put the baby under the table for safety. She insisted that she couldn't mistake the sound, however improbable it seemed to me, and, of course, she was proved right. The newspapers next day carried the story that a V1 had come down in Lancashire after crossing the Pennines.

In the spring of 1945 I made a third attempt to find a home for the Cairncross family by renting a first floor flat at 43

Kensington Park Gardens, Notting Hill. By that time housing was not too easy to find and I have a vivid memory of talking to the owner with quite a number of others clamouring for the same flat. In the end he decided, rather to my surprise, to let me have it and we remained there until we were able to resume possession of the repaired maisonette at 84 Philbeach Gardens towards the end of 1946.

## The Board of Trade June-December 1941

But I have run on well beyond 1940. A few days after the cleavage with the statisticians I was in Liverpool as secretary of a group under Sir Cecil Weir charged with reporting on port congestion. Weir, of whom I was to see a great deal in 1941 and later, was a successful Glasgow businessman who had played a leading role in organising the Empire Exhibition at Glasgow in 1938. I found him congenial, sensible, but often a little vague. Liverpool handled about half our imports. We very quickly drafted a report — my first experience of preparing a government report — which was presented to the Cabinet, on methods of ensuring faster clearance through inland sorting and other devices.

I was interested to see the Liverpool docks because I had long thought that if the Germans had selected them as their prime target they could by continuous bombing have done more than in any other way to shatter our war effort. Inspection of the docks made me more doubtful of this judgment, because the extent of the docks brought home the difficulty of knocking out a major port completely. But I am still rather astonished that the Germans refrained from concentrating on Liverpool.

A month or two later I was given a second assignment under Cecil Weir, this time on the need to make sure there was enough factory and warehouse space in reserve in case of blitz . We prepared our report without any formal evidence and I can remember asking myself as I wrote how far we should go in seeking powers over commercial and office as well as factory premises. It was perhaps my first experience of drafting a scheme for resolving a social problem, and the scope of the proposed agency seemed to extend further with every paragraph I put on paper. With some hesitation I decided to leave offices out and what eventually came into existence was a Control of Factory and Storage Premises with Cecil Weir as the first Controller. I was offered a post in it and finally agreed, moving to the Board of Trade in late May or early June 1941.

I had assumed that my post was at the level of Principal and it was a long time before it emerged that it was not. These things were rarely the subject of clear written agreements. When I moved over, later in the year, to the Industrial Supplies Division of the Board of Trade to take on from Richard Kahn (as I understood the matter from him), I found again that I was neither assuming his duties nor given his grade. I left the Board of Trade in December, still not graded as a Principal. But that played no part in my decision to move.

That decision had its origin in an inquiry undertaken along with John Jewkes and Norman Chester in May 1941 into planning in the Ministry of Aircraft Production. As soon as Beaverbrook ceased to be minister, Archie Rowlands, the Permanent Secretary, invited Jewkes to prepare a report on the case for setting up a planning department. We approached this issue with an open mind since Jewkes was even then no great admirer of plans and none of us had a very concrete idea what planning aircraft production would involve.

The evidence we heard was sufficient to convince us of the case for planning of some kind but conveyed little to us of the true state of affairs. This did not reflect any deliberate attempt to withhold information. It was more that a department that had lived for a year on improvisation, and had presumably faced one crisis after another, could hardly imagine — any more than we could — what central planning would contribute to overcoming a chronic state of muddle. It is also likely that nobody realised just what a muddle it all was — certainly nobody conveyed to us what was instantly apparent once we were inside MAP and observing what went on.

The upshot was that Jewkes was asked to set up a planning staff in the department. He quickly decided to accept and handed over the Directorship of the Economic Section to Lionel Robbins. Devons joined him shortly afterwards, sharing Jewkes's feeling that the time had come to move to more positive tasks and perhaps also a little doubtful whether he would have as free a hand if second-in-command in the CSO.

When I moved to the Board of Trade I served first under Bay Kilroy (later Lady Meynell). Together with her close friend

Evelyn Sharp, who was to appear memorably in Richard Crossman's diaries as his formidable permanent secretary, she was the outstanding success among the first women entrants to the Home Civil Service in the pre-war period. Bay had enormous charm, good looks, acute intelligence and occasional waywardness of judgment, in evidence of which most people pointed to her introduction of utility cups without a handle in an effort to achieve a small economy in manpower. I found her a most pleasant boss and she left me free to follow my own judgment. Others in the office included Sir Thomas Barlow, the Factory Controller, who was a successful businessman from Manchester, had written the standard book on Rhine wines, and had a wonderful cellar; Sidney Offen, a young economist-administrator who was later killed on war service; and Mary Wise, a daughter of a Labour MP, E.F. Wise.

My job was two-fold. I had to build up a "blitz reserve" of factory premises to which firms could move if bombed out, or to which stores could be moved for safety; and I helped to prepare schemes for the concentration of industry so as to release factory space and labour. Most of the premises of interest were in the textile areas of Lancashire and Yorkshire, so that I had to make journeys there from time to time in order to see what was available. The most useful premises were the Lancashire spinning mills and weaving sheds, and many of these were quickly occupied by aircraft firms and their sub-contractors: so quickly, indeed, that it became apparent to me that a separate reserve to be held empty in case of a major blitz was likely to prove a will o' the wisp.

The work of industrial concentration was rather different. It proceeded by way of circulating files relating to so-called "inessential" undertakings. Many of these were companies which were working below capacity and so had space to spare. If they could arrange to rehouse themselves in joint occupation of another under-utilised factory, so much the better. Where no such proposal had been made, the Factory Control might arrange to requisition the premises, thus speeding up the process of concentration. For in Lancashire it was quite clear that the rehousing of one textile firm by another was most unlikely ever to be reversed, and the looms and spindles in the vacated mill were almost certain, therefore, to be broken up.

In the middle of all this I received my calling-up papers and presented myself at the recruiting station where I spent an agreeable morning on a new-fangled intelligence test in which one was asked to complete certain geometrical figures in keeping with the picture of some comparable design. We were also stripped, weighed, medically tested and interviewed. I remember only the refrain of the officer who interviewed me, Sidney Offen and others: "Do you have a good mechanical sense?" To this thinly disguised invitation to join the Royal Tank Regiment, put in a variety of ways, I could not honestly answer "Yes" but did not think it honourable to return a "No". So, with a little havering, I found myself endowed with gifts no one else had ever perceived in me and added firmly to the strength. But nothing followed. The Department insisted that I must stay where I was.

Shortly after this, Richard Kahn approached me with the news that he was leaving for the Middle Eastern Supply Centre in Cairo. Rather reluctantly I agreed to move over and work in the Industrial Supplies Division which was in some ways the key policy section of the Board of Trade: for example, it dealt with the allocation of labour and materials and had been the source of new ideas for the limitation of civilian supplies, rationing and so on. Richard Pares was in charge of the division. He edited the *English Historical Review* in his spare time just as Austin Robinson had done his share of editing the *Economic Journal* from the War Cabinet Offices. But I saw little of him and was not sure what my duties were. I can recall little of value that I accomplished before I rejoined Jewkes, now in the Ministry of Aircraft Production, early in December.

It was not geographically much of a move since the Board was in the ICI building at Lambeth Bridge and MAP was in Thames House just across Horseferry Road in Millbank. For the better part of seven years in the 1940s I worked in one or other of these office blocks. Throughout most of those years I occupied a room above Millbank with a commanding view of the Thames where I could look out on the barges moving upstream and downstream and see the occasional aircraft leave its spoor in the evening sky.

But in other respects, the difference was considerable. I was moving from a department that was reasonably orderly to one in a chronic state of muddle. I was to spend the rest of the war years helping to impose some order on that disorder.

## 7

## *Planning Aircraft Production, 1941–45*

I was with the Ministry of Aircraft Production, which I joined in November 1941, for almost four years. It provided me with an apprenticeship in planning that has stood me in good stead. When I arrived, a couple of weeks before Pearl Harbour, the situation had something in common with the one I recalled at the beginning of 1940 when I entered the Cabinet Offices. Important issues were being neglected, co-ordination was poor and the collection, circulation and use of statistics was primitive.

Yet, if I formed a low impression of MAP, I subsequently came to recognise that it was the way of the world. I little thought in those years that the time would come when MAP would be represented to an admiring British public as a model of careful planning: still less that I should look back myself on MAP — as I did when I worked in post-war Germany — for guidance on how to proceed.

The disarray at MAP was hardly surprising. The Ministry had been under Lord Beaverbrook until May that year. He simply did not believe in planning. Improvisation? Yes, of course. Priority? Yes, provided it was priority for MAP. But to lay out production programmes over a period two years ahead would have seemed to him futile, if not downright sabotage. For him, the only production programme was "all that can be done". Nor was John Jewkes, who had prepared the report on the advisability of setting up a planning department that I had helped with, a great admirer of plans. Indeed, none of us who worked on the report had a very concrete idea what planning aircraft production would involve. But the evidence we heard convinced us of the case for planning of some kind.

When Jewkes had submitted his report, he was asked to take on the job of organising a new department of planning and statistics within MAP. By mid-1942 this directorate was to be the central body formulating production plans.

Its title was important, because it brought together responsibility for statistics, the information on which planning rested, and programmes, the shape that planning took. The power of the department to co-ordinate activities within the Ministry rested first on the range of information available to it and second on the official production programmes which it was authorised to issue. There were times when the departments in charge of the production of aircraft components sought to maintain that the preparation of "their" programme was entirely their responsibility. That made no sense: the production programmes for aircraft components had somehow to reconcile outputs with requirements, and requirements were interconnected. In addition, the aircraft programme itself had to be consistent both with what the Air Ministry needed and with the prospective supply of aircraft parts. The planning department's power to issue or refuse to issue the programmes that represented marching orders for the firms making aircraft and aircraft components was a highly effective instrument for procuring co-ordination.

The situation at MAP was not unlike the one in Whitehall generally at the beginning of the war. Then, one of the main tasks of the Economic Section had been to assemble, in the form of time series, the statistics of current production and consumption, which were usually scattered through policy files, and issue them in a succession of secret statistical digests. Only when the information had been brought together *in this way* was it possible to judge what was happening and what most needed to be done. In MAP, as in the War Cabinet Office, Ely Devons took on the brunt of the work of collection and setting out the numbers. He prepared a statistical digest of aircraft production for distribution every month. It went to not far short of 200 people, to the horrified disapproval of people like Lord Beaverbrook, who were more shocked that top secret figures should reach so many people than that anyone should have imagined it possible to co-ordinate aircraft production without them.

After our arrival, we began by preparing production programmes for aircraft, engines and propellers, showing the planned output by type over the next 18–24 months. Each of these was printed and circulated within (and beyond) the Ministry as top secret documents. They were revised from time to time, but not altogether simultaneously, the normal interval between successive programmes being three or four months.

All this seemed so obvious once done that it was natural to feel puzzled that it had not been done before. But there were three reasons for the absence of production planning. First, we were working on a scale far beyond that of pre-war years. At the peak, MAP employed nearly 2m men on aircraft production, bombs and other accessories. It would have been impossible to organise their work satisfactorily without some form of systematic co-ordination. In pre-war days, by contrast, the RAF could keep track of every single aero-engine by sticking coloured pins in a board. When planning was talked of then, it was only the airframes that figured in the plan; and attention was concentrated on the capacity needed to meet the expected peak. Such a plan had been drawn up shortly before the war by Sir E.H.Lemon, and although it had been almost completely forgotten in the excitements of 1940 and the Beaverbrook regime, the level of production in 1941–42 was, I believe, quite close to what Lemon had originally scheduled.

A second reason was the need in 1940 to change priorities abruptly as the war changed course. Beaverbrook was in any case no believer in planning, nor in paperwork when the house was obviously on fire. He was essentially a privateer who did not in the least mind a little piracy if it served some immediate need at the expense of another department. In his view, MAP was entitled to an over-riding priority and on the whole he had quite a good eye for priorities. But except in the very short run it is allocation, not priority, that must govern the distribution of resources in wartime, and Beaverbrook had no intention of abiding by any allocation if he could find a way round it.

A third reason for the lack of production planning was quite simply that British industry had little experience of it. Long after the war, there were plenty of British firms that treated production planning in the manner of a small builder who can never stick to the date he promises and meets a request for a production schedule with a vague promise to "see what can be done". Indeed, much the same was true of research and development, which few firms in pre-war days undertook on any scale; Rolls-Royce was fortunately one of the few and ICI another. Both production programmes and R&D were associated mainly with the mass production of consumer durables. In pre-war Britain the capital goods industries, like shipbuilding, were geared to the production of one-off items and to development by progressive modification in succeeding orders. Large sections of the consumer goods industries (other than durables) had to meet rapidly varying requirements and were so laid out that there was little economy in long production runs. The way in which the manufacture of standard items in long runs transforms production methods is familiar from the textbooks, but the historical development of production planning is a subject that has not been studied very fully.

## Life in the planning department

Jewkes was the head of the department (which eventually became a directorate general) until he left to join the Ministry of Reconstruction in January 1944. Under him came Devons who was responsible for statistics but had a very active interest in programmes as well, and took over general responsibility for the Directorate after Jewkes's departure. Frank Paish, an economist from the London School of Economics, shared with me responsibility for programmes, Frank concentrating on aircraft, undercarriages and turrets while I took charge of propellers and most other components. Among my colleagues were Brian Tew, a future professor of economics at Nottingham University, who ran the engine programme and Marjorie Craigie — who later married Brian — and who took over the propeller programme from me.

All members of the Directorate without exception held degrees in economics and seven held chairs in economics after the war. I brought into the group no fewer than four women ex-pupils of mine at Glasgow of whom two married colleagues in the Directorate before the end of the war. We were a close-knit group, although each of us was very busy with our own affairs. We were all young, high-spirited, and not lacking in a sense of our collective importance. The Ministry was our oyster to which we provided the necessary intellectual grit for the cultivation of those pearls of higher logic — the production programmes. We observed other departments with amused detachment and reported to each other on the latest absurdity. Life was frantic, nonsensical, but above all hilarious. We were endlessly preoccupied with complex and important issues and yet endlessly entertained by paradoxes and trivialities.

We wrote little and spent hardly any time in committee meetings. What we did was endless arithmetic and endless telephoning. Now and again we tried to rationalise what we were doing. Frank Paish did an anatomy of planning and we mulled it over. I tried to establish principles by which to decide what items should be supplied on "embodiment loan" (ie, at government expense) to aircraft manufacturers and what items they should be left to procure. But these excursions into theory were rare.

The use of technical jargon intrigued, baffled and amused me. We took great pleasure in finding some new term or phrase with which to mystify even the supposed experts. I remember a cable from the United States, the source of a jargon with the special piquancy of a foreign language, in which reference was made to "cold shuts" in the engine castings — a phrase that seemed made for repetition and appears to be unfamiliar, to this day, among British metallurgists. Another expressive American term was "choke-points", meaning bottlenecks. Our satisfaction in using cabalistic phrases of this kind derived in part from the tendency of our less expert colleagues to take refuge in jargon whenever we asked awkward questions.

We spent long hours in the office in Thames House and slept there (in the basement) when on fire duty. We usually took our lunch there too and often dined in the appalling canteen in the basement of the ICI building across the road. We could rarely get away from it except on Sunday, when I made a point of cycling out of London or walking in the Chilterns. And in 1943 I found time somehow to complete the last two chapters of my textbook and get it off to the printer. I also found time to get married.

## Planning propellers

When I joined MAP, I was completely ignorant of the aircraft industry. I was not even aware that an airscrew was another name for a propeller, nor that some propellers were fixed pitch and others variable pitch. It took me some time to unravel these and other mysteries because, as was gradually born in on me, many of the staff of the production departments were almost as much at sea in the technicalities as I was, while others had the greatest difficulty in communicating what they took for granted that everyone must already know. It was only when I made contact with De Havillands, one of the two propeller manufacturers, and could discuss matters with John Parkes (later Chairman of Alvis) and his assistants, Val Cleaver and Stephen Appleby, that I began to fathom what the effective options were. Indeed, there came a time when this knowledge allowed me to suggest a way of providing a new propeller for the Lancaster that got us out of an awkward situation — I could even claim to have invented a propeller made up of an American hub and English blades.

Jewkes had asked me to take charge of propeller planning. He put it to me that if I could increase the output of aircraft propellers even by two, I should be adding an entire aircraft to the RAF and that alone would make the move from the Board of Trade worthwhile. There were, he said, 300 propellerless Wellingtons on the beach at Blackpool, and the whole propeller programme was in a frightful mess.

Certainly, at the end of 1941 propellers were the major bottleneck. Rotol, one of the two manufacturers of variable-pitch propellers, was far behind programme, particularly on the electrical propellers fitted to Wellingtons, and the other types of propeller could not be used as substitutes. All that one could do was to juggle the current output to meet immediate requirements and make sure that future needs were fully reflected in production programmes.

At first this seemed a highly complex task since there were many aircraft types and an equal number of different propellers. But I learned gradually that there were in fact only a small number of hubs; that the difference usually lay in the blades; and that there was rarely an insuperable problem in machining the blades to meet specific needs. For example, the Mosquito and the Lancaster, which both used single-stage Merlin engines, took the same propeller hubs and, in some variants, the same blades.

I eventually discovered that Beaverbrook had placed large orders in America for Hamilton propellers for the Lancaster. A major problem arose when these American propellers started to arrive. They turned out to have stubby blades, intended for use on aircraft fitted with *American* Merlin engines and we were unaware that they were unsuited to the many Lancasters fitted with *British* Merlins. Since we had planned on using the American propellers on all Lancasters, we looked like having an enormous surplus of American propellers and a disastrous shortage of propellers for the Lancaster. Fortunately it proved possible, once I had grasped the problem, to arrange for the removal of the American type blades and their replacement with British ones. This relieved the shortage of hubs, and we had no lack of machining capacity for blades. But, of course, a great stock of useless blades accumulated, and although I sought to check the inflow, my colleagues took the view that we would be wiser to let it continue rather than attempt the impossible task of changing American production schedules at so late a stage.

In 1941 the entire aircraft industry was still suffering from the improvisations of the previous year and was doing its best to produce aircraft without much co-ordination from the centre. The propeller situation was an extreme example of the general muddle.

Up to the end of 1941, no one knew how many propellers were produced each week or even each month. There were figures for deliveries against each contract, but there were usually several contracts for any one propeller, and nobody took the trouble to aggregate the deliveries by type. In addition, while orders for propellers for new aircraft were placed by MAP, spare propellers were ordered (through MAP) by the Air Ministry which had a large Directorate of Equipment (D of E) in Harrogate. This meant that firms had to draw up their production programmes on the basis of requirements calculated by two different authorities, usually from quite different information. D of E at Harrogate worked from hypothetical calculations of future squadron strength. MAP, on the other hand, adopted a simple rule — named after its inventor, the Champernowne Rule — which called for the delivery of an extra 20% as spares one month before the delivery of the corresponding aircraft. This was a rule based on calculations made by David Champernowne, a leading mthematical economist who worked with the department, after a visit to Harrogate, where he witnessed dozens of squadron leaders trying to work out engine requirements.

The next difficulty was that MAP did not know the production programme — if there was one — of the propeller firms. I remember asking on my first visit to Rotol to be shown the production programme and being handed a sheet of figures extending over the next 18 months. On inspection they proved to be MAP's estimates of propeller requirements, based on an (out-of-date) aircraft programme with spares added in accordance with the 20% rule. When I pointed out that this could hardly express the firm's production intentions, especially as their current output was well below the figures shown, it became apparent to me that MAP contractors regarded a programme either as a device for showing that they did not have enough capacity to meet requirements, or as a proof of their (inflated) demand for materials. In fact, the figures I was shown were wildly misleading for either of these purposes. But that did not seem to trouble Rotol at all.

What puzzled me was how they decided what to produce from month to month. But it became apparent that they (and de Havilland's, the other producer) took instructions from the main airframe firms they were supplying and that such planning as occurred was a response to the pressure of so-called "chasers" in these firms or from D of E in Harrogate.

Once we had issued programmes for the production of aircraft and engines, we went on to produce programmes for other important items for which the government was paying directly, such as propellers, undercarriages, turrets, wheels, constant speed units, spinners, bombs, radio valves. In the case of contractors' parts, however, the aircraft manufacturers were responsible for meeting the initial cost of manufacture, and we had no powers to issue programmes. However, we were not just asked but harried by manufacturers to produce programmes for many items, such as radiators: they despaired of establishing in any other way what requirements they ought to be meeting and in what order.

Some of us felt that we should go further and prepare programmes for major items like wings. Jewkes (and Devons, who succeeded him early in 1944) took the view that the more programmes we prepared, the more we were bound to dilute the effectiveness of our planning. While I fundamentally agreed with this view, my own experience was that anyone engaged in propeller planning could hardly avoid planning the output of the key accessories, in order to avoid awkward bottle-necks later in apparently minor items.

On one central point, we were all united. There could be no effective planning of aircraft production unless we had control of the aero-engine programme. The hard core of the problem of co-ordination lay in the scheduling of engine requirements, and this was eventually recognised as the undisputed responsibility of the Programmes Department.

But this was one of several areas where the need for the Programme Department to play its central role inevitably involved friction with the production departments. There were times disgruntled members of one production department or another accused us of depriving them of their functions; and at first I was not too sure what answer to make.

We learned gradually to insist on our co-ordinating role and to identify planning with co-ordination. This meant that the production departments had to guide us, particularly at the beginning, on the scale of output consistent with available capacity, and of course they worked with us to draw up each production programme. But that done, there was still plenty of work for them to do in assisting firms to meet their programme and arranging for further expansions in capacity where needed. We, for our part, had to keep track of the changes that were in the wind in, for instance, the aircraft and engine programmes and of the pressure on spares and the likely demands of the Air Ministry. We had to have the best and most up-to-date information on output and requirements. In short, we had to function like a kind of Stock Exchange of the aircraft industry, registering the pressures of supply and demand and issuing buying orders in the form of production programmes.

It would be idle to pretend that this was uniformly successful. Our turret programmes, for example, made little impression on the production department concerned. They preferred to go by what the Air Ministry told them, however often this proved to be based on out-of-date information. They took the view that their obligation was to the RAF and that they could not afford to disregard what the ultimate user said was needed. Similarly, we made no progress with the radio programme because the production department was not interested in educating us in the intricacies of radio valves and because radio requirements were less intimately linked to the aircraft programme itself.

At each stage our information was incomplete, often suspect and uncertain or contradicted by other information from normally trustworthy sources. The situation was changing in unexpected ways, and at an unpredictable pace. One day the Spitfire would be on top of enemy fighters; the next, we would find that a Spitfire had been shot down by the FW190 and the whole fighter programme would be in doubt; the next again, Rolls Royce would mount a new and high-powered engine — the two-stage Merlin — in the Spitfire by extemporised methods and its ascendancy over enemy fighters would be restored. Research would reveal that the Halifax did not compare with the Lancaster in its ability to deliver bombs and return safely to base. But, before we could begin to fade out the Halifax and use the capacity to build Lancasters, we would be asked to replace the Merlin engines on the Halifax with Hercules VI engines, so transforming the performance of the Halifax but throwing the aero-engine programme into confusion. Or in 1944, shortly before Arnhem, we might suddenly find that the Albemarle, then at the very bottom of the Air Ministry's priority list as a light bomber, suddenly shot to the top of the priority list as a glider tug.

Moreover, each time manufacturers made an improvement in one component, changes were likely to be required in associated parts. So other aspects of design had to be changed as well. In particular, as engine power increased, the main components had to be adapted. The propeller had to be capable of taking up more power and this usually meant longer blades. This in turn meant that the aircraft had to stand higher off the ground so that a new undercarriage might be required. The extra engine power might put a premium on cooling and this meant a new radiator. The change in propeller carried with it a change in spinner and constant speed units. So the very success of manufacturers in their endless quest for increased engine thrust guaranteed plenty of headaches for anyone planning aircraft components.

Nor was it only spares that created problems of this kind. The need to use aircraft abroad might involve major changes in aircraft design or in engine accessories. "Tropicalisation", as it was called, affected radiator, turret and other requirements but the decision to tropicalise often reached us from the Air Ministry in Whitehall long before D of E in Harrogate were informed or had time to revise their orders. Co-ordination, to be successful, meant that we had to be even better informed about what one department of the Air Ministry had in mind than some other departments of that ministry were. And, of course, within MAP, we had the same problem, since the production departments were not always well informed about developments in progress.

The case of aircraft wheels may serve to illustrate some of our problems in gaining accurate information. About 1942 or 1943 the Air Ministry submitted large orders for spare aircraft wheels. To meet them would have meant building two new factories when the strain on manpower was already at peak. MAP was not disposed to agree, pointing out that spare aircraft wheels should be needed only in the early life of an aircraft. Indeed, our information was that it was normal for a stock of wheels to accumulate once an aircraft had been in service for some time, since wheels were recovered when the aircraft crashed. It seemed likely that the Air Ministry's figures were defective in some way. They were calculated on the basis of returns from maintenance units, and it was known that one maintenance unit might issue spare wheels to another before they finally went to the squadrons. That might lead to two or more entries, in place of one. The scarcer any item of equipment became, the more likely it was that units would run out of stock, leading to some such duplication. In our experience, any shortage always appeared greater than it really was, whatever system of recording was used.

Fortunately it proved unnecessary to engage the Cabinet in speculation on the meaning of Air Ministry statistics. On the morning when the issue was to be discussed, a clerk in Harrogate confessed to an error in the figures, and this, when corrected, was sufficient to deprive the Air Ministry's case of any foundation. We had no more trouble on wheels.

Another example was propellers. I remember discovering early in August 1945 that the Air Ministry wished to place large orders for Hurricane propeller blades for use in the Far East. At that time, the Hurricane had been out of production for years and the spares requirements were enormous in relation to past experience — the total bill ran to over £2m. I spent the morning with the Air Ministry and found that provisioning for the limited number of Hurricanes due to be sent to the Far East covered every possible contingency. There were spare aircraft in case of damage to the front line Hurricanes; there were spare propellers in case of damage to the propeller when the Hurricanes landed on the aircraft carriers; then there were spare blades in case the damage was only to the blades. Damage was thus covered three times over, in spare blades, spare propellers and spare aircraft. The risk of damage was also put very high and no account seemed to be taken of the accumulation of semi-obsolete spares for the Hurricanes at home base. An hour's discussion cut the order by more than half.

These arguments about spares were typical of many. The American practice was to calculate the spares likely to be required over the lifetime of the new equipment and produce them at the same time. The UK divided the responsibility between two ministries, one dealing with new equipment and the other with spares. It was virtually impossible to get the Air Ministry to place orders for spares for equipment that was so new that they knew little of what replacement parts they were likely to need. But if MAP had to wait until the Air Ministry put in orders for spares, they tended to arrive — in large quantities — when the aircraft needing them had almost disappeared from service. Either way, it caused headaches for the manufacturers. Firms which we were urging to introduce new equipment as fast as possible might thus find themselves held up or planning too modestly for lack of orders; or they might plead that they had no spare capacity because of large and urgent orders from the Air Ministry.

I cite these examples of the casino-like atmosphere of MAP, not as evidence of the incalculability of requirements and the importance of luck but to demonstrate how, as Per Jacobsson used to say, one must always be ready for the unexpected. We were forever exploring and weighing up contingencies in order to decide where to have a margin in additional stock-building and how large it should be. But we also needed help in assessing contingencies, particularly those involving changes in technology. How could we hope to know whether liquid-cooled engines were more promising than air-cooled? Or what chance there was that the jet engine would supersede both before the war was over? Or at what point a limit would have been reached to the development of the Merlin? Or when a new engine like the Griffon would reach the stage in its development when it would be ready to go into production?

On questions of that kind, there was only one way to proceed: find someone of unquestioned standing, consistent good judgment and a reliable track record. We put our trust in Ernest Hives (later Lord Hives) of Rolls-Royce. He was an engineer who had both a remarkable flair for business and an extraordinarily accurate judgment of the potentialities for development of the engines his firm was producing. It was Hives who saved Rolls Royce from heavy losses in the United States by winding up in the 1920s a branch of the firm that was trying to pit British one-off craftsmanship against American mass-production of motor cars. It was also he who took Rolls into the manufacture of modern aero-engines just when rearmament was about to begin in the 1930s and built up the powerful development team that gave Rolls the edge on German aero-engine firms. We felt we could trust Hives for an honest and competent opinion on the development prospects of the Rolls family of engines and on these difficult technical issues we were never disappointed. Hives was not, of course, our only source of technical guidance. We had experienced engineers within the Ministry to whom we could turn, such as Air Commodore Banks, Director of Engine Production. For propellers and accessories I made great use of Parkes, Cleaver and Appleby, of de Havilland's. But there were other components where I can recall no adequate source of technical comment and no expert whom we could consult with confidence when in difficulties.

I have laid stress on Hives's contribution — which in my view was equal to that of anyone in civilian life towards the winning of the war — because the aero-engine lies at the heart of aircraft design and production. In the summer of 1945, I was to visit German aircraft factories with the Farren Mission. I found that the German designers were puzzled as to how our fighters had always managed to produce the extra power to keep ahead of theirs. Practically all our fighters had Rolls-Royce Merlin engines, and Rolls had found ways of modifying the Merlin on the production line, with or without a change in the formal designation of the engine or Mark number, to yield more and more engine thrust. Their opposite numbers at, say, BMW, had relied on discontinuous changes in specification as one Mark of engine replaced another in the production line. Thus the Germans improved performance in jumps; and, as they did not have an

engine as capable as the Merlin of further development, any lead
they established in one of those jumps did not last long.

## The Farren Mission

When war with Germany ended in May 1945 I was still in MAP.
I was in some doubt what to do next, until Geoffrey Crowther
persuaded me to join the staff of the London *Economist*. But
before I joined, in April 1946, I made two visits to Germany.
One, discussed in Chapter 8, was as Treasury representative in
the discussion on reparations in Berlin between October 1945
and March 1946. The other was in July 1945, as a member of the
Farren Mission.

The Farren Mission was composed of a group of aircraft and
other designers under the leadership of W.S.Farren, Director of
the Royal Aeronautical Establishment at Farnborough. They
were asked to visit some of the chief manufacturing and research
establishments connected with the German aircraft industry and
report on the way new developments were planned there. They
were all technical experts, but Devons suspected — rightly, as it
turned out — that their interests would inevitably veer in the
direction of production planning, and suggested that I should
therefore be added. The suggestion was not, I think, initially very
welcome but it was pressed, and I was finally accepted as a
member.

So we all set out, kitted in RAF uniforms from head to foot,
and landed near Kiel as our first step. We stayed there only one
night before going on to Plon but we had time to take in the
appalling devastation of the town. The sight was one to which I
gradually became accustomed as we moved on to Brunswick,
Munich and other towns. I was, of course, already familiar with
bomb damage on the grand scale in London. But the visual
impact of Kiel was shattering and unforgettable: mountains of
rubble between which the roads flowed like a river; houses sliced
in two, with the furnishings open to the air; pedestrians emerging
from nowhere, spick and span, with every appearance of normality;
and nowhere in sight a shop, a hotel, or even an undamaged
house. It looked uncomfortably like the shape of things to come.

As we motored to Plon we passed a number of large open
trucks, most of them carrying human cargo — presumably
demobilised soldiers or refugees — and there were many people

trudging along the highway, but no public transport. Our first visit was to the Waltherwerke, a private research establishment, financed by the government, and occupied in the latter stages of the war in developing launching aids for the VI. Herr Walther gave us a full account of the various chemical compounds that were in use as rocket fuels — *K-stoffs* and *T-stoffs* and sundry other *stoffs*. What I carried away was first of all an appreciation of the importance of hydrogen peroxide as a booster, whether in submarines, rockets, or any form of propellant. Added to this was an appreciation of what research and development had contributed to Germany's war machine and of the early date at which it had been brought into play. Walther had set himself up in the 1930s and had engaged the interest and financial support of the German Air Force more or less from the beginning.

We went next to Hamburg where the destruction was far more massive but, as in London, there were areas that seemed comparatively unaffected. I walked round the Alster to visit a German family with whom Mary had stayed before the war and found that all of them had survived.

The most interesting part of our journey was the visit we paid to Garmisch-Partenkirchen and Oberammergau. Here we discovered that Messerschmidt aeroplanes had been produced in the exact location where the village's Passion Plays were normally staged. We heard also on the radio broadcasts by the Russians addressed to the scientists from Peenemunde, Germany's main military research institute, inviting them *by name* to come and work in the Soviet Union.

From Garmisch we went on to the Heinkel factory beyond Innsbruck to inquire into the development of the Heinkel 162, a single-engined jet fighter that was put in the air in the spring of 1945 within a matter of weeks straight from the drawing board — too late, however, to check the Allied air supremacy. It was an aeroplane of which I heard much in later years because other countries sought to take advantage of the design, especially the Russians. But, as the Germans had found, it was unstable and the design faults were hard to cure. Years afterwards in Paris in 1950 I recall coming on an article in *Figaro* about a pilot released by the Russians from internment there who had flight-tested the Heinkel 162s in the USSR and commented on the number of pilots killed in the tests.

As we returned along the valley of the Inn, we could see a long line of railway vans moving up towards the Brenner, with men in holiday mood waving to us from the open doors. I assumed that they must be Italians on their way home from the wars and hitching a lift on what may well have been Italian rolling stock also on its way home. All Germany that summer was full of people on the move, many of them going back to other countries while others were returning from abroad. There were many contrasts on the road but none as great as I remember on the road between Munich and Patton's headquarters in Freising. We had just left the BMW works which was equipped with the most sophisticated machinery for making jet engines and found ourselves on a long straight road passing fields in which oxen were the only source of motive power. In Freising itself we enjoyed American army rations, unparalleled luxury to a Londoner in 1945 but even further removed from the meal I had shared in Munich with the family of Herr Frydag, the Chairman of the Sonderausschuss for aero-engine manufacture under Speer.

I found our interrogation of German aircraft designers and manufacturers very revealing. They complained bitterly of interference by government just as their British counterparts would no doubt have done. But in some respects they had more cause. We were told that Goering had suspended work on jet engines in 1940 after the French debacle on the grounds that the war would be fought and won with piston engines. This had greatly delayed the production of jet-engined fighters like the Messerschmidt 262 which might have played a decisive part had they been available a year earlier. It appeared also that the German firms had no contact with the front line in the way Rolls Royce, for example, had, so that operational experience did not feed back so readily into new design.

What most impressed me was a copy of the BMW engine programme which I picked up at random from documents that were being bundled into huge packing cases for transmission from Munich to America. This showed the German airforce's engine requirements fluctuating wildly between 3,000 a month, zero and back again to 2,000 a month. How the firm coped with such violent changes I cannot imagine. That piece of paper punctured completely the inflated esteem in which I had previously held German planning. The Germans chose methods of planning new engine production that simplified production at the expense of delaying what might be important operational modifications. But so far as I could judge, this did not spare them acute production problems later: if an aircraft was too slow, it might have to be scrapped together with its engine. We had tried to deal with such problems on the production line; they, by aiming to maintain output instead, had been liable to suffer far bigger losses later. Whatever the cause of the erratic fluctuations in the production programme, they were far beyond anything I had come across in MAP.

A fortnight was, of course, far too short for an investigation of the strengths and weaknesses of German methods and I had little opportunity of following up, amid the highly technical discussion that took up most of our cross-examinations, the points that interested me most. From my point of view, the questions were how competition operated under the compulsions of war; what made for success in outdoing the enemy when so much hung on it; and what contribution could the State could make: how could the State improve its chances of picking winners? Above all, how could one find and encourage those rare spirits on whose imagination and drive, experience and leadership everything ultimately hung? The aircraft industry had many lessons for peace as well as war, for economists as well as engineers.

**Planning in wartime**

But much of the MAP material for those lessons is lost. Some years after the war, when I was working in the Board of Trade, I had a visit from a lady who had served with us in MAP during the war and was horrified to find that it was intended to destroy all the records of the Programmes Department. This news astonished me too, and I assured her that all the threatened documents would be preserved. I had them put in two sacks (formerly used by the Bundespost) which I found in one of my cupboards, and handed them over on condition that I was told where they could be found. I am fairly sure that they were sent to Cardington (the airship base), but when I came to make inquiries a few years ago, they had disappeared without trace. Some files that I had myself preserved I deposited in the Public Records Office but, these apart, nothing of DDG Stats P survives among the official records — not even a specimen of the *Monthly Bulletin of Statistics* whose circulation of 200 had aroused such strong disapproval from Lord Beaverbrook.

When I look back on those four years in MAP, what is it that stands out in my memory? First and foremost, the incessant uncertainty and confusion. Our world was in constant change, we knew very little of what was going on, and what lay ahead was hard to foresee. No one could be sure how well an aircraft would perform until it had flown: even then, as was the case with the Lancaster, its merits might not be fully recognised until later. No one could be sure what the enemy would put into the air: German jet-engined aircraft might have wrought havoc in 1944. We had to be ready for unexpected changes of mind in the Air Ministry and equally unexpected changes in technical requirements.

But when I think of the confusion it is not these uncertainties that I have in mind: it is the difficulty of agreeing on a course of action that makes sense; the different levels of competence and knowledge in those who decide; the incalculability of the path towards a decision when it is almost a matter of chance who is consulted; the lack of continuity and the wide scope for rumour. At the time, MAP seemed to me one gigantic muddle. Nobody who served in it would pretend that MAP was a particularly efficient body. The speed of change, the scale and variety of MAP's activities, the low calibre of much of the staff, all told against a really high level of performance. Of course it would have been possible to do better. But if it had been less frustrating, it would probably also have been less fun.

A second reflection is how alike communist and wartime planning are. Both rely on controls and suppress the price mechanism. Both replace monetary by physical indicators. Both profess a single objective to which all else can be subordinated. Even the disorders of the one have much in common with the disorders of the other. A good example is what the Russians call "storming": trying to push through everything at the end of the month so as to meet the target. Or the difficulty of devising an appropriate target for an assortment of items (for example, spares), some of which are easy to produce and not much needed, while others get in the way of new production and are badly needed. The parallel struck me forcibly in Moscow in 1952, when I was able to distinguish those who did from those who did not understand planning by the importance they attached to stocks (which of course play the role of prices in a competitive system).

This leads on to another reflection. War is a great centraliser, since it is fought by governments which, in conducting the war, readily use their powers of control. But centralisation implies a multiplication of interrelated decisions and requires far more decision-takers: decision-takers, not as consumers or producers on their own account but as officials acting as part of the government. The decision-takers or officials who are washed into government from civilian life are likely to be a mixed bag, and those who enter late (as with MAP) will not be the ablest, nor will they be accustomed to the kind of decision-taking that government normally requires. MAP was a process of acculturation to which some took and some did not.

Another lesson I learned was the supreme importance of technical change. It dominated my life for four years and largely determined the balance of air power. It was impossible not to take away a sense of its equal importance in economic development. I could never believe, after watching the struggle between rival designers of aircraft, that capital investment, management, or any other factor ranked equally with technical change in its influence on competitive success on the one hand and the standard of living on the other.

At the same time it was impossible not to become aware of the many snags in giving effect to new techniques and introducing new designs. Again and again firms proved to be too optimistic about the time it would take to gain technical clearance or to introduce a new model. Similarly they nearly always underestimated the loss in production in a changeover from one model to another. It was a simple corollary that in the absence of technical change productivity would be much higher — but only by forswearing all the advantages of change.

It is common among scientists to read into wartime achievements (and later events, like putting a man on the moon) the lesson that men have only to put their minds to a problem for the thing to be done. This is not the conclusion that an economist would draw. It is easier in wartime to know what the problem is and find a market for the solution. There is a narrowing of the range of problems, a concentration of talent on them without regard to cost, and above all a known requirement in almost every case. This is not true of economic problems in peacetime where consumers' wants are far wider and new wants frequently emerge only after new products are put on the market. Cost plays a much larger part in controlling development to meet a specific civilian want than in development of weapons indispensable to the larger aim of victory. This is not to decry the great importance of research and development. But its role in improving the standard of living is very different from that in improving munitions of war — as is indeed only too obvious when one looks at what happened in the transition from the atomic bomb to atomic energy.

My immediate impressions were more of what went into planning: the narrow margin between shortage and surplus; the importance of the trend in stocks as an indicator of how the margin was changing — an indicator rarely understood by those with no experience in planning; the tendency to overreact so that, as we were constantly reminded, "there's nothing like a shortage for creating a surplus or a surplus for creating a shortage".

We were of course, engaged only in *production* planning, like any very large firm, and that is a more limited form of planning than trying to plan the whole wartime economy. That the planning we did helped to raise the level of production of aircraft, I have no doubt. The big question, in the light of foreign experience, is not whether we should have done less planning but whether we should have done more: whether, without damaging loss in aircraft performance, we (or some other group with more knowledge of engineering problems) could have taken firmer control over modifications in design and reaped the impressive advantages of standardisation that Speer achieved in Germany. Personally, I attached more importance to expanding the output of proven aircraft and cutting out what I thought of as junk. Above all, I think that there was not the close collaboration that was needed between the staffs engaged in development and the staffs dealing with planning and production.

I could see the need for more planning in the firms with which I dealt. But central planning of the entire economy such as we engaged in during the war seemed to me inappropriate for a free civilian economy. It was obviously reasonable to carry over some wartime controls for a time while various shortages persisted and the government ran down its demands on manpower and other resources. The role of government, too, might be enlarged compared with pre-war years. Policy to co-ordinate economic activity necessarily incorporated a form of economic planning. But that it should supplement, not supersede, the planning engaged in by businesses in response to market pressures and price signals seemed to me almost beyond question.

# 8

## *German Reparations: a Country to Play With*[1]

I spent the winter of 1945–46 in Berlin, negotiating on reparations and the future level of German industry with the Americans, the French and the Russians. The episode was of critical importance to the relations between the Great Powers. The war-time allies held very different views about the future of Germany, and it was over reparations that disagreement went deepest.

At Yalta, the Soviet Union had demanded $20 billion from Germany, half for itself and half for its Allies. The Russians, not unnaturally, wanted to ensure that their country would never again suffer such terrible losses from a German invasion and sought to destroy even the vestiges of Germany's war potential, whatever the cost in German living standards. The Americans in 1944 had gone even further and talked of "pastoralising" Germany, a proposal they later quietly abandoned. The British were more hopeful of a Germany that would live at peace with its neighbours and were concerned to leave Germany with the means of earning a reasonable living. As for the French, their interest was in keeping Germany weak, by detaching territory, resisting central control and building up their own steel, chemical and pharmaceutical industries to take over markets the Germans would no longer supply.

In the summer months of 1945, there had been preliminary negotiations in Moscow between officials from the United States, the United Kingdom and the Soviet Union, with little agreement between the three powers. This had been followed by

---

[1] I have provided a fuller account of the negotiations (and atmosphere) in Berlin in 1945–46 in "The Price of War" (Blackwell, 1986) and (from a more personal point of view) in "A Country to Play with" (Colin Smythe, Gerrards Cross, 1987).

a major conference at Potsdam at the end of July 1945, from which the French were again excluded. Agreement had been reached between the three powers represented there that Germany should be allowed to retain just enough of her equipment to permit an average European standard of living, while any excess could be taken in reparations. The implications of the formula were to be worked out over the next six months and a reparations plan prepared by February 2nd, 1946.

Talks between representatives of the occupying powers (now including the French) began in September 1945. The task of the experts in Berlin, as I discovered in due course, was to draw up a "plan" showing what equipment might be taken without encroaching on the requirements of a peaceful Germany. This was not intended to be a plan for the future of the German economy, but might serve to indicate how the equipment remaining after reparations had been paid could support a standard of living comparable with the European average. It was therefore necessary first to lay down what this standard of living implied in terms of levels of industry, and subsequently to compare them with the surviving industrial capacity in Germany. The excess capacity revealed by such a comparison could then be translated into actual industrial plants and removed in reparations.

By the end of September, the Americans had produced a draft plan on what reparations might be provided, and the British were hard at work on one. Austin Robinson and Donald MacDougall, two distinguished British economists, had completed most of the preparatory work but they had to return to England to take up other duties. In those circumstances, Sir David Waley, head of the Overseas Finance Division of the Treasury, turned to me as I was winding up at the Ministry of Aircraft Production and asked me to take over as Treasury representative in the Berlin talks.

I did not give Waley an immediate reply. A year previously my wife and I had been bombed out of our London flat, and Mary had sought refuge with her parents in Yorkshire for the imminent birth of her first baby (Frances). It was not many months since she had rejoined me, and I did not welcome the prospect of a renewed separation, especially as she was again pregnant. After six years of war I felt stale, exhausted and diffident. I had neither experience of diplomacy nor the patience and self-control that it requires; no acquaintance with the earlier history of the negotiations; only a superficial knowledge of German industry and of the German language.

These were not, however, the main reasons for my hesitation. I doubted whether anything I could do would be worthwhile. It seemed to me as plain as a pikestaff, after my three-week tour of Germany with the Farren Mission (described in the previous chapter), that any sensible man, asked what industrial plant was surplus to the requirements of a peaceful Germany, was bound to reply, "None." When I said as much to Waley, he asked, "What about steel?" I thought it just possible that there might be some surplus steel capacity, but if there were, it was likely to be in poor shape and of doubtful value to anyone else.

The one positive advantage I foresaw, and what finally persuaded me to accept, was that Berlin was the only place in the world where it was possible to meet Russians on equal terms. I was curious to do so, not merely because I knew absolutely nothing of Russians at first hand but admired their literature and took a professional interest in the mechanics of their economy; mainly, it seemed supremely important to make ordinary human contact with them while the opportunity lasted. People did not talk at that time about an iron curtain. But they were conscious of the segregated world in which the Russians lived and of the clash that had begun to be felt between that world and ours.

I had another motive for going. I had believed since 1941 that the only two world powers remaining at the end of the war would be America and Russia, and that there would ultimately be a conflict of interest between the two. The relations between them at the time of Potsdam were highly unstable and artificial. The honeymoon between America and Russia had ended with the dropping of the first atomic bomb, but divorce proceedings had not yet started. Britain was leading the attempt to limit Russian expansion in Europe, but was in acute economic distress, and hardly likely to be able to sustain an active and independent foreign policy on borrowed dollars. Sooner or later, Russian propaganda, stridently anti-British in the summer of 1945, would be aimed across the Atlantic. Sooner or later, a third world war, with Britain a mere nut in the nutcracker, would become a real danger. If that danger was to be averted, it was in Berlin that a beginning would have to be made.

The Farren Mission in Germany, July 1945:  W S Farren is hatless in the middle of the group on the left.

Berlin, when I got there in late October, was a scene of desolation and destruction. Scattered throughout the city were perhaps 100m tons of rubble. Where other towns had acres of ruins, Berlin had square miles of them. Sir Walter Layton, the former editor of *The Economist*, visited the city while I was there and declared, "It will take 11 years to clear the rubble: ten years of occupation, and one year after the Allies leave for the Germans to do the job." Superficially, life was normal. People went about their business, the children played in the streets, shops were open, trams running. The theatres were open and well attended; and there was free movement from one zone of the city to another. Yet at night there were frequent gunshots, and regular kidnappings. Moreover, I learned in due course that the death rate in Berlin during the second half of that year was averaging over 50 per 1,000, or about four times the normal rate, a sure sign of starvation and disease.

I had been accorded the rank of a Brigadier: it had been felt necessary to give me some appropriate military rank, and I had been issued with an army uniform. (This was to give much amusement to my Russian opposite numbers; I could hardly explain to them that the main reason I had been given a uniform was because it was supposed that anyone not wearing one would be likely to be attacked and robbed by them.) In spite of my exalted rank, it soon became clear to me that I had extremely modest powers.

I was a relatively junior official with no place in the hierarchy of the Control Commission and the most tenuous links with London. Formally, I was head of a body called the economic advisory panel which was attached in the UK Delegation to the Allied Reparations Commission. But both the delegation and the reparations commission were phantoms.

My panel, which was housed in a large building on the Kaiserdamm, in the British sector of Berlin, worked as a group of consultants alongside the economic division of the British Control Commission. This body was one of four which administered the country's four zones. My immediate staff consisted of six female economists, two extremely capable secretaries, a security officer trained in the raiding of night clubs and a Treasury staff officer with the promising name of Gambling. They had all been working on the plan and knew far more about the issues than I did. Because I was so busy, the day-to-day running of the office was handled by Captain Hodd, a young soldier who was also an economist — a rare combination at the time.

My life passed in a furious dichotomy between meetings and preparations for meetings at the lowest possible level — that of the Technical Staff. This was a quadripartite group of experts where the bargaining process over implementing the Potsdam agreement began. It was separated from the Allied Control Council, on which sat the zone commander, Field Marshal Montgomery, by three layers of committees.

To an extraordinary degree, I worked on these negotiations, so central to the future of Germany — and thus of Europe — in a vacuum with no contact with senior officials in Berlin and no guidance from the Foreign Office or the Treasury back in London. I was thrust into taking responsibility for strategy by being obliged to make the first move without direction, but with no control over tactics.

In Berlin there were no meetings of British officials except to consider tactics, and even these were rare. As British representative on the lowliest committee, I had an extraordinary amount of responsibility: the British never repudiated at a higher committee what was put forward on their behalf at a lower committee. I thus found myself, like the tortoise in Hindu mythology, supporting a series of more and more elevated British spokesmen, each tier of which stood on a policy originating further down.

London, too, largely left me to shape my own course. In general, the Foreign Office and the Treasury rarely intervened: the former limited its advice to underlining the folly of being in a minority of one (the worst possible advice, as events proved); the latter was anxious only that a plan agreed upon for Germany should be "viable" (a proper, if largely meaningless, aim). As for the higher reaches of government, visiting officials were rare birds. And, apart from the unfortunately named J.B.Hynd, the junior minister in charge of the Control Office, the department of state in London which at that time dealt with German affairs, no minister ever set foot in Germany that winter. Indeed, I began to wonder whether there was such a thing as British reparations policy, beyond what was in the Potsdam agreement. Incredible though it may seem, not a single Cabinet meeting on the subject of Germany occurred between September 1945 and March 1946 — throughout the entire period when I was in Berlin.

Moreover, as I later discovered, the arrangements for communicating with London were far from satisfactory. The minutes of meetings even of the Control Council, which was after all the top body, took days to reach London, and its agenda even longer, while in some cases the Control Office (the department in charge back in Whitehall) received no copies at all. Papers from the committees dealing with reparations, including those of the Technical Staff, got through only if they were despatched by the admirable Gambling, and we made sure that the Treasury had a complete set. But I doubt whether they were obtainable anywhere else in Whitehall.

The press, too, took little interest until the negotiations were over. When the key decision on the future level of the German steel industry was taken at the beginning of January 1946, no mention of it appeared in the British press until a short piece in *The Times* over a fortnight later.

But I must not exaggerate my independence. It was severely limited by a number of factors. I could not seriously depart from the British plan, already in draft when I arrived. I in turn was influenced by the climate of opinion in the Commission, which tended to be that Germany should be left with a reasonable economy, and I was far more the spokesman of that opinion than the creator of an independent view. We were all bound by the Potsdam agreement itself. We were not in a position to start from scratch, and work out a rational assessment of the margin of capacity available for reparations. Instead, we were presented with a ready-made formula and we had to work out what it meant. It might be challenged if it added up to something obviously absurd, but not if it merely added up to an economy on the borderline of sense and solvency.

## The Delegations

The Russians, whom I so much wanted to meet, were at first represented by individuals who frequently did not appear at the meetings of the Technical Staff, and when they did, were clearly out of their depth. The atmosphere changed with the arrival in early November of the new and colourful group drawn from the Russian Ministry of Commerce, and led by a Mr Kolpakov. It soon appeared that, unlike their military predecessors, these men were accustomed to economic argument and, indeed, willing to proclaim more loudly than we dared a suspicion of the incompetence of the military to resolve economic problems.

Mr Kolpakov later explained to me that the arrival in Berlin of Western experts who raised unexpected difficulties in the interpretation of the Potsdam agreement had obliged the Russians to assemble his little team by way of reinforcement. He himself was a man of about 40, short and stocky. His features had an Irish cast: the mouth firm but humorous, the eyes alert and imaginative. With him came a Professor Petrov, who held a chair in statistics at Moscow: round-faced and solemn, rather stout, fond (like most Russians) of proverbs and giving a first impression of pomposity that his sallies and good humour soon caused me to revise.

Then there were three experts in industrial economics. The most lively was Mr Piskopell, a Balt, with a face even rounder and spectacles even thicker than Professor Petrov's. He was a short, slightly round-shouldered man, with fair hair, a reddish face and a broad mouth, often extended in a smile. Improbably, he turned out to be a parachute colonel with over 40 combat jumps to his credit. He looked on our discussions as something of a game in which he quite liked to join, and had a habit of adding up our figures to see whether our arithmetic was right. He had learned English by picking up "The Wealth of Nations" and making his way steadily through its pages with the aid of a dictionary. It said much for him that it was the dictionary that he discarded first. In our discussions, he used his English to add some necessary levity: he would enliven a meeting on binoculars by peering through his massive spectacles and delivering the words, "Bathing beauties" with an incredibly bad accent and much pantomime, to show that binoculars had important uses, even in time of peace. Out at Flotow, a suburb of Berlin, dining with the French, he had been known to put away so much neat rum that before the evening was over he was toasting everyone imaginable, including "the King of America".

Professor Menshinsky was of a more retiring disposition, precise and sceptical. He shared with me an interest in international trade and a dislike for the title of statistician. He had written a book on Joan of Arc which had not been published because it was thought to be offensive to Russia's British allies to allow such a work to appear in 1942. I doubt whether he was much comforted when I told him that the British tended to see her as a great English patriot, since but for her we should all be talking French. Finally, there was Mr Chermensky. If any peculiarly obscure idea was put forward, you could be sure he was the author, and that when he came to develop the idea it would grow fainter and more obscure than ever. He moved with a kind of far-away cheerfulness, like a Cheshire cat, listened patiently and talked little. I saw him again at the Moscow Economic conference in 1952 (see Chapter 11) and sought news of his colleagues by uttering their names in turn. He said never a word but smiled and shook his head at each inquiry.

The Russians certainly knew their Dickens. Our colleagues called themselves the Pickwick Club. One Sunday morning Kolpakov came to lunch at our mess. Professor Petrov had been invited too, and we were all to have gone skating, but there was no sign of him, much to our disappointment. Kolpakov explained how, while on the way to Berlin by aeroplane with his staff of experts, they had been obliged to come down near Minsk. They had been held up there for three days, and had formed themselves into a Pickwick Club, with Kolpakov himself as Mr Pickwick. There was, he reminded us apologetically, one member of the original Pickwick Club who, when the party goes skating, first boasts of his skating prowess and then turns out to be unable to meet his boast. Professor Petrov, said Kolpakov, was the Mr Winkle of the Club and had rung up that morning withdrawing from the party.

Of the Russians at grander levels in the delegation, I saw nothing. I heard descriptions of the Russian generals in all the splendour of uniforms and medals, self-confident, upstanding, unsophisticated: a new governing class, that showed its proletarian origins most unmistakably in its women-folk. Many stories were told of the richness of their receptions, the interminable toasts, the vodka baiting. At one reception, one of my colleagues saw a French general pinned against the wall with a glass in his hand, with a Russian general from a tank regiment, one of the best drinkers in the Red Army, shouting toasts at him. "Here's to the French! I like the French! They know how to die!" When my friend offered to translate, the Russian general seized him instead

and began again: "I like the French! They know how to die!"
When it was explained to the general that it was an Englishman
that he was clutching, he still held up his glass, shouting, "Here's
to England, the birthplace of the tank!" At this point, he was
called away by the aide de camp of Marshal Zhukov, the head of
the Russian army, and marched to the room where the Marshal
and his wife were assembled, threw open the door and called in
a voice of thunder, "Comrade Marshal, I have the honour to
announce that all is well with the tanks!" Zhukov promptly sent
him off again before he had a chance to say anything else.

The other delegations were more humdrum. The French
kept a low profile in the negotiations until near the end, where
their spokesmen seemed to voice French commercial interests
conveyed to them from Paris and usually at variance with the line
they had taken during technical discussions in Berlin. Their
delegation had inadequate staff, inadequate data and little weight.
For most of the time I was in Berlin, they were represented by a
M. Lazard, a member of the French banking family, who had
spent a good part of the war with the Maquis in Savoy. Rather
an old-fashioned gentleman, I thought, liberal in temperament,
but conscious of being rather out of fashion and out of date.

The Americans had a large delegation under General Clay.
He was not a man I took to. He had a wizened, wary look that
put one on one's guard and was at first, I was told, very pro-
Russian. He seemed to me responsible for the bungled agreement
on steel, reached at the start of 1946. No doubt Clay will look
different to posterity. But there seemed to me some justice to the
crack by one of our delegation that he was a Brooklyn Jew of Irish
extraction who hated the Germans for his father's sake and the
English for his mother's. His number two, General William H.
Draper, had a much more attractive personality: easy to talk to,
intelligent and entertaining. And my opposite number on the
Technical Staff, Benjamin Ulysses Ratchford, was also easy to
deal with. He was an academic, and there was little on which he
and I disagreed.

Sir Percy Mills, who led the British delegation, had been in
charge of the machine-tool industry during the war, and later
became a cabinet minister in the 1950s. He was a boor, ill-
tempered and over-bearing. But his redeeming virtue was his
pugnacity. He did not easily give way on anything. He had two

second-in-commands. One, Brigadier Bader, was a jaunty South African engineer who had a good, sharp mind but was a little out of his depth on economic problems. The other was Eric Seal, an experienced civil servant who had served as one of Churchill's aides in the war. He told me how Churchill would wake him up in the middle of the night, saying, "Seal, get down off your iceberg", to hear him rehearse his speeches.

The wide differences in point of view that separated members of the Technical Staff gave rise to no personal animosities. When I lamented to Kolpakov that we should be in such deep disagreement, he said comfortingly, "Mr Cairncross, we are playing chess." Although I thought of myself as the spearhead of the opposition to their line, the Russian team gave me a party when I left Berlin and loaded me with presents of vodka and caviar. Kolpakov assured me that it would fall to me one day to write the history of our negotiations, and clearly felt that I would do justice to all parties.

## The Negotiations

In an idle moment I wrote a few lines of verse that summed up the nature of what took place in Berlin in those winter months. They began:

> If four should join to frame a plan
> For taking all the loot they can
> While leaving to the fifth enough
> Of all the necessary stuff
> To just maintain, but not exceed,
> The average of Europe's need
> Always omitting from the sum
> (What may appear a trifle rum)
> The Bear and Lion, as extremes
> Beyond the reach of Europe's dreams....

Under the terms of the Potsdam agreement, Germany was to be allowed to retain just enough of her equipment to sustain an average European standard of living, while any excess could be taken in reparations. The calculation may sound straightforward, given agreement on the necessary statistics, and one not requiring negotiation. But it turned out to be extraordinarily complex.

To try to establish the average European standard of living, we had first to designate a year. Potsdam gave no guidance. The natural year to select was 1938, because that was not only a year for which the figures were available, but the last peacetime year which had been reasonably normal. However, the German standard of living in 1938 had been well above the level of the rest of Europe's, and if it had to be reduced to Europe's 1938 average, it would have to be cut to the level Germany had been at in 1932. In other words, it would mean reducing Germany to the conditions that had brought Hitler to power.

Other questions arose. How were the efficient Germans to be limited to the European average per head unless many of them were unemployed? If unemployment were imposed on them, how would it help to make the Germans live at peace with their neighbours?

Was the plan to relate to the whole of Germany, or only to the Western zones? Potsdam laid it down that Germany was a single economic unit to be treated uniformly for the purpose of reparations. But, even at Potsdam, a deal had been done allowing the Russians — without consulting the other Allies — to remove what they chose from the Eastern zone (the future East Germany), where they were, and remained, the occupying power. They had already begun to take advantage of this, although how much had been taken or could be taken, no one knew. How then could one include East Germany in the calculation?

Then there was the question what to do about the Russian insistence that each German industry should be limited to the European average, regardless of the macro-economic consistency of a collection of such averages? Moreover, what guarantee was there that, if every German industry was limited to the European average, with some falling well short of it, the resulting standard of living would also reach the European average?

Finally, there was a more immediate problem. In the British zone, the industrial heartland of Germany, the terms of the Potsdam agreement were bound to cause severe unemployment. The Western zones were also likely to be deprived of the inflow of grain from Eastern Germany on which they had depended in pre-war years. This would particularly affect the British zone. Britain would then be obliged to provide hundreds of thousands of dollars, of which it already had an acute shortage, to pay for American grain to keep the population of the British zone alive.

As the negotiations progressed, disagreements were chiefly between the Americans and the British on one side and the Russians on the other, with the French keeping a low profile most of the time except when they saw a possible commercial advantage, as they did mainly in the future of the Saar and the Ruhr.

The first serious tussle was over steel. It happened to be almost the only industry on which the Americans took a position radically different from the British. Their delegation was full of steel men anxious to boast on their return that *they* had settled the future of the German steel industry. They paid no attention to their economists who held views close to ours.

The British had argued that Germany should retain 9m tons of steel-making capacity to meet domestic needs, and a further 1.5m tons for exports. They were conscious that these amounts were below what was likely to be required but well above what the other delegations were likely to accept. The matter came up at the end of December when it was the Americans' turn to chair all meetings of quadripartite committees, and when most of the senior British negotiators (including Percy Mills) had left to spend Christmas in London, insisting nothing would happen in their absence. A British general drafted in from the British zone at one day's notice accepted a limit of 5.6m tons without any appreciation of what this meant. In effect, the Americans thus contrived to reach an agreement with the Russians on a figure well below what three out of four delegations originally proposed and roughly half of what the British cabinet had agreed to support.

Confronted with this unsatisfactory figure, the British subsequently insisted that it related to the level of output, not capacity; and that 7.5m tons of capacity should be retained. They stuck to this in spite of the common sense — and contrary — view of all the other delegations. In fact, since most of the steel making capacity was in the British zone, the British could resist dismantling capacity beyond what they thought acceptable. But the incident did not give the British a reputation for straight dealing.

After the steel decision I felt I had had enough and meditated return. I rang Waley at the Treasury. He insisted that I should, in Berlin, give my loyalty to Percy Mills, a man for whom I had no great regard. But Waley urged me to stay on when the negotiations were already so near completion. I decided to stick it out for another month and in the end stayed until the final meeting at which an agreed plan was adopted, early in March.

The steel decision settled the level of one, but only one, industry. The Technical Staff continued their wranglings over all the other industries, with each country submitting a different figure for the capacity to be retained. Austin Robinson had provided a consistent plan — what economists would call an "input-output" plan — showing what plausible combination of outputs from the main German industries would allow Germany to balance her international accounts and maintain a standard of living equal to the European average. But his plan did not take us any nearer agreement, since each of the other countries was preparing their own plan and had yet to debate the British Plan (if, indeed, they could be induced to do so).

The Russians held to a fixed bargaining position with sharp changes at long intervals if we were patient. When we reached an impasse in meetings of the Technical Staff, with no way of deciding among four suggested levels of industry, they urged us to reach agreement by applying what I called the "Rule of Four": with each industry in turn, they suggested with every show of sweet reason, add up the four submissions and divide by four to reach an acceptable average. Unfortunately, they were likely to repeat the process at each stage on the way up the hierarchy of committees, advancing their original figure in opposition to the new average and suggesting a fresh averaging to resolve the difference. This meant that eventually figures were discussed that differed little from the Russian starting point which invariably lay at one extreme of the range.

I had much pleasure in bringing out the weaknesses of the Rule of Four. For example, at a meeting called to discuss Germany's eventual oil requirement, General William Draper, the American chairman, was just about the invoke the Rule when I drew his attention to the fact that, in spite of the chaos of late 1945, Germany was already consuming more oil than the average of the four figures proposed. Electric power illustrated the same point: the level of consumption, even in the chaos of the October of that year, was already close to the Russian estimate of Germany's peace-time requirements in the years ahead.

Early in February there was a sudden change in the bargaining posture of the Russians. Broadly speaking, they seemed prepared to come about two thirds of the way if the other delegations would come the remaining third. As a result, agreement was soon reached on all points except one: whether the agreed levels of industry constituted a plan that Germany should be required to adopt (with fixed upper limits for all industries, peaceful or warlike) or merely a indication of how what was retained in Germany could provide an average European standard of living.

Some time later, after I had returned to England, I was told that a more fundamental issue had only just surfaced. In many industries, a given output could be produced by working one, two, three or even four shifts. Agreement on the future level of output did not, therefore, imply agreement on the equipment required to produce it. We had taken it for granted that shift-working would remain as in peace-time Germany before 1939. Not so the Russians. They insisted that we must assume the maximum double-shift or treble-shift working.

There were times when it looked as if the Russians desperately wanted German equipment for use in Russia to help them in their own recovery from the devastation of war. Naturally we sympathised. But we found that they took particular care when dismantling factories that made equipment of military value, such as aero-engine factories, and transporting the plant. Other equipment was carelessly dismantled and despatched in a way that made it almost inconceivable that it would ever be used again. It was routed via the Berlin canals and on the way a fair proportion was tipped overboard. A great deal more was abandoned in Polish railway yards.

When I got back to London Sir Wilfrid Eady, one of the second secretaries at the Treasury, asked to see me and inquired whether I thought the British government should accept the Plan. I was a little taken aback: in all my months in Berlin not a word had ever reached me from the Treasury to suggest such doubts. On the one hand, the Plan was a nonsense; on the other hand, we had already gone a long way to approve the nonsense and appease the Russians. Could we afford to take a stand on our own and defy Russia? I found it hard to imagine the government unilaterally repudiating it after our delegation had accepted it in Berlin. But I was also unsure what approach to Russia the government was prepared to adopt and how far it would be willing to refuse Russia reparations that the Russians might reasonably claim to be in keeping with the Potsdam declaration.

Fortunately, the Americans had moved fast into a position indistinguishable from ours. They could claim — and at the beginning of May General Clay did claim — that the Russians had ceased to treat Germany as a unit and were stripping their zone of equipment regardless of their obligations under Potsdam. The Americans had a pretext, and they had the power we lacked. So, when they announced the suspension of reparations within two months of the Berlin agreement, we were able to follow them and spared the need to act alone.

Back in London, halfway through March, I set about preparing a full report on the Plan agreed in Berlin and submitted it to the Treasury and the Control Office at the end of the month. It sank out of sight for a year until, a little to my surprise, I was asked by the Control Office for a fresh copy in February 1947, presumably because no copy could be found. But it rapidly disappeared again. I have been unable to trace it in the Public Record Office. Some years later, I wrote a brief sketch of my five months in Berlin, calling it "A Country to Play With", a phrase used by Austin Robinson when I encountered him in a London street soon after my return.

What was most extraordinary about the whole exercise was how little attention the post-war British government paid to the negotiations in Berlin. Nobody ever invited me to come and discuss my report. There was no de-briefing. I did not set eyes on any minister from start to finish, either in London or Berlin, never exchanged a word with General Robertson either in Berlin or afterwards. Yet our relations with Germany after the war should surely have been one of Britain's most important considerations.

The Reparations Plan may have been no more than a brief moment of illusory agreement between allies who were never likely to see eye to eye. It had little observable effect on Germany's economic recovery. But the long negotiations helped to keep the future of Germany in play until the United States adopted a position very different from that initially supported by American public opinion and by General Clay in Berlin. As the months slipped away, they gave each side time to take stock of the other, to recognise more clearly what was at stake, and to ensure that, if Europe was to be divided, the dividing line would not move steadily westwards.

9

## Advising the Board of Trade 1946–49[1]

When I returned from Berlin to London in late March 1946, we went first for a family holiday to Polperro in Cornwall, worlds away from the atmosphere of Berlin or even London and nearer in spirit and institutions to Queen Victoria than to the mid-20th century. Thus fortified, I presented myself for duty at *The Economist*. It was the only period in my life when my employer was a company in the private sector. It did not last long.

*The Economist* at that time was edited by Geoffrey Crowther, from whom I learned much of the journalist's craft. My first assignment when I arrived was to draft an appreciation of Keynes, whose death had just been announced. I soon found that journalism did not come easily to me and was interested to see how Crowther completely revamped my inadequate first draft and extended it to form the first leader.

At that time *The Economist* had a distinguished staff that included Barbara Ward, a veteran environmental campaigner; Wilfrid King, the leading expert on the discount market; Paul Bareau, who also wrote on City matters; and Donald MacLachlan, later editor of the *Sunday Telegraph*. We all assembled once a week for an editorial meeting in Geoffrey's room, some of us sitting on tables or on the floor, while Geoffrey suggested what should be the subject of the leading articles and who should write them. There was a certain rivalry (which continued in later years) between the paper's front half (political) and back half (industry and finance), with occasional incursions by members of either group into the province of the other, either by way of developing

[1] For a discussion of economic policy in those years, see my "Years of Recovery" (Methuen 1985).

themes normally handled by the other group or by providing articles for inclusion in the other half of the paper.

My closest association was with Roland Bird, who was in charge of the back half of the paper. Normally my role was limited to writing notes, usually on Wednesday or on Thursday morning before we went to press, and as often as not to fill space and allow the text to match the pagination. But every now and again I did a leader as well, rebelling a little at the need to show a degree of omniscience I did not lay claim to, and ending reluctantly with a rounded conclusion as if I had a superior understanding of the appropriate action to be taken. I suppose that in those days I had neither learned to assemble facts and opinions quickly by telephone nor developed the strength of conviction to advance views of my own. I have always suffered from an inability to take sides on issues on which I have had no time to inform myself thoroughly. In journalism, this is a major drawback.

But there was another more serious one. Shortly after my return from Berlin I received an invitation from Stafford Cripps to join the Wool Working Party. This was one of those committees made up in equal numbers of employers, workers and independent members that were set up to examine 17 of the industries for which the Board of Trade was responsible — all of them industries making consumer goods and nearly all of them contracted and concentrated during the war. There was no intention of nationalising any of them, but Cripps appeared keen to find some way of making them more responsive to the public interest.

Membership of this committee involved travelling to Bradford every Sunday evening and spending two days there hearing evidence. This left only Wednesday to prepare comment on current affairs before the usual Thursday morning scramble to fit the text to the space available at the St Clement's Press. The remainder of the week was of limited value to a journalist writing for *The Economist* (although some of my colleagues used Friday and Saturday to help bring out *The Observer*). I could sometimes prepare a leader for the back half at the weekend, but for much of the time even that was difficult as I found myself compelled to draft the Report of the Working Party.

In short, I felt I was proving a bad bargain for *The Economist*, from which I drew my salary. I was therefore quite a willing listener when in September I was approached by Sir John Henry Woods, the permanent secretary of the Board of Trade, with a proposition that I should come back into government service as Economic Adviser to the Board. This was a post which Austin Robinson had held since he left Berlin shortly after I got there in 1945. I had no doubt that there was an important job to be done. Some years earlier I had been summoned to see Sir Arnold Overton, the then permanent secretary, who wanted my opinion on the merits of Sir Henry Clay, with whom I had worked in the Economic Section in 1940, as a possible Economic Adviser to the Board. Sir Arnold felt the need for someone fierce enough to defend the policies in vogue among the department's officials from attacks from the Treasury and elsewhere. I did not carry away from that interview any hankering for the kind of job that I imagined Clay would be asked to do. But I had seen enough of the Board in 1941 to appreciate how much it stood in need of economic advice; and enough of John Henry Woods to be confident that he was not another Overton and that I could enjoy working with him.

So I agreed to join the Board for a period of three years. I felt that, if most of my time was being devoted to the service of the government already without pay, I might as well give the rest of my time too and ask the government to foot the bill. Remembering, however, that I had been misled about my status when I last worked for the Board and that throughout the war I had drawn a salary lower than I had earned in Glasgow in 1939, I tried to make sure that the terms on this occasion were reasonable. I was not very successful, and was given a salary slightly lower than I had on *The Economist*. I put it on record without rancour but with some regret that on every occasion on which I have left a job to work for the Government it has involved a sacrifice of income.

### The Wool Working Party

My early months at the Board were partly taken up with the concluding stages of the Wool Working Party whose report was submitted in November 1946. It was an interesting group. Of the 15 members, I was the youngest and am now the only survivor. The chairman, Sir Richard Hopkins, had been head of the Treasury and since his retirement had been prevailed on to take on more duties than he would have liked.

Berlin, January 1946  left to right - Kolpakov (USSR);  Anne Romanis (UK);  Soviet Aide;  General Draper (USA);  US Aide;  M Lazard (France - looking away from camera);  Brigadier Bader (South Africa).

Among the independent members was W.T.Astbury, a well-known crystallographer, who enlightened me on many matters such as the way in which hair grows sporadically in different places on a baby's skull. For him, wool was simply a protein fibre to be thought of in terms of amino acids and likely to be subject to competition from fibres still unknown. "Look out for the polypeptides," he would tell me. "You'll hear more of them in time." But when we come to discuss industrial organisation he was a little out of his depth, and would ask me to provide "the" answer to unanswerable posers. When I demurred and indicated that there were just as many ways of organising an industry as of constructing tribal lays, he wagged his finger at me and delivered what I would call the scientist's war cry: "But there must be an answer, Cairncross, there must be an answer."

Another of the independents was George Dickson, a Scottish engineer, who had strong views on industrial democracy and insisted throughout that what was needed in the wool textile and every other industry was a "common objective". This objective had to be one of full employment and on this basis there could be "full and regular consultation between management and workers" covering productive efficiency, working conditions and welfare generally. The other independent members were sceptical in varying degrees of the attainability of any such objective, but they allowed themselves — as often happens on committees of this kind — to be talked into subscribing to a recommendation in keeping with Dickson's views. All that came of our recommendations was an advisory committee which made a modest contribution to the affairs of the industry in post-war years.

The two other independent members were Fred Burgess, an able and active member of the London metal market, and John Pears, who was already a dominant figure in the accountancy firm of Cooper Brothers, and of whom I saw a great deal in later years. Since all of us except Astbury lived in London while the five employers', like the five workers' representatives, lived in Yorkshire, we travelled every week together by train to and from Bradford, talking endlessly on the way there and back, debating the evidence submitted to us as well as much else.

The experience did not fill me with confidence in tripartite committees as a means of coping with Britain's industrial problems. It would have been much quicker and cheaper to commission a study of the industry by a professional economist and issue it to a committee of industry representatives (and any independent members thought necessary). Then they could be left to debate the issues arising, concentrating on the central political issue of the future role of workers' representatives in their dealings with management. But governments have taken a different view. Throughout the post-war period they have appointed one body after another with various permutations of management, unions and others, on which first independent members and later an independent chairman and civil servants have provided a buffer between the representatives of management and unions.

I found an interesting contrast between the wool and cotton textile industries — a contrast that has persisted in spite of predictions that the future of one could be no more lasting than that of the other. For many years, the British wool industry continued to flourish and contribute significantly to exports of manufactures, while the cotton industry faced increasing difficulties. I do not know why this was so. But it would seem to me that wool textiles call for more craftsmanship than cotton, make particular demands upon design and marketing ability to which Yorkshire employers learned to respond, and do not lend themselves so readily as cotton textiles to large-scale manufacture with long runs and a high degree of mechanisation. Thus the typical small mill was less vulnerable because it was making a luxury product, often to the design of a manager with artistic leanings who took a personal interest in his customers' requirements. Not surprisingly, for many years after our deliberations, the West Riding remained one of the world's most important producers of wool textiles.

### The Board of Trade
All this was not a bad introduction to my duties in the Board of Trade. I was then 35 years of age, had specialised in industrial economics, both in writing my textbook and in my contacts with the aircraft industry, and was in general sympathy with the free-trade, consumer-oriented philosophy of the department. At first, it was not altogether clear where I fitted into the hierarchy. Most of my colleagues were only dimly aware of the economic

aspects of what they were doing, while I did not know enough about the specific issues that occupied them to be in a strong position to comment on them. What I could do was to bring home to them the importance of more general issues, some of them handled by the Treasury or some other department, some essentially interdepartmental. But there were also plenty of issues (such as those of commercial policy) where the Board of Trade was in the lead and in which I could hope, given a chance, to make some contribution.

In fact, as I came to realise, the Board of Trade was one of the key departments in the shaping of economic policy. As one of the very few professional economists in it with any influence on policy, I had quite an important role to play. This expanded steadily as I came to learn where the action was and as my colleagues came to see how I could be of assistance to them. Precisely because I did not fit readily into the hierarchy and was as much in contact with those well down it as with those at the top, I could provide a useful channel of communication, passing upwards advance warning of new developments and conveying downwards the state of thinking on urgent policy problems. The Treasury might be in a far more powerful position in shaping economic strategy, but the Board was in close touch tactically with the forces at work: with the operation of many of the controls (on imports, raw materials, clothing rationing, factory construction, etc., etc.); with the ways in which the balance of payments constrained economic activity; and with all the aspects of industry and of commercial policy.

For a year after I entered — until his appointment as Minister of Economic Affairs at the end of September 1947 — the President of the Board of Trade was Sir Stafford Cripps whom I had already got to know as Minister of Aircraft Production. I had followed his career with interest before and during the war, not least because his personal assistant for much of that time was David Owen, with whose family I had shared 11 Bute Gardens when we were both lecturers on the staff of Glasgow University. Cripps was about as different from some of his Labour Party colleagues such as Ernest Bevin as a man could be. His tall, thin figure, rimless glasses and severe features lent themselves to the caricaturist's picture of him as austerity personified. It was hard to conceive of him addressing a miners' gathering or cracking jokes with his working-class constituents. But with a different audience, he could establish an easy *rapport*. I can recall Freddie Bain, then vice-president of the Federation of British Industries (now the CBI), coming away from a meeting with him in the President's office in 1947 and asking me with unconcealed admiration whether Cripps might accept an offer of the presidency of the FBI.

He was a man of extraordinary powers. Once I was summoned, not long after 9am, to the private office, where I was asked to read the draft of a speech in Cripps's own hand to be delivered in Glasgow, and I found myself sitting beside two officials: a Yorkshireman (Herbert Andrew, a future head of the Education Department) and a Lancastrian (Raymond Baldwin). Each was occupied in reading similar speeches in Cripps's handwriting for delivery in Leeds and Manchester respectively. All three speeches had been written that morning. What astonished me was that so practised a speaker should need to write out more than a few notes or, if drafting the whole text, should not dictate it. Once, when I had observed that my own drafts seem to be little used by Cripps I inquired of the private office whether an outline of the argument would suffice. The reply came back that the President would still appreciate receiving a full text, since he liked to follow the development of an argument.

On another occasion, I remember reading the draft of a speech that was to be cleared for delivery in the House of Commons. It seemed to me clumsily written, full of tired phrases and claptrap, with the wrong emphasis or phrasing, and reflecting no credit on the draughtsman. Who could have written it and was it too late to re-write the whole thing? When I went along to the House later to sit in the officials' box, I was taken aback to find that it was Stafford himself who was the author; and still more surprised to observe how successfully the unchanged text was delivered and how warmly the House reacted.

Yet at the back of my mind was the recollection of Cripps's failings as Minister of Aircraft Production. He had that kind of powerful logic that reminds me of the definition of theory as "an organised way of going wrong with confidence". If, for example, aircraft output was rising too slowly — as invariably it was — he wanted to be shown what was holding things up. He would go round the chart room and, when told that aero-engines were the bottleneck, would look at the graph of output and ask what limited the output of aero-engines. This in turn would take him to carburettors and so to carburettor castings — as if changing the capacity to make carburettor castings were the bottleneck in the whole business. It was hopeless to explain that the limiting factor was management, since there was no chart to correspond. Failure to place orders at the right time, for example, did not lend itself to quantitative measurement or pictorial illustration.

So I did not look for miracles under Cripps. But in my year with him he seemed to me to fight courageously on the right side: first over the fuel crisis early in 1947 and later over the need for austerity in the face of limited importing power. There was at least one occasion on which I heard him say, when it looked as if he might not prevail on his colleagues to accept the restrictive measures we were urging on him, "If I am unsuccessful I shall have to consider my position." (i.e., threaten resignation).

He was already concerned at that time with the problem of wages under full employment. How could manpower shortages be got rid of? How should wages be fixed in conditions of general labour shortage? These were perhaps the only questions that he spontaneously put to me; but I was not able to provide any satisfactory answers. Later, as Chancellor, he was to secure from the Trade Union Congress (TUC), almost single-handed and by sheer force of personality, their agreement to a wage freeze in the period following devaluation.

The Permanent Secretary, Sir John Henry Woods, was as different from Cripps in temperament and philosophy as in figure, but proved an ideal foil to his minister. He was a large, stout man who expressed himself stoutly and had all the bonhomie and common sense that Cripps appeared to lack. He was jovial and good-natured, as clubbable a man as you could find. But he had no great sympathy with socialist ideals and a strong preference for market forces over bureaucratic paternalism. He was particularly troubled by the reliance put by the government on voluntary conformity with what it represented as the national interest, even when this ran counter to self-interest, or where the response by different businesses might be very unequal. Over and over again in wartime, the government would assume that individuals or businesses would voluntarily do what it wanted them to do. He christened this "voluntaryism" — a phrase which suggested to him "the occupational disease of a church organist". It was remarkable to me that he and Cripps, so far apart in outlook and experience, got along so well together.

The Second Secretaries, when I joined the Board, were James Helmore and Harry Lintott, both of whom had distinguished careers elsewhere in later life. Helmore headed the domestic side of the Board, while Lintott was in charge of external relations. For a time in 1949, when Woods was ill, Helmore acted as permanent secretary, and in 1951–56 he was head of the short-lived Ministry of Materials, and then of the Ministry of Supply until he left the civil service for industry in 1956. He was a forcible but not always convincing character, with a keen sense of humour, and combined a natural forthrightness with a relish for bureaucratic manoeuvres. I was never quite sure that I knew what Helmore was up to, but he was a useful man to have on one's side.

Harry Lintott, the son of an artist, had a gentler and more subtle approach which I came to appreciate in Paris, when he was one of my colleagues at OEEC. I don't recollect much contact with him in London, since he was away a good deal of the time at one conference or another, and left to become Deputy Secretary-General of the OEEC in 1948. He was succeeded by Stephen Holmes, who joined the Board from the Commonwealth Office. Lintott had been at the Board when I was there during the war, but I had had no previous contact with Holmes, and it took me correspondingly longer to establish a working relationship with him. In fact, since I had so many friends in the Board, it was usually more convenient to work through them than to approach a comparative stranger.

Among those friends were Douglas Carter, whom I had known at Cambridge as an economics undergraduate; Jack Stafford, a lecturer in economics at Manchester who succeeded Leak as head of statistics; Eric Wagstaff, with whom I had been on a walking tour in Germany in 1936; and a host of others. I saw something of my old boss, Bay Kilroy, who was now Lady Meynell and an undersecretary. But I spent most of my time with the assistant secretaries and principals.

There were two others at the Board whose work was of special value to me. One was Laszlo Rostas, a refugee economist from Hungary who had become attached to Cambridge University and had given more time to the measurement of changes in productivity and comparisons of productivity in Britain and America than anyone else. He it was who first brought to my attention the undervaluation of the Dmark after the German currency reform in 1948.

The other was my assistant Polly Hill, a niece of Keynes, who had helped Austin Robinson to produce a monumental report on British export prospects. Polly was a splendid research worker and keenly aware of the significance of research for economic policy. She did some particularly good work on estimates of the level of manufacturing investment in relation to the pre-war period and as an element in total engineering output. This was long before the Central Statistical Office took on the work, and at the time we had very little idea of the claim on resources made by post-war re-equipment. Polly rightly felt that the government seriously undervalued the indispensable need for a continuing supply of economic information in the conduct of export and investment policy. For that reason, she was not content with her back-room duties, but wanted to sally forth and agitate for more attention to be paid to research and its potential. She had my full sympathy; but I was so occupied in fighting my own battles that I hardly had time to see her, much less to promote her views. In due course, not surprisingly, she left, and the work she had begun never developed in the way she had hoped it would.

With the junior ministers in the Board, I had very little to do. I never so much as set eyes on Barbara Castle, who was to be easily the best-known woman minister in the Labour government of the 1960s, even though she had a room a few doors away from me and was then Parliamentary private secretary. John Belcher, the Parliamentary Secretary, made little impression on me, but his successor, John Edwards, who joined the Board in the spring of 1949, was an old friend to whom I could talk openly. As it happened, the politician I saw most of was Arthur Bottomley, who took over from Harold Wilson as Secretary for Overseas Trade in 1947. Out of the blue he asked me, in January 1949, to join a mission to Burma and as a result I spent five fascinating weeks in India (see below).

I have left to the last the most important figure in the Board after the departure of Cripps: Harold Wilson. I had seen him at the British Association Meeting in Dundee in 1939; worked with him in the Economic Section in 1940; recommended him to the Ministry of Fuel and Power when they were looking for a statistician in 1941. I had been in touch with him from time to time thereafter. In 1944, he told me that he was dividing his time between his duties as a civil servant in the Ministry and addressing miners' gathering in the North at the weekend. In 1945, he made the transition from civil servant to politician, and enjoyed a meteoric rise. In March 1947 he joined the Board as Secretary for Overseas Trade, and just over six months later, he was appointed President at the age of 31.

Although I thought I knew Harold fairly well, I had not suspected any political ambitions from my early contacts. Others were more sceptical than I. John Fulton, who was later to become the first vice chancellor of the University of Sussex, is reported to have said, coming down the steps of the Athenaeum in 1945: "Some people have no conception of their own strengths and weaknesses. Look at Harold Wilson who talks of going into politics. Of course he'll be no good at politics, no good at all." Yet here he was, three years after his first election campaign, the youngest member of the Cabinet this century.

Knowing the President was of no particular help to me. Although I saw him from time to time, I have no recollection of any occasion on which he sent for me for a personal discussion of economic issues. Even on so important a matter as devaluation, where I thought that his political career might be transformed if he took the lead in Cabinet in supporting it, he refrained from any discussion and, as happened again in the 1960s, never once asked for a professional exposition of the case for and against. This did not prevent him from putting it about subsequently that he had been a leading supporter of devaluation and was entitled to take the credit for bringing it about. What emerged during the summer of 1949 was Harold's fondness for keeping his options open, his disinclination to say unpalatable things to his colleagues, his tendency to see economic issues in purely political terms (in this case, the date of the next election) and, most of all, his deviousness. One characteristic he shared with Stafford Cripps was a preference (most evident when it came to devaluation) for the use of administrative measures to put things right rather than make adjustments to market signals.

I find an entry in my diary for October 12, 1949 — shortly after devaluation — that says a good deal about Harold:

> Michael Halls (assistant private secretary) at lunch described to me the President's exertions, including about six successive nights in the train, and his astonishing resiliency and good nature. Never angry. (I said I thought this was in part his weakness also, as it prevented in him a certain forthrightness.)

> In Oxford (where he addressed the Institute of Bankers) he dined with Michael on fish and chips and went to Christ Church with a bag of chips, much to the surprise of his hosts.)

I spent most of my time at the Board on domestic affairs. Almost any paper with an obvious economic aspect began to come my way. Papers that fell outside the normal ambit of the Board were also apt to come to me: the President might want briefing on a Cabinet paper by another minister such as the Chancellor on general economic policy or the dollar drain, or the Minister of Agriculture on the extermination of rabbits. At the height of the debate on devaluation, I was also preoccupied briefly with the case for building the Channel Tunnel. Then there were papers to prepare for the Permanent Secretary's weekly office meetings. These provided me with an opportunity to draw the attention of the Board's senior officials to emerging policy issues or to expound the doctrine bearing on them. After devaluation, for example, I circulated two notes, one seeking to explain what I took to be the strategy and another examining the load on the export industries and arguing for cuts in government expenditure to make the load easier to bear. Activities of this kind led me to explain subsequently to academic colleagues that my duties had been essentially those of staff officer to the Permanent Secretary.

Some of my most important duties were interdepartmental. I served as a link with the Economic Section, then still attached to the Cabinet Office, and to a lesser extent with the Treasury. For example, I represented the Board on committees preparing the *Economic Survey* or dealing with the balance of payments, and would be asked to brief on issues such as the future of the sterling area or the recovery plan submitted to OEEC.

My most important interdepartmental duty, however, was in my individual capacity as a member of the Investment

Programmes Committee, a small but influential group which scrutinised the main programmes of capital investment by the public sector and by private industry submitted by Departments and prepared a report for ministers on the position in the coming year. The Committee obliged departments to keep their forward commitments under review, to consider their options and to examine both against a comprehensive picture of what was proposed for the economy as a whole. Its members tried their best to take a detached non-departmental view, although there was inevitably some tendency for them to view matters in terms of departmental interest. When I left, the Board of Trade promptly replaced me.

I became increasingly dissatisfied with the group's proceedings on a number of grounds. It did not seem to make much sense to concentrate on the coming year when investment commitments often had a much longer time horizon. I also doubted whether we were right to rely as heavily as we did on the inadequate technical expertise of departments when some of the programmes might be open to challenge on technical rather than economic grounds. In addition, we were often very much in the dark as to what was actually happening. I distrusted recommendations that investment be held to a given programme when we did not know, for example, whether aggregate industrial investment was rising or falling or what the current level really was.

The government's control of investment during this period was often attacked in later years on the ground that the level of industrial investment in the early post-war years was much too low to maintain the competitive power of British industry. It is sometimes alleged that the government held down the level of investment and that additional investment would have transformed the long-term prospects for British exports. My time on the committee, and all my subsequent experience, convinced me that both propositions are extremely doubtful. Since there was already full employment, additional investment, unless financed from abroad, would have added markedly to inflationary pressure. At that time, only the government was saving; and by bringing the budget into surplus in 1949–50, the government did more than any of its successors in the next 20 years to make additional savings available for the finance of investment. It also embarked on a much expanded programme of public investment. The only way it could have boosted industrial investment was by limiting other kinds of domestic investment, as indeed it did, except in the case of housebuilding, which by 1948 had reached over a quarter of the total. It is also a gross oversimplification to assume that a higher level of industrial investment was crucial to success in meeting competition in foreign and domestic markets, although it would no doubt have been helpful.

Looking back now, I have the impression that the Board made less use of me on the external than the domestic side. Although the department that dealt with commercial relations and exports was the central policy department and I had many friends working in it, I was not much involved in specific issues of commercial policy. In all the negotiations over the International Trade Organisation (the ITO: the ancestor of today's World Trade Organisation), the Havana Charter on the rules of international trade which was agreed a few years after the war and the formation of the General Agreement on Tariffs and Trade which paved the way for the post-war liberalisation of trade, I was hardly ever involved. Indeed, I can recall a visit from Helmore to express outrage that I had dared to suggest in a minute that we could not afford to sell anthracite to Canada even for hard currency. I also recollect expressing — in vain, as it happened — strong views on the political danger of discriminating against Japanese exports. And on one occasion, a fellow official dealing with commercial policy showed me a minute denouncing Franco-German efforts to achieve what would subsequently have been called a common market, but I could understand neither the source nor the strength of his indignation.

However, twice during my three years in the Board I spent some weeks abroad with an official economic mission. The first was to Canada at the end of 1947 as a member of an interdepartmental group whose primary task appeared to be to reconcile the Canadians to the cancellation of contracts to buy their bacon and eggs. It left me fearful that the British market would never resume its importance for the Canadian farmer. It also introduced me to many of the leading Canadian Ministers and officials, including Lester Pearson and Mitchell Sharp, who became respectively prime minister and foreign secretary of Canada in the 1960s.

My second and much more exciting trip was to Pakistan and India, just after Gandhi's assassination, en route for Burma. Civil war had broken out between the Burmese and the Karens, Chins and other groups in the interior of the country. Arthur Bottomley who had succeeded Harold Wilson as Secretary for Overseas Trade, led a mission which was intended to go to Rangoon and try to restore peace. But this intention was not to be made public; instead, it was announced that he would be making a survey of the trading facilities enjoyed by British exporters in the main ports in India. I would have no part in the negotiations in Burma, but would provide Bottomley with a kind of beard-and-whiskers disguise.

We never got as far as Burma[2], but I was able to acquire some education in Commonwealth affairs. We spent an evening in Karachi with the Pakistani president, Liaquat Ali Khan, sitting with him in his library surrounded by his books. When we moved on to New Delhi, we stayed there for several weeks, while telegrams arrived from all over the Commonwealth, many of them unenthusiastic about our intervention in Burma. I saw a good deal of my friend V.K.R.V.Rao and his family, learned the Indian way of taking a shower by ladling cold water over one's body, and had time to look round Delhi. Bottomley took me with him to meet Nehru; and when we went to call on the Indian President, Rajagopalachari, I can still recall my astonishment at his first words: "I've been reading your book." I looked at Arthur Bottomley in some surprise, since I knew nothing of his venture into authorship. But the President exclaimed, "No, no, *your* book on economics," making it clear that my "Introduction to Economics" had not only reached India but had somehow come to the attention of the President.

## The bonfire of controls

While I was not much involved in the external side of the Board's work, I was very much in the picture in efforts to promote

---

[2] The name of the leader of the Karens, General Ne Win, lingered in my mind. I assumed at the time that he was a statesman-like representative of his people, defending them against their Burmese oppressors. Bottomley, who had met Aung San, the Burmese prime minister, before his assassination, took a more balanced view of the position. I learned to regard Ne Win in a very different light when, many years later, I met Aung San's daughter in Oxford; and when Dr Solomon Suvi, a distinguished Burmese surgeon and a fellow student of my wife's brother in the 1920s, described to me how, in the 1980s, he had been stripped of all he had and put on a plane, penniless, to India for no offence except a refusal to take the General as a patient.

exports. I encouraged the preparation of an illustrative table showing how different industries might contribute to a level of exports 75% higher than before the war — the level said to be required in order to balance our international accounts. This table came to the attention of Cripps, and excited him greatly. To the astonishment of us all, he made it at once the basis of a system of publicly announced export targets — without any effort to establish by what means we could assist or direct industry to achieve them. One such means was the allocation of materials and this was used, for example, to bring pressure on the motor-car industry to develop its export markets and to allocate to those markets at one stage no less than 75% of its output. But this case made it abundantly clear that we were living in a world of excess demand and that better results might be obtained by fiscal action to reduce demand rather than by the use of controls to direct supply.

Most of the controls introduced during the war were continued for a time when it ended. There were many different kinds of control: consumer rationing which covered, at its most extensive in 1948, less than one-third of consumer spending; price control which covered about half, or perhaps 60%, of consumer spending but did not prevent prices from rising in line with costs and was largely abandoned in 1952-53; building and investment control, one outcome of which was that over half the value of factory construction was in the "development areas" — regions of high unemployment which normally employed about 5% of the working population; raw material allocation, where decontrol was arrested after the outbreak of the Korean war and many controls re-imposed; and finally labour controls which were removed after a couple of years; and import controls, which affected 90% of imports up to 1950.

I accepted the need to retain import controls for a time, in order to allow our limited supply of foreign exchange to be used to the best advantage. I also thought that until industry had recovered nearer to peace-time levels of production, the removal of controls in face of excess demand ran the risk of promoting inflation. As I saw it, as production for civil consumption recovered and exports grew, we would be able gradually to equate supply and demand without violent changes in relative prices (or in the price level), whereas if we tried to let the price mechanism take over too soon, there would be large swings in prices that would complicate and delay the process of adjustment and were likely also to cause public irritation. For example, a premature devaluation would undoubtedly set off dangerous inflationary forces. Those who protested against austerity and its hardships overlooked the fact that shortages in some form were inescapable until output for civil consumption had returned to normal levels.

This is not to say, however, that I was in sympathy with the apotheosis of a system of central planning. I had seen enough of the limitations of central planning and the crudity of most controls in my time in MAP to have no wish to perpetuate them. The Board generally took the same view: as soon as controls had served their purpose over the period of transition, they should go. And go they did, in a series of bonfires under Harold Wilson.

These bonfires were widely endowed with ideological significance, as if they expressed a conscious decision to revert to an uncontrolled economy. But it makes no sense to go on rationing when there is enough to go round. What *is* true is that there was sometimes excessive eagerness to remove a control (for example, the rationing of sweets had to be resumed) and there was often room for disagreement whether the underlying balance of supply and demand (for clothing, for example) was such as to make decontrol feasible. It is also true that there *was* a presumption in favour of a move from physical controls to financial controls. Certainly, no one in the Board tried to work out what controls were likely to be required under a peace-time system of central planning.

The most vivid illustration I remember of different attitudes to controls was the exchange between Ludwig Erhard and Cripps, to which I listened after bringing Erhard, then a professor of political science in Munich, to Cripps's room. I had been asked to devise a programme for Erhard's visit to London in 1947 — a visit promoted by the British Government at a time when Erhard was still a rather obscure German politician, holding no federal or state office. He had hardly been in my room for two minutes before I realised that his economic philosophy was already familiar to me as that of John Jewkes (although I should have been surprised if either had ever heard of the other) and I felt a keen sense of transmigration to a tubbier carcass.

I took him to two factories which I thought might be of interest to a German economist worried by the need to dilute industrial work so as to make more use of female labour and by the equally pressing need to economise on imported materials. The first factory was a Dunlop tyre-retreading plant at Greenwich which employed a high proportion of women; the second was the Harris Lebus factory in Tottenham, making utility furniture out of indifferent timber. Erhard expressed disappointment, if not contempt, that we had nothing better to show him than this. The tyre factory was obviously run down and dirty, while the furniture factory was turning out shoddy goods. It was apparent to me that he envisaged the reconstruction of German industry not in terms of "make do and mend" but in a very different spirit of: "Let us have nothing but the best."

When we went to see Stafford Cripps, the President stressed the need for a system of planning and control which he saw as the British way to recovery and Socialism, while Erhard listened quite unimpressed. When his turn came, he dismissed the Crippsian remedy in a sentence. "Control may have worked successfully in this country, Mr President, and no doubt you have good reason to be satisfied with the way your economy has performed; but in my country the public associates control with Hitler and has had enough of it." He then developed views that were the antithesis of Cripps's. But when he came to describe what his government actually did, it bore a striking resemblance to British measures. I was asked by Cripps to explain the advantages of our utility programme. When I had finished, Erhard merely nodded approvingly: "Ach ja, das Jenemann program — das haben wir auch." It was the same with control of investment, import quotas and so on. Similar situations dictated similar policies even if ministers represented their actions in a quite different light in different countries. It was my first experience of what was later christened "Butskellism".

## Coal and devaluation

Of the events of those years, the two that stand out most prominently in my mind were the fuel crisis and devaluation, and I was closely involved with both. I had gone through the arithmetic in 1946 while I was on *The Economist*, comparing the expected output of coal with the expected requirements for it in

1947, and I had seen how a dwindling labour force in the coal mines had been reflected in a fall in the level of coal production. It seemed quite obvious that supply and demand were not balanced and that shortages were bound to develop as the winter advanced. What nobody could foresee was that the winter of 1946–47 would be of record severity and that the long freeze would begin only once stocks were at their lowest.

The Ministry of Fuel and Power had made no adequate preparations, either by cutting consumption so as to balance the coal budget or by bringing before the Cabinet plans for action should the shortage develop on the scale that seemed likely even before the freeze. The policy adopted in February 1946 was to close down factories wholesale in order to build up stocks at the power stations and gas works. I thought this plain crazy and said so. But the Ministry officials appeared to take a fatalistic if not complacent view of the situation and were unwilling to alter their priorities. They had their eye on one set of risks while we were obsessed with very different risks. It made no sense, in our view, to shut down British industry in order to add to the stocks of coal for electricity generation. Many factories used little electric power and still held some coal in stock.

When the matter was reconsidered early in March, Cripps was successful in obtaining a change in policy. Aneurin Bevan, who was then Minister of Health, took the sensible view that he would rather run the risk of being hung in October than commit suicide in March. On this basis it was agreed to let industry resume working with such stocks of coal as it had , and on the whole, industry found it not too difficult to get going again. But as a test case of efficient planning, the fuel crisis found the Labour Government wanting. I estimated that it lost us £200m in exports (I should now put it at £100m) when foreign exchange was our worst bottleneck. My estimate was given unexpected publicity by the President who cited it in one of his speeches[3].

I have less bitter recollections of devaluation[4]. I took the view in late 1948 that external balance had been restored and the time

[3] For a full account of the fuel crisis of 1947, see Chapter 13 in my "Years of Recovery" (Methuen 1985).

[4] I have published several accounts of the devaluation of 1949, the fullest of them in "Sterling in Decline" (with Barry Eichengreen: Blackwell, 1983).

was approaching when the exchange rate should be reviewed. It may seem paradoxical to think of exchange depreciation *after* exports had climbed to equal imports, but the issue was not how to restore British trade to balance but how to respond to the so-called dollar shortage. At some stage in the post-war period, it was obviously necessary to reconsider the relationship between sterling and the dollar, and the time to do this was when the recovery of trade was no longer a matter of logistics but depended again on relative prices. We needed to redirect not only British trade but the trade of the sterling area and of Europe so that deficits in hard currency and surpluses in soft, inconvertible currency no longer existed side by side; and the way to do this was to make hard currency dearer and soft currency cheaper until the first softened and the second hardened into convertibility.

There were, of course, people who thought that devaluation was intended primarily to improve Britain's export prospects in the American market and reduce our dependence on American imports. They judged on this basis that the devaluation of 1949 was a failure; and many economists have argued in somewhat similar terms that it did little good because it left British exports no more competitive than before. All this is largely beside the point. The devaluation of 1949 had a much wider significance and was an indispensable step towards the removal of the dollar shortage and the substitution of financial for physical controls over international trade.

Not that anyone in the Board of Trade asked me whether I thought that we should devalue the pound. But the matter arose in various areas that came under the sway of the Board, including the misuse of commodity markets through a practice known as "commodity shunting". Holders of sterling who were not allowed to convert their holdings into hard currencies but needed dollars would sell their pounds "cheap", and use the proceeds to acquire commodities that could be sold for dollars with a profit for the commodity trader and a loss of foreign exchange to the British reserves. Commodities could be turned into hard currency, even if sterling could not.

In December 1946 I sent a minute to the Permanent Secretary suggesting that the time had come to consider devaluation and that we should do so before the issue came to be publicly debated. In my view we had six months in which to act. Three months later, having failed to convince the Permanent Secretary, I arranged that the President should see a copy of my minute. It read as follows:

"Now that we look like having a favourable balance of payments in 1949 I suggest that we ought to have another look at the sterling-dollar exchange rate. My reasons for thinking this are:—

(1) Everybody thinks the issue is now dead. If it were alive and under public discussion we should find it very awkward to take action. The very fact that action would come as a complete surprise is one of the strongest reasons for re-considering our policy now.

(2) Up till now we have had no exports to speak of that could be regarded as surplus. Diversion was, therefore, liable to cost us just as much as we gained. Now we have an unmistakable margin on which to operate.

(3) Our relations with Canada seem to be going from bad to worse. The real cause of this is our inability to expand exports to Canada. This in turn is linked with the rate of exchange which is either an immediate stumbling block or a discouragement to exporters looking at their long-term prospects in the Canadian market.

(4) The chances that US costs will rise sharply relative to British costs now look a little remote — at any rate in the industries competing with British exports.

(5) Since our dollar expenditure is financed largely out of Marshall Aid it would be unaffected by depreciation. A heavy debtor position in relation to Canada and the US means that we have much to gain and little to lose from a change in exchange rates.

(6) The contribution made to economising on dollars by the rest of the Empire over the past year cannot be consolidated unless British products are fully competitive with American. It is futile to expect that the controls that have been imposed to force importers to buy from the UK rather than from the US will be retained indefinitely. There is little prospect of a marked gain in competitive power vis-à-vis American exports without exchange depreciation.

(7) Many other countries (including some of the European countries) are prevented from doing their share to increase

exports to North America by high exchange rates and are inhibited from taking independent action to vary these exchange rates. If we took the lead they would be likely to follow.

(8) Finally, there can be no question that the hard currency markets are much the least attractive to British exporters at present because of the difficulty of competing on price. But if in the long run we hope to increase substantially the proportion of our exports going to hard currency markets we must assume that the prices in those markets are more, not less, attractive than elsewhere. I see no possible way of achieving this (apart from further inflation in the US) except by exchange depreciation."

I was not at all sure that I had any right to go direct to the Minister on any issue; but I regarded this as a unique occasion on which hierarchical considerations did not apply and I was entitled to give my professional opinion without going through the usual channels. I was not aware at that time that my view was shared by anyone else: it was certainly not the view of any of the senior officials of the Board. It was also apparent that the President had no enthusiasm for the idea. Since I had no opportunity of discussing it with him, I had to rely on Max Brown, his private secretary, to keep me informed about the state of his thinking.

In the spring of 1949 John Henry Woods was ill, I was in India and the proposal seemed to have fallen by the wayside. But as the spring moved toward summer, there were indications of a recession in trade that might have serious effects on sterling. At the beginning of May Cripps, now Chancellor of the Exchequer, reacted to rumours of a possible devaluation by a speech in Rome that slammed the door on any such suggestion. It seemed to me that, whether he was right or wrong, he had gone much too far in his anxiety to strike at speculation against the pound, since anyone could see by now that there was at least a possibility that devaluation might become inevitable.

About this time I found others in Whitehall were strongly of my opinion, especially Robert Hall, who had taken over the Directorship of the Economic Section from James Meade. On the other hand, most of the Bank of England was ranged against us and the Treasury was divided. Robert Hall had converted Edwin Plowden, who was Head of the Planning Staff and Roger Makins, then a senior official in the Foreign Office. But had I, he asked, had any success with my colleagues in the Board? My advice from Max Brown was that Harold Wilson had not made up his mind, but Robert Hall's information was that in Cabinet he took the other side. John Henry Woods was still away (and not sound on this issue) and James Helmore was inclined to sit on the fence while Stephen Holmes, in charge of commercial policy, was dead against devaluation. So, although I kept hammering away, I was not confident of contributing much to the battle.

The big change came in July. In mid-June the dollar drain had increased and the Chancellor put round a paper asking what could be announced in July after the figures were made public. At that stage nobody seemed to be taking devaluation seriously and the President had actually come out against it in a report on his recent tour of Canada. A few days later, a draft came to us from the Treasury of a paper, presumably by Otto Clarke, a senior Treasury official on overseas finance, forecasting that we would have no dollars left by January 1950 or at latest by March. It was proposed that dollar expenditure should be cut by 25% on July 5th, when the quarterly statement on the dollar drain was due for release, and that a Commonwealth Conference should be summoned at once. Meanwhile, no fresh dollar expenditure should be authorised before September 30th.

Proposals of this kind spelt crisis and in the crisis, opinion changed quickly. I began to meet people who assured me that we were bound to devalue, such as Paul Bareau, my old colleague from *The Economist*.

In the first week of July, John Snyder, secretary of the U.S. Treasury, arrived with Averill Harriman, who was then adviser to the American President, and Lewis Douglas, the United States' ambassador to Britain, for talks with the British government. The press took it for granted that he had come to urge devaluation on the government, but the word was not mentioned in the talks, until a draft communiqué came up for consideration. The very fact of the absence of discussion of devaluation delayed the issue of the communiqué while first officials and then Ministers argued for an hour and a half each — three hours in all — over its inclusion or exclusion from the text. Snyder was petulant and angry. As there had been no discussion of devaluation, why should it be mentioned at all? Stafford

Cripps replied that all he wanted to say was that it had not been discussed. After a 30-minute adjournment, Snyder reluctantly agreed. He obviously felt caught in a logical trap. Stafford could argue that, if they made no reference to devaluation in the communiqué, everybody would say that Snyder had been urging devaluation on the Chancellor; but Snyder, who had come at the request of the British government to listen to what they had to say, resented the innuendo that, because he had failed to express his views, they would be inferred from his silence.

A few days later, Cripps, who had been in poor health for some time, was in a nursing home and Hugh Gaitskell took over the responsibilities of Chancellor. Before the end of the month, a firm decision to devalue had been taken. The sudden change of front puzzled me at the time, and over the following year so many people came into my room to explain how they devalued the pound that I doubt to this day that they can all have been right. The most convincing account was one I was given in early August: Gaitskell was converted by Rosenstein-Rodan, a professor of economics at Harvard University, in the course of a long walk on Hampstead Heath. Rosenstein-Rodan later confirmed this tale.

In any event, Gaitskell's conversion was the turning point. By then Douglas Jay, the Economic Secretary, who had been hitherto a strong opponent, had already been persuaded by Robert Hall and others. These two set about bringing their colleagues round, and found them responsive. Aneurin Bevan and Herbert Morrison, the Lord President of the Council, were already predisposed to agree. Harold Wilson was also by this time in favour, although without real force of conviction, contending characteristically for making devaluation the subject of a bargain with the United States.

So in the end, almost by accident, we devalued in September 1949 — three months later than the limit I suggested in the previous December. Had Gaitskell not taken over from Cripps there would have been a further delay and we should have faced the Korean War with reserves still less adequate to our needs. And had there been no exchange crisis and no anxiety to sell more in the US, the case for devaluation would have gone unexamined. Of such quirks and coincidences is history composed. At least the issue had been settled before I left the Board at the end of

November, and there was already some evidence that the pound was strengthening.

## 10

## *A year in Paris at OEEC, 1950*

In the autumn of 1949, shortly after the devaluation of sterling in September, I was on the verge of taking up an appointment at the University of Glasgow as the first holder of a new chair in applied economics. My wife had travelled north to look at a house I had already inspected, when I was approached by Robert Hall, the government's Economic Adviser, to ask whether I would go to Paris and take over once again from Donald MacDougall, this time as economic adviser to the Organisation for European Economic Co-operation, the body that eventually became the OECD.

When Mary came back, we talked the proposal over and agreed that I should decline. I knew little about the set-up in Paris, feared it might be more productive of paper than anything else, and was impatient to get back to academic life. I was also conscious of the problems for Mary in piloting three small children (all under five) first to Paris and then to Glasgow or (if I went alone) in coping with them in my absence. I told our lawyer to buy the house that Mary and I had seen in Lenzie near Glasgow, and Robert that I would not go to Paris.

Next day I was requested to call on the Chancellor, Stafford Cripps, at 11 Downing Street. He looked ill and leathery in complexion, and I could not find it in my heart to refuse a direct appeal from him to go for a minimum of six weeks, deferring my move to Glasgow. I was conscious that, with devaluation an accomplished fact and an election in the offing, I might have little of importance to do if I stayed at the Board until April. OEEC was then at the centre of the international stage. It had been set up in 1947–48, to be an intermediary between Europe and the United States on Marshall Aid — and was in the final stages of completing its second report on that subject. This document was, in effect, Europe's bid to the United States for aid with post-war reconstruction. Only a few weeks were required to complete the Report, and most of the job had presumably been done.

I decided that if I was going for the six weeks that Cripps indicated as the minimum, I might as well go for six months and take the family with me. I did, however, insist that my successor at OEEC should be appointed in good time. In fact, this proved a vain hope. In the end I had to set about finding my own successor, Brian Reddaway, and it was not until January 1951, more than a year later, that we were able to leave Paris for Glasgow.

I made a preliminary visit to Paris in mid-November, and called on Robert Marjolin, the OEEC's first Secretary General. He was a remarkable figure: he had all the gifts — of administrative ability, and of political leadership — that would have made him prime minister of France. But, when he stood for Parliament, he was not returned. The OEEC was lucky to have him as its leader in those early years.

When I saw him, I explained that I was very ignorant about OEEC and had read little or nothing of what it had published. He laughed at this. "You're in good company. We have a large printing works over there," he said, pointing to the office across the road, "but we're too busy to read what we publish. It's like Alice in Wonderland. You remember how all the jury scribbled away and then threw their scribblings out of the jury-box into the court without anybody taking the trouble to read them? We're like the jury. We have one reader — a member of the Turkish delegation. He gets up at 5am to read our papers and stays up late to read more of them. At meetings he quotes from document after document, including some that nobody present has ever heard of. But all his quotations refer to dried fruit and tobacco."

When I got back to London, I had a busy time ahead of me and felt exhausted. John Edwards, a junior minister, had asked me to deputise for him at a meeting in Copenhagen and I had been looking forward to this trip. But in the end it was agreed that he should go and I was left to prepare a draft for his address, submit it to departments for comment and rewrite and edit it. At that point, Stafford Cripps, the Chancellor, weighed in with his own amendments, some of which surprised me — as when he wanted it said that the expenditure cuts that followed devaluation had been decided upon "side by side with it". (We all knew perfectly well that the cuts were quite insufficient, bitterly contested and very much an after-thought.) After the first batch of amendments, the Chancellor's secretary rang up with yet another suggestion for an extra paragraph to the effect that the dollar problem was America's as much as anyone's.

This and other business occupied me over my final fortnight at the Board. I said my farewells on December 5th and left for Paris the following day. Six weeks later the family joined me in an apartment off the Avenue Mozart.

In the development of OEEC, 1950 was a year of critical importance. It was the year in which France put forward the Schuman Plan, a plan to bind together the coal and steel industries of Western Europe, signalled a further stage in the development of close relations between France and Germany, and was to prove the starting point of the European Union. The year also saw the creation by the OEEC of the European Payments Union — a kind of clearing union that superseded the many bilateral payments agreements between member countries and opened the way to a sustained expansion in trade without constant crises in payments arrangements. I was not involved in setting up either institution, but I recognised at the time their importance to the reconstruction of Western Europe.

As Director of the Economics Division, I was responsible also for statistics (after I left, the two responsibilities were split). There were some able statisticians among the staff, but no systematic machinery for issuing statistics in a convenient form: no statistical bulletin or authoritative document to which all administrators could have recourse for up-to-date information and a view of current economic trends.

I insisted that there should be such a bulletin, little thinking of the flood of publications that would issue from the rock I was striking with such vehemence. Since progress was slow, I turned for help to Ely Devons, my closest friend in Whitehall, who had done the same job twice over in wartime, first in the Economic Section of the War Cabinet Offices and then in the Ministry of Aircraft Production. A dummy bulletin of what was to become the OEEC's General Statistical Bulletin was prepared under his direction while I was on a visit to Washington with Marjolin. Some of the younger statisticians were unhappy with this "invasion", but although I had some doubts how successful Ely would be, I got back from my trip to America to find that he had completed his assignment to everyone's satisfaction.

This was only the beginning of the OEEC's ventures into the field of statistics. During the summer, I was asked to secure agreement from statisticians in the OEEC's member countries for what is now familiar as the Standard International Trade Classification of imports and exports. This was intended to replace the Brussels classification, and allow international trade statistics to be presented in meaningful economic categories, acceptable to all countries, thus facilitating international comparison, aggregation and analysis. Once I was convinced of the case for this, I agreed to take the chair at a meeting of statisticians from the leading countries and was successful in securing unanimous acceptance. Rather to my surprise, the agreement stuck — and figures began to reach OEEC on the new basis. We issued them monthly in a new series of bulletins which occupied a vast amount of library space, but were quite invaluable in providing data on the commodity structure of international trade, on trends in that structure, and on the volume of trade by commodity group. Most trade analysts have used these SITC figures ever since. Indeed, I am still using them today, for my forthcoming book on post-war trends in international trade.

As the months passed, I began to wonder whether this accidental foray into statistical engineering might not be my most important contribution to OEEC. I had slogged away at the almost-complete second report, but the key opening section, which was in effect a manifesto bidding for more aid from America, was produced literally out of Otto Clarke's pocket in the course of a flying visit in January. A former journalist turned Treasury official, he had dashed off what I had struggled to put together for weeks.

Thereafter, for most of the year, we were meditating the Third Report, which was eventually issued in 1951, and trying to give meaning to integration, harmonisation and other approaches to international economic co-operation. All this was against the background of the Korean War, the scramble for raw materials and the world-wide inflation of 1950. Then, in late October, something else happened that affected me much more intimately.

## A German crisis

In the late autumn Germany had developed a balance of payments crisis — the only one in post-war years. The country had increased its imports, mainly of raw materials, on a scale that it could not afford, and was running out of foreign exchange. Germany appeared to be on the verge of suspending the measures to liberalise trade it had taken earlier. The issue was the first serious test of the newly created European Payments Union, which had come into operation in July.

I became involved in Germany's balance of payments crisis when, at the end of October, I was rung up by Marjolin in Geneva, where I had gone for talks with the Economic Commission for Europe, and asked whether I would act alongside Per Jacobsson, then the economic adviser to the Bank for International Settlements — the central bankers' bank and the operating arm of the EPU — in advising the EPU on the German crisis. A few days later, I left Paris by train for Frankfurt, with a mind about as blank on the whole subject as it would have been possible to find in OEEC. I received no papers until the day before my departure and knew nothing of the background to the crisis. I was accompanied by two colleagues, one of whom was Otmar Emminger, a future President of Germany's Bundesbank. When we reached Frankfurt, we were met by Dr Albrecht and Dr Wolf, two of the most senior officials of the Bank Deutscher Laender (or BDL, the forerunner of the Bundesbank), and taken to lunch with the governor, Wilhelm Vocke and several of the directors, including Karl Bernard, the president of the bank's board of directors, and Karl Blessing, who eventually succeeded Vocke as governor.

At that stage Per Jacobsson had not arrived. His plane from Stockholm was delayed and did not reach Frankfurt until lunch time. He then proved to be suffering severely from oyster poisoning, and for the first day or so he was unable to play an active part in our inquiry. Indeed, initially it was by no means certain he would be able to do so.

Jacobsson, however, had already exercised a decisive influence on subsequent events. Many of Germany's bankers were

Jacobsson's personal friends, and he was listened to with attention by its politicians. He had discovered to his surprise and dismay, when he had passed through Frankfurt on his way to Stockholm a few days earlier, that Dr Vocke, although a firm believer in liberalising trade, had decided on suspension of existing measures of liberalisation. The managing board of the EPU, to which we were about to report, had already taken the same decision, without communicating the decision to Jacobsson and me or waiting for our views. The American mission to Germany on Marshall Aid was also pressing for the suspension of liberalisation and seemed quite oblivious both to the consequences for American prestige and to the desirability of avoiding the suspension of existing import contracts.

All this dismayed Jacobsson, who wanted at all costs to avoid the suspension of liberalisation. Suspension would be a first-rate piece of propaganda for Eastern Germany, a blow to the policies sponsored by the United States in Western Europe and a most discreditable outcome for the first serious problem to be dealt with by the EPU managing board.

An increase in Germany's discount rate had previously been under discussion by the BDL, and Jacobsson had accordingly spent some time with Vocke, arguing in favour of such an increase as a way to choke off imports, and for the retention of the liberalisation measures along with the higher discount rate. In the discussion with Vocke, he happened to have the support of a senior official from the Allied Banking Commission, a body set up by the Allies, whose advice would obviously be given quite independently. Other countries, Jacobsson pointed out, had had to raise their discount rates in similar circumstances, and had found it a successful solution to a balance of payments problem; he, as an expert, would inevitably recommend it, and it was better to act independently than under pressure from outside; finally, the state of the money market seemed to him to be now sufficiently flexible for movements in discount rates to begin to take effect.

The meeting of the Bank's Central Council, at which the Bank rate decision was taken, was attended by the prime minister, Konrad Adenauer, as well as several cabinet ministers: a very rare thing to happen. Adenauer was against an increase and so were the other ministers, except Ludwig Erhard, who was then

Federal Minister of Economics, and most of the members of the central council, apart from Vocke. The members of the cabinet had no idea how serious the situation was. Despite this lack of enthusiasm, the council decided to raise the discount rate. I was told subsequently that the reluctance to raise the rate sprang mainly from the fact that the measure was widely associated with Vocke's known deflationary leanings.

I did not see the issue in the light of my talks at the BDL in quite the same way as Jacobsson. I saw no need for the adoption of his favourite medicine, a stiff dose of deflation. But I accepted that Germany had embarked on stockbuilding of imports, mainly raw materials, on a scale that she could not afford, and no doubt the stockbuilding rested heavily on bank credit. On the other hand, German exports had already begun their headlong expansion, doubling in the course of 1951. It was likely that, as the expansion proceeded, imports would come back into line with exports, and the external deficit would prove no more than a temporary hiccup.

The technical difficulty facing us was that Germany relied on a system of import quotas to control the volume of imports, and that the import licences outstanding were large in relation to one month's imports. It was not possible to estimate with any confidence the rate at which these licences would be used and hence the prospective scale of imports over the next few months. But, with raw materials shooting up in price after the outbreak of war in Korea, importers had every reason to use their licences as quickly as possible.

We spent three days in Frankfurt, analysing the figures and talking things over with the able officials of the BDL. We then motored to Bonn to see the Ministers immediately concerned. We soon found ourselves involved in not one but two issues — the immediate problem, the balance of payments crisis, and the question of financing German rearmament, which was a long-term matter. With the beginning of the Cold War, the United States was pressing Germany to raise more taxation to pay for a substantial army. Several of the German ministers we saw attached more importance to the rearmament issue, and the taxes it would entail, than to the balance of payments.

An example was Fritz Schaeffer, the Federal Finance Minister, whom we saw in Bonn. Everyone explained to us, including

Schaeffer himself, that the Finance Minister was not to be thought of as the Chancellor of the Exchequer, but had a humbler role. Nevertheless, he seemed clearly the most powerful personality in the Cabinet after Adenauer. Schaeffer was not averse to some increases in taxation, (although he insisted to the contrary in a speech he gave while we were in town) and indeed told me and Jacobsson independently that he thought he could raise an additional DM2 billion. But he, unlike us, was clearly thinking of taxes in terms of rearmament. Our feeling was that he could do more but probably not very much more; and that he would wait until an agreement with the Allies had been reached on rearmament, and use the announcement as a screen for a tax increase. Neither he nor his advisers seemed to have a particularly profound understanding of public finance.

When we saw Erhard, he was as eupeptic as ever and did not seem at all chastened by what must have been a narrow squeak in his political career: had liberalisation been suspended, he would almost certainly have had to resign. He gave us a long talk on liberalisation and chain reactions — if one country suspended liberalisation, others might do the same. We then saw Franz Bluecher, the founder of the Free Democrats and deputy Federal Chancellor. He had opposed the increase in the discount rate, on the grounds that it made the capital market work less efficiently and might drive up rents. Finally we visited Cologne to get Adenauer's views from Dr Pferdemenges, his chief adviser.

We later entertained Schaeffer, Bluecher and Erhard. Throughout our time in Bonn, I was a little at a disadvantage because the conversations took place almost exclusively in German and my spoken German is decidedly weak. Schaeffer, however, had a reasonable command of English and described how his dismissal by the Americans in 1945 from the post of prime minister of Bavaria was effected in three peremptory words: "You are dismissed."

Subsequently, we saw Hermann Abs of the Deutsche Bank, at that time the most powerful private banker in Germany, who was widely (but wrongly) assumed to be Vocke's successor. He had come back specially from Rome to see us, and was intelligent and shrewd and probably more flexible than Vocke, although he did not convey the same impression of sincerity. He provided us with information about the various ways in which the terms of payment had moved against Germany (thus contributing to Germany's current financial difficulties), and about the extent to which exporters had concluded long-term contracts (which might imply that the payments problem might be receding).

We then saw two of the most senior Americans in Germany: Jean Cattier, who was head of the body that administered Marshall Aid on America's behalf, and J.J.McCloy, who had been the second head of the World Bank. Cattier was unimpressive: he was inclined to blame the Germans for, as he put it, "throwing caution to the winds" in issuing import licences, and was rather surprised to hear that imports into Germany had not risen out of proportion to industrial activity.

Our discussion with McCloy was mainly on the need for Germany to spend more on occupation costs and rearmament. He kept telling us that Eastern Germany had managed to put together 27 military divisions and that he saw no reason why Western Germany should not do the same. If this meant running a government deficit, why not? If it were necessary to go back on liberalisation, he argued, it might ease the problem of finance. This we could not see. But he was insistent that, in any recommendation we made, we should not side-step the question of occupation costs.

These interviews were sandwiched in between some frantic scribbling while Jacobsson and I tried to prepare a document for circulation to the Managing Board of the EPU on our return to Paris on November 3rd. This should have been entirely possible, but our respective methods of work differed so greatly that in practice we did not come within sight of a completed document. What was perhaps more important was that we both reached a similar diagnosis of the situation and were prepared to make similar recommendations. This was to some extent a fluke: in other circumstances, I could imagine there might have been a real difference of view. I saw no overwhelming need for deflation: exports were rising so fast that they would bridge the gap. But fortunately, we agreed that Germany would be able to combine credit restriction and liberalisation with increasing economic activity and employment by the spring of 1951.

I was allowed to attend the meeting of the EPU Managing Board, the first time somebody not attached to the EPU had been allowed this privilege. Jacobsson and I made an oral report to the board, in which we recommended a credit to Germany of $200m. Guido Carli, who was then an official of the Bank of Italy and later became its Governor, was in the chair. After a brief discussion, which unfortunately did not mention our proposed figure, Hubert Ansiaux, a senior official at Belgium's National Bank who was one of the most influential figures in central banking circles at the time, cut the meeting short by proposing a credit from the EPU to Germany of $120m. No one demurred and the meeting turned out to be short and businesslike.

Not so the subsequent meeting of the OEEC Council, the body to which the EPU's Managing Board was responsible. When the matter came up for approval there, the occasion reminded me forcibly of the story of the elephant as variously described by people of different nationalities. Each delegate saw the German case in terms of the situation of his own country, and spoke of Germany as if discussing his own government's behaviour. Thus Arne Skaug, the official who led the Norwegian delegation, insisted on the virtues of strict import licensing: on his last visit to Germany, he said, he had been able to buy bananas but in Norway there were none, thanks to import control. If the Norwegians could do without bananas, so could the Germans. The British saw the advantage of buying raw materials from abroad cheaply, but didn't see why a country should be allowed to do so with other people's dollars.

In the end, however, the Managing Board's recommended credit was approved. The fact of the matter was that this was a unique opportunity for the Europeans to show that they could rally to the support of a European country in difficulties without turning to the Americans for help. Not only was this the first occasion since 1945 when self-help was practised by Europe on a Continental scale. It was help to a country of first importance to the future of Europe, and one that was almost pathetically grateful for a gesture which, in financial terms, was astonishingly cheap. The EPU credit paid off handsomely in terms of German dedication to the OEEC throughout the next two decades[1].

Not everyone agreed. The decision that Jacobsson and I had promoted was attacked both by Thomas Balogh and by

---

[1] In 1951, on my return from Glasgow to Paris for a short time, I wrote a note on "The Handling of the German Case in the EPU" which goes over the ground in detail. This and a short account of events I wrote for my own use, "The German Balance of Payments Crisis 1950–51", appear (in German) in *Die Korea Krise* (Gustav Fischer Verlag 1986). The

Nicholas Kaldor, two Hungarian economists of Labour sympathies who were to cross my path many more times in future decades. Nicky Kaldor argued, in effect, that there should be no financial brake on expansion in a country suffering from heavy unemployment[2].

This view, however, took no account of purely organisational limits on the *rate* of expansion. It was true that Germany had a high level of unemployment which was not showing any perceptible tendency to disappear. But if one looked at output rather than unemployment, the whole economy was booming as it had never boomed since 1914, with exports doubling in a single year in 1951. Given the rapid growth of output in Germany in 1950, it might well be advisable to moderate the pace a little, even without the need to take account of the balance-of-payments constraint. There was bound to come a time when such expansion would be reflected in the demand for labour. In fact, it was not many years before Germany began to suck in labour from surrounding countries to maintain an extraordinary rate of industrial expansion which was to continue for more than 20 years.

### Life in Paris

On the whole, my year at the OEEC involved far less pressure than I had become accustomed to, and left far greater opportunities for recreation. For the first and only time in my life we had a brand new car — a Citroen Onze légère, my first car since 1939. Our weekends were free, so that we could drive out of Paris in a different direction every Sunday — to Fontainebleau, Chartres or Versailles. And not only drive, but move at speed, since in those days car ownership in France was still very limited. Indeed, when I first arrived, one OEEC colleague had taken me through the streets of Paris at 100 kilometres an hour and thought nothing of it.

second of these and "The Economic Recovery of Western Germany" are reprinted (in English) in my "Economic Ideas and Government Policy" (Routledge 1995).

The episode is covered from a different angle in Erin Fleetwood's "A Life for Sound Money. Per Jacobsson: His Biography" (Oxford University Press 1979)

[2] A highly critical pamphlet issued by Balogh prompted me to write, not a rejoinder, but "The Economic Recovery of Western Germany" for *Lloyds Bank Review*:

Then there was the OEEC store where excellent wine was to be had for a song and no coupons or other rationing limited purchases. The shops were stocked in a way inconceivable in the London of the 1940s. For example, a housewife wanting to buy liver or kidneys was offered several different varieties — not just an occasional supply from under the counter.

We had rented a flat in the Avenue Mozart from a member of staff of the World Bank. This led to complications, culminating after some months in a visit from the bailiffs, and an SOS by telephone from my wife, while I was at work: our landlord, who was not the owner of the flat (landlords in Paris hardly ever were) had omitted to pay his bills. When we moved after six months to another flat, the landlady turned out to be a duchess who ran a chocolate factory. We were all anxious that the concierge should not know the true nature of our arrangement. I was to write to the duchess in the character of a Scottish cousin and enclose for her signature a letter beginning : "Mon cher Cousin, Je vous confie mon apartement…" Rent was to be paid three months in advance, in cash — also a familiar habit in post-war Paris, particularly when dealing with foreigners. All of our belongings had to be carried up the main staircase, and it must have surprised the concierge to see us move in mattresses, pots and pans and three small children. In the event, the concierge turned out to speak fairly good English.

This flat had several memorable peculiarities. The duchess's son lived in a maid's room on the top floor of the building, and its electric wiring system was connected to ours. As he had a habit of going out in the evening leaving his electric fire switched on, and the electricity automatically turned itself off if the load exceeded a set limit, we were frequently embarrassed to find the lights going out whenever we tried to heat water for the children's baths. The flat also had a bullet-proof front door, dating from the time when it was occupied by a Minister of the Interior in the wartime Vichy government. On Christmas Eve there was an almighty banging on the door. When we opened it apprehensively, we found a group of *sapeurs-pompier* who had come to warn us that the chimney to the floor below was on fire.

Mary's experience of Paris, with three children under five, was coloured by the domestic help she had, some of whom seemed characters straight out of a Russian novel. We inherited

Lydie, a forceful woman from the Dordogne, who had once worked for a motor-car manufacturer called M. Panhard. Lydie was obviously disappointed that Mary did not keep house in the stately fashion of the Panhards. So from time to time, I was let loose on her as a kind of pseudo-Panhard, to restore her confidence in the pre-eminence of her employers. This routine, which Mary claimed was highly effective, came to be known as "Panharding". Effective or not, Panharding did not free Mary from a sense of inferiority in the presence of this dominant female, and it was with relief that we parted company with her when, after six months, we moved from the Avenue Mozart to the Rue Octave Feuillet.

Life in Paris was largely bounded by the organisation with which I worked. There was little time to make personal contacts with the French, whether in academic life, in business or in government departments: our leisure was simply saturated by the obligations of official and family duties. The rich web of personalities among whom we moved held us back from seeking friendships elsewhere. I cannot remember a single occasion on which we dined with a French family unconnected with OEEC and only one lunch of this kind, when our landlady invited us to meet an ex-ambassador. For me, the most lasting influence of this period in Paris was the experience of working with colleagues from many different countries, with many of whom I remained in personal contact long afterwards.

## 11

## *A visit to Moscow*

Towards the end of 1951 a letter arrived from Lord Walston, a Labour peer with a special interest in agriculture and foreign policy, inviting me to join a group that was due to attend an international economic conference in Moscow in April 1952. We were to pay our way to Prague, but the rest of our expenses would be met by the Soviet Union. This was an extraordinary opportunity for foreign economists to catch a rare glimpse of the Soviet economy at first hand. The letter made clear that those who were invited would be able to express their views freely, and would not have to vote on, much less subscribe to, resolutions of an embarrassing kind. Invitations were not limited to Communist sympathisers, but included the right wing as well as the left, businessmen and academics as well as politicians.

However, when I attended a preparatory meeting in Lord Walston's rooms in the Albany shortly before we were due to leave, I arrived a little late to find him announcing that, after searching his conscience, he had decided that he ought not to go to Russia. He implied that the rest of us would do well to follow his example. When he sat down, there was consternation. After a few moments, however, Sidney Silverman, a Labour member of Parliament, rose and declared that he at any rate still proposed to go and could see no reason why others should change their plans. So rallied, the rest of us fell into line. Some time later, we heard that Lord Boyd Orr, Chancellor of the University of Glasgow, would lead the party. In the event, we were a politically somewhat unbalanced group, since no Conservative MP defied his party in order to join us. However, the Conservative MP for Ilkley arrived just as the conference ended. He claimed that, although Churchill had had him on the mat, he had come with the Whips' agreement. At this early point in the Cold War, with Russia still under Stalin, relations between Britain and the Soviet Union were extremely frosty.

The subject of the conference was trade between east and west — an odd choice, given that freedom of trade was the last thing Russia wanted. I never understood why the Russians ran it. It had been a long time in the making. Was it all propaganda? Was it from weakness or self-confidence that we were invited? Was it in preparation for a post-Stalin regime? Or to break the partial blockade operated by the West? I never knew, but it was to provide a fascinating glimpse of Russia in the early years of the Cold War.

As we drove in from the airport, the conversation in the car — as so often happens on one's first visit to a foreign country — threw a flood of light on Soviet life. We had arrived on April 1st, the day when consumer prices had just been cut by government decree[1]. What prices were people most interested in? Without a doubt, vodka! Perhaps, we thought, things had not changed much since Tsarist days, when the tax on vodka brought in about half the revenue of the state. One of the signs along the highway urged, "Drink more champagne" which seemed an odd injunction in the Soviet Union. We were told that this particular bit of advertising was intended to convey the message "…and drink less vodka". It seemed to have little effect. We were to see later that there was vodka on tap and some citizens tapping it for all they were worth at 11 in the morning.

The conference was a large affair, with delegations from 46 different countries and a total of 450 delegates. The French delegation was the largest; there were about a dozen Americans, but no Germans. It appeared to be promoted partly by Oskar Lange, a well-known Polish economist, and partly by Nesterov, the chairman of the USSR Chamber of Commerce. There were many speeches, few of which I listened to. Our hosts stuck to their promise not to involve us in embarrassing resolutions, but many of the delegates freely expressed Communist views and sympathies.

---

[1] We were amused to find that it was Soviet practice to pick on April 1st as the date for the annual announcement of changes in prices.

The conference enjoyed lavish hospitality, which jarred with the evidence of poverty around us. A brand new hotel, the Sovietskaya, had been built to house the delegates, who were luxuriously fed, provided with chauffeured cars, offered free seats nightly at the Bolshoi, allowed to travel to other parts of the USSR and flown, if they wished, across Siberia to leave for home from China. My chief recollection of the Sovietskaya, however, is of the long interval before the food that was ordered appeared, and the absence of telephone directories, railway timetables, and newspapers in English or French.

At that time in Moscow good clothes were scarce and dear, and queues formed readily wherever they were put on sale. There was a good deal of interest among the delegates in Russian nylon stockings, which were available and of good quality (while in Poland they were still unobtainable). There were also shortages of durable goods, such as watches and television sets. The delivery date for a private motor car was about three months. At the time, I was reminded of the four stages in the post-war recovery of Western Germany: one year for the Germans to fill their stomachs, one to replenish their wardrobes, one to stock up their homes and thereafter, the export drive. At that point, the Soviet Union appeared to be some way into the second stage; as it turned out, the fourth stage was to wait for more than 40 years.

I took the opportunity to see something of Moscow and the region around it, and to learn what I could about the economy. I also, in the course of the conference, learned a great deal about the way communists from many countries saw the world at that time. I walked through the streets in the vicinity of the hotel, noting what was on sale and at what price, travelled on the Underground, and observed the crowds camped at the railway station. There was little sign either of acute poverty or of affluence. The atmosphere was, not surprisingly, proletarian, and reminded me far more of a Lanarkshire mining town than of a great capital city.

With other economists in the delegation, including Piero Sraffa and Maurice Dobb, both of them Cambridge economists, I arranged for a visit by car to Klin (originally Tver), a town about 100 miles from Moscow, as a way of seeing something of the surrounding country. Our interpreter was a young man who had fought in that area, but was unsure how to read a map: when we stopped on a straight road and I asked him how near we were to our destination, he plucked a piece of grass and laid it on the map in Sraffa's *Guide Bleu* as if this would conjure up an answer. In Klin itself, we visited a damaged church where at the same time as builders hammered away at the bidding of the state in order to preserve an ancient monument, a choir sang imperviously in praise of higher powers.

Later we made a visit to the Lenin Library in Moscow which housed books by the million. As Maurice Dobb was a well-known Communist, we thought it interesting to see whether his works appeared in the catalogue and were amused to find no reference to them. From this we deduced that he was not regarded as "safe" reading, for it was probable that his books were in some part of the library, presumably with limited access. A brief look into the library's large reading room made it clear that foreign journals were extensively consulted, but so far as I could judge they were nearly all on various branches of science and technology, and predominantly American.

I was able to use my time to explore how the Soviet economy really worked — or rather, was supposed to work. I visited a number of factories and factory clubs, checking my impressions with others in the delegation who were either employers or trade unionists. I went to the Moskvich car factory in Moscow, which employed some 6,000 workers. It was scheduled as a Stakhanovite plant. The Stakhanovites — workers with a record of high productivity — were much in evidence during our time in Moscow: there were portraits of Stakhanovites prominently displayed, and a much higher rate of pay was offered to those classed as Stakhanovites, as we were told that more than one in three of Moskvich workers were. To a layman like myself, it looked like an oldish British engineering factory with a rather inferior layout. Certainly the workers did not seem to be exerting themselves much more than workers in a similar British plant — my trade unionist colleagues thought rather less. I later heard it suggested — not in relation to this factory — that it would probably be true to say that about half the workers in a Russian factory were putting their backs into their jobs. Some large British factories would at that time have regarded such a proportion as by no means unsatisfactory.

Even at this high point of the communist era, there were areas of the economy over which the state had little control. It was already customary in Moscow for those workers who had an opportunity of doing so, to add to their earnings "on the side".

These earnings added up to something quite large, and were a normal feature of the functioning of the economy, although less important than in the days of rationing. Journalists engaged in freelancing, doctors carried on a private practice, plumbers would come quickly only if they had reason to expect a good tip, taxi drivers would turn off the meter when they had a fare and so on.

I was interested to exchange experience on hoarding, which is endemic in any system of planning under inflationary pressure. Wherever factories are held to a rigid programme, they will hoard everything they can — labour, materials and even finished goods — so as to be able to guarantee delivery to schedule. A Russian engineer to whom I put this point was scandalised, and indignantly denied that Soviet factories hoarded anything. But from other sources, I gathered that my inference was well-founded. The Chinese delegation at the conference made no bones about their drive against the hoarding of materials, They agreed that there was a constant tug-of-war between the central departments, battling against shortages, and the factories, determined to hold as large a stock as possible to keep production running. How else, indeed, could a factory beat its programme by 20% or even 50%? And how else could a motor-car factory claim to change over to a new model without loss of production? The history of economic planning is largely the history of stocks, which register the ebb and flow of demand and supply just as prices are supposed to do in a market economy. It was surprising, therefore, how rarely Soviet economists and engineers showed any understanding of the role of stocks.

I learned more about the Soviet economy from applying my experience of wartime planning than from what I was told by Soviet economists, with whom I had several conversations. The best-known among them was Eugene Varga. I recall his comment on the writings of Gunnar Myrdal, the famous Swedish economist: "das Papier had viel geduld" (paper is very patient) — a dig at the length of Myrdal's books. Varga also scoffed at our faith in market forces. There was no need to let prices reflect demand as well as supply: if demand increased, the right thing to do was to hold prices steady until the supply could be expanded to the level required.

However, I found it hard to believe that prices in the USSR were never varied to encourage or check demand. We had quizzed our interpreter on the cut in food prices announced on the day of our arrival. Did this mean, we had asked, that the turnover tax on food had been cut? Apparently not. Then was the Soviet farmer being paid less? Certainly not. The young man was appalled at the very thought. Perhaps the distributive margin had been reduced? No, that did not seem plausible. By further cross-examination we elicited that the fall in food prices was intended to re-align them with *long-term* agricultural costs, which slid down progressively throughout the year as they did everywhere else in the 1950s, while cuts in food prices were made at intervals.

Subsequently, I noticed further evidence to suggest that prices were sometimes used to change demand. I asked whether it had been the practice with television sets to begin by charging a high price, lowering it gradually as larger supplies became available. I was assured that scarcity would not be allowed to affect prices in this way: a high price would put television sets "beyond the means of an average working man". In fact, television sets were first marketed at 4,000 rubles, the equivalent at that time of a little under £360. They had a small screen and were technically mediocre. They proved unsaleable and stocks accumulated in the shops. The price was subsequently reduced, first to 3,000 rubles and then to 2,000 rubles, at which price they went "under the counter". Nevertheless, the price was lowered to 1,000 rubles, and the shortage increased.

Taxation in the Soviet Union, I established, served its classical purpose of raising funds to meet the needs of government. It was not complicated, as in "bourgeois society", by egalitarian sentiment. The government did not seem to be seeking to reduce class differences, since in theory there were none. Class was conceived of solely in terms of the ownership of the means of production, not of wealth or political power. There was no nonsense about regressive taxation; the turnover tax brought in half the national revenue. There were no death duties, no taxes on savings, no prohibitive levies on excess profits (all familiar in the Britain of that day). I came away almost tempted to think of the Soviet economy in its attitude to profit and to wealth as much nearer to 19th-century capitalism than to the twentieth-century welfare state.

I asked whether my hosts were not afraid that inheritance might give rise to a new wealthy class. This question amused them and the answers were instructive. They pooh-poohed the idea that people might use inherited wealth in order to relax or cease from work, saying that in the Soviet Union everybody liked to work too much to want to be a parasite. They pointed out that there could be no private ownership of the means of production and that there could therefore be no exploitation in the Marxist sense. I reflected that this offered the main clue to the communist outlook. For the communists, the essence of capitalism was private profit; and the necessary consequence of a system of private profit was war and unemployment. This was what made them discount any professions of friendship by capitalist countries, and distrust the intentions of their governments. They felt in danger, not from the measures devised by particular statesmen, but from the inevitable operation of a particular system.

It would have been comic to find men so much in the grip of a fantastic logic, if so much had not hung on bringing them to contemplate other assumptions. They were not prepared to think of an evolution of the capitalist system: the system had been analysed for all time by Karl Marx, and could alter only in conformity with the laws governing its motion that he put forward. The fact that these laws were absurd and that capitalist society had evolved rapidly and was still evolving did not interest them because, having one religion, they were not anxious to embrace another.

All this was impressed on me time and time again in conversation with communists of various nationalities in Moscow. An Austrian communist babbled to me about centres of power in capitalist society as if private industry had some secret hold on the government — so much a travesty of life in Whitehall that one could only laugh out loud: he felt no need to examine the centres of power in communist society, or to consider the hypothesis that there might be no *centres* of power at all. A Canadian communist was fearful of the intentions of American steel makers, as if they had some special influence on American foreign policy. This same man — a journalist whose profession it was to observe things accurately and without bias — assured me that the standard of living in Russia was already higher than in the United Kingdom and that in 10–20 years, it would be as high as that of the United States. In fact, as far as I could judge, real wages were about half the level in Britain.

A young Russian asked me how much unemployment was needed to run *the* capitalist system. Another Russian — a man of obvious intelligence and wide experience — assured me that, under capitalism, economic development was naturally controlled by private profit. He seemed a good deal surprised — and it was one of the few occasions when I saw a Soviet economist register real interest — when I told him that on average 75% of the profits made by a firm in British industry went to the government, and that I should be very happy to think that private incentives exercised any real influence on the pace and direction of economic development in the United Kingdom. I suggested to him that, in contrast to the situation in his country, British firms had far less interest in the making of large profits than had the British government.

All those to whom I spoke at the conference appeared to have a passion for systematising economic and social forces far beyond the limits of ordinary observation; and to want the simplicity of a label to attach to each system once their minds had embraced it. I had a long discussion (in French) with one Soviet communist who, when I spoke of the differences between one capitalist country and another, and between 20th-century and 19th-century capitalism, asked me to give our present economic system a name. In desperation I gave him the only label I could think of: "the Welfare State". Unfortunately I could not translate this into French and had to write it down for him, so he was probably no further on, even with those mysterious hieroglyphics in front of him.

The calibre of the older Soviet economists was a little disappointing. I was not surprised to hear that there had been complaints that social and economic research was lagging behind technical research in the Soviet Union. I can recall no powerful analytical minds able to fight their way out of an old system of thought. Those whom I met seemed far more at home in the field of applied economics than of theory.

The questions which were asked of us by the economists were significant. The younger men — the interpreters — generally asked political questions. What did Britain think of the Americans? What attitude did Britain take towards a united Europe? How did people feel about the rearmament of Germany. And so on. We also had a special round-table discussion with some senior economists (in which Joan Robinson, the distinguished left-wing Cambridge economist, took part). This was one of the few occasions on which *we* were asked questions. Usually it was the other way round: we asked all the questions, and *they* were liable to tell *us* what was going on in the United Kingdom.

Several of the questions addressed to us dealt with the British balance of payments, trade and devaluation. I was struck by the limited understanding that Soviet economists had of the rest of the world. When, for instance, we discussed Britain's trade with the Far East, they thought Britain's trade with China was substantial and not (as I subsequently verified) less than 1% of our total trade. Even after the meeting they came back to the subject, asking us to make sure we had not got our figures wrong.

Several questioners asked about what was done in Britain to "plan the work of private enterprise". Another questioner wanted to know why prices were still rising. Mrs Robinson replied that, in the British economy, prices rose as wages rose, and with full employment, wages showed a tendency to rise progressively; in this there was a fundamental difference between the British and Soviet economic systems.

In some ways I was more attracted to the younger interpreters who expressed themselves more freely and had views of their own. One young graduate student lamented the mass of reading he still had to do: this included 2,000 pages of Marx, 1,000 pages of Lenin and 7,000 pages of selected texts. I asked him what foreign economists he had read, but although he was familiar with the name of Keynes, he had clearly read little or nothing by any bourgeois economist since the time of Marx. He was making a special study of the United States, but the only book that he had read by an American economist had been issued by the American Labour Research Department — and was one that I had never heard of.

I came to the conclusion that the job of Soviet economists was to preach theory: to be Stalin's hot-gospellers, and say what was supposed to happen, not what did in fact happen. Again and again, my British colleagues and I would ask questions relating to the short-term, to the improvisations that are the stock-in-trade of the planner; back would come an answer that made sense only in relation to the long-term, the paradise of the classical economist. How rigid, we would ask, was the five-year plan?

How often did it alter and how was it altered? Who took the initiative in altering it? Who took the knock if things went wrong? Something had to give if there was a muddle. Under capitalism, it was employment that suffered; what was it under the five-year plan? After all, if there was never a muddle, then in effect there was no plan either, economic planning in practice being an endless battle with change and the muddle that arises out of change.

The questions with which I went to Russia remained largely unanswered. Sometimes, they were met with a circumstantial, textbook account of planning, which might do service in the lecture room. I was too old a hand at the game to be impressed. Sometimes, they were met with slogans: "it's planned"; "this is a developing economy"; or "everything is taken into account". Their minds were riveted, as so often happens in social philosophy, to the stiff models of past thinkers. The world had moved to a new orbit; but no one hastily discards a cherished model. Let me say, in justice to them, that a collection of British academic economists might have done little better if cross-examined on the British investment programme, import licensing, purchase tax and so forth. But they would, I think, have been quicker to recognise that the only satisfactory and meaningful answers must be in terms of administrative procedures with which they were unfamiliar.

My overall impression was that Russia was doing some things well. The social services were highly developed, communal facilities for entertainment and recreation were good, and the men in executive positions seemed competent, level-headed and of a practical turn of mind. On the other hand, there was appalling over-crowding, clothes were expensive and lacking in style and real wages were far below the level in Britain. More important, I found hardly any of the self-criticism which is natural to healthy government. Only once did I talk to a Russian who was prepared to poke fun at any side of Soviet life. Self-assurance tended to be carried to the point at which it became complacency.

This was most obvious in the younger generation. I asked one young man whether he would favour student exchanges between Russia and Britain. He asked me if I wanted a frank answer and I encouraged him to give one. He then said that he thought the

Soviet students would have nothing to learn. It was the same young man who was studying the American economy without having read a single book by any American economist of repute.

When the time came to leave Moscow , I had an unusual opportunity to make a link with the future. Among those attending the conference was a young Canadian journalist on *Le Devoir* called Pierre Trudeau whom I got to know quite well. He decided to take advantage of the offer to fly delegates to other parts of the USSR and on to China. That left him short of rubles, and since I had to return directly and had no particular use for mine, I naturally handed them on. I was delighted to hear him speak of me many years later to Harold Wilson, by then British prime minister, as "my benefactor". I can claim to have advanced money in my youth both to a future Canadian Prime Minister and to a future president of KLM. But only the first remembered.

I retained about 80 rubles, and when we touched down at Minsk on the way home I divided them between a small bar of chocolate and a bottle of perfume. This price relationship seemed a little unusual until my wife came to use the perfume. She found it admirable: so much so that when I went on a trip to Budapest some years later, she insisted that I must at all costs bring her some more. My Hungarian hosts were mystified until I explained that my wife had found Russian perfume perfect for visits to the Scottish west coast — as an insect repellent.

The conference had been a unique chance for a few British economists to learn more about the workings of the Soviet economy. We had opportunities of informing ourselves on some aspects of the country that were much superior to any enjoyed by the officials to whom we talked in the British Embassy in Moscow. Yet what struck me when I returned to Britain was that, although the American Consul in Glasgow visited me to discuss my experiences, no one connected in any way with the British government took the least interest.

I had reached an agreement with *The Times* before leaving for Moscow that I would write an account of the conference for them. I sent it back with a delegate who was returning early. I returned a few days later, via Prague, and was a little surprised to gather from some chance remark before we left Moscow that there has been an article in *The Times* dealing rather favourably with the conference. I could only assume that it was mine. But how did one obtain a copy of *The Times* in Moscow, or for that matter Prague? Copies were not on sale in either city. In Prague, we were taken to the Communist Party headquarters where I tentatively asked for a copy of the newspaper. To my surprise, one was promptly produced. There was the article on the middle page.

It was quite a scoop, since no other paper had any news of the conference. But its publication infuriated Anthony Eden, who was then Foreign Secretary, and made immediate inquiries as to its authorship. I suspect that this was the reason British Intelligence started a file on me — of which, of course, I know nothing except its existence. A few years later I found myself lunching with Harold Wilson at the Savoy, and he told me of a passage at arms he had had with British Intelligence over this file. He had insisted on seeing it and was able to point out that it made no reference to many events in my career, such as my four years in the Ministry of Aircraft Production, that seemed at least as significant for the purposes of MI5 as my participation in the Moscow Economic Conference.

## 12

*Glasgow 1951–61: Establishing a Research Department*

In early January 1951 I finally returned to academic life in Glasgow after 11 years' absence. I was to remain there for a decade, setting up one of the first research departments of applied economics in the country. It was a period that sealed the fate of many Glasgow industries, and as my Department specialised in industrial and regional economics, we devoted much attention to studying some of the causes of later decline, but failed to attract the attention of the people that mattered in the city.

My time in Glasgow was broken by an 18-month interlude in 1955–56 during which I went to Washington, DC, to set up the Economic Development Institute for the World Bank; and I combined my academic duties with sitting on several committees, of which the most important was the Radcliffe Committee, and with a great deal of travelling. All these are covered in later chapters.

Our arrival in Glasgow came at a time when there seemed to me good reasons for despondency over the prospects for peace in Europe. Russia had done remarkably little to demobilise, had taken a very aggressive attitude towards her former allies and in one country after another, from Czechoslovakia to Korea, was seizing power or extending power by murder, subversion and war at second-hand. I feared that nothing might now interrupt a build-up on both sides towards a Third World War, and felt some relief in moving my family off the continent to the comparative safety of Glasgow.

We drove to Glasgow from Paris, not in the Citroen, which we had sold, but in a Hillman Minx which I had bought from a fellow economist, Wassily Leontief. The house we had bought before leaving for Paris was in Lenzie, a small village to the east of Glasgow on the Glasgow-Edinburgh railway line. It was well located for getting in and out of Glasgow to the university on Gilmorehill, and there were the Campsie Hills and the wonderful country beyond almost on our doorstep. When we first arrived, it had stood empty for a year on what our lawyer described as "a cauld soil" (it stood near the edge of what must once have been a bog), but apart from the damp it was a good choice of home. We also, during this period, acquired an old gypsy caravan in Galloway and later a more substantial hut, so that each year we were able to return to enjoy the most attractive of sights to a Scot: the English coast with the Lake District hills rising behind it — from the safe distance of the other side of the Solway Firth.

Academic life offered great variety. Over the decade, I lectured in many different places. Although at the University I held a research chair, I taught from time to time, conducting seminars in my final years, and collaborating in launching a one-year course on industrial administration for graduates contemplating a career in industry. I helped to found and edited the *Scottish Journal of Political Economy*. I attended conferences at home and abroad. I did my stint of examining in Glasgow, Cambridge and elsewhere. I wrote other articles from time to time. In short I was for the most part a typical academic working among academics.

In the 1950s I found myself turning more and more to economic history for guidance on how the economy worked, and downgrading a little the importance I had previously attached to theory. When, in the course of the decade, I published the gist of my doctorate thesis of 18 years previously, I cut out the theoretical treatment and confined myself to the more statistical parts. I included in the volume articles that I had hoped to expand into books.

### Establishing a department

I had come to Glasgow to build a new department, in applied economics. This set two initial tasks: assembling a staff and deciding on a programme of work in which the new department should engage. I was fortunate in being able to recruit an extremely able staff, of whom half a dozen were selected in due course for chairs. Work on industrial relations was in many ways the most lively element in the research the Department undertook.

One of my staff, Donald Robertson, took over the direction of the department when I left in 1961 and made it one of the leading centres in Britain in industrial economics. Donald was an economist of invincible common sense, with a rolling nautical and nonchalant way, who taught me a vast amount about the functioning of the labour market and the limitations of national wage agreements. He had shown an interest in occupational pay differentials during his post-graduate studies in Oxford, and pursued this in studying earnings in the shipyards on his return to Glasgow where he had been an undergraduate. One of the more interesting conclusions he drew was that the unskilled men often earned as much as the skilled men by working longer hours; but I was never able to fathom why there was so much overtime working on offer for the unskilled when the chronic shortages seemed usually to be among the skilled.

Donald would almost certainly have been Principal of the University had he survived, but he was cut off in his early forties. He worked closely with Tom Paterson, who was an explorer and geographer turned sociologist who combined entertainment and erudition. He had been with me at Trinity College, Cambridge, and was for many years a Fellow there before returning to the North. Tom was always bubbling over with ideas which, although they baffled most of us, obviously excited the younger managers he taught. One of the most interesting things to emerge from his books, such as "Glasgow Limited", was the pathology of industrial morale. He showed that various apparently unconnected phenomena — low productivity, high absenteeism, high accident rates, strikes — tended to fluctuate together. Strikes, he argued, reflected earlier tensions and had a cathartic effect, so that it might be better to precipitate one and get it over.

Tom Brennan was another sociologist-raconteur who bred Welsh ponies and had an inexhaustible supply of exotic anecdotes of life in the Glasgow slums where he had carried on much of his research. Tom became interested in the plans for rebuilding Glasgow and wrote a book on the subject, "Reshaping a City", whose conclusions have stood up remarkably well to later events. He could see no sense in pulling down acres of tenements in the inner city when it would have been possible to install modern plumbing in them and throw adjoining flats together to provide satisfactory housing. He was even more sceptical about the consequences of turning out scores of small businesses with no provision for their replacement. When he looked at what uses were proposed for the inner-city space thus released, he found that one-third of it was for new schools, which seemed the last thing to put in what was no longer the Gorbals. The only substantial point he missed in his work was the eventual cost of pulling down one-third of a major city and then trying to replace it. No balance sheet of eventual outgoings and revenue was ever constructed, as far as I know, for an operation whose cost dwarfed that of developing Concorde and came near to reducing Glasgow to bankruptcy. Disappointingly, this work attracted very little public interest, on the part of the City Chambers, government departments or local industry.

In considering the programme of work in which my Department should engage, it was easy to see that our comparative advantages should lie in the examination of regional problems on the one hand and industrial problems on the other. We had a laboratory on our doorstep and it would be foolish not to use it. We should, however, take care not to adopt too narrow and specialised an approach. If we studied local industry, it should be against the background of industrial economics, with a full understanding of the technical and market forces at work to produce growth here and decay there. Our analysis of labour problems should be grounded in current work on wage theory, pay structures, and industrial relations and should be capable of throwing light on national or even international trends. Regional policy should embrace social as well as economic analysis and take account of population movements and the reasons behind them.

I recognised that I could not simply draw up a research programme and then parcel it out in individual assignments. That is not how successful research proceeds. I had instead to recruit staff who were anxious to undertake research within the areas I had selected, and leave it largely to them to choose specific themes. Sometimes it was possible to be a little more precise: for instance, Jack Parkinson came specifically to do work on the ship-building industry, Tom Brennan to undertake a social survey of Govan and Peter Hart to specialise in the movement of profits.

At an early stage I looked around for a subject that would bring together the whole of the Department and allow them to co-operate on a project. At first I thought of a highly statistical volume along the lines of "The Social Structure of England and Wales", a work by Sir Alexander Carr-Saunders and D. Caradoc Jones which had been published before the war and was widely used for teaching purposes. But I felt that something a little more analytical would be preferable, and so conceived the idea of a volume on "The Scottish Economy" with chapters by different members of the staff examining the different aspects of the economy[1]. It might have an incidental advantage of pouring a few hard facts on the fires of Scottish Nationalism, though whether as cold water or fresh fuel we should discover as we went along. I had arrived in Scotland just after the "Covenant", a kind of Nationalist manifesto, had attracted over 2m signatures, and the nationalists appeared to be on the way to exercising great political power. They seemed, however, to have little or no grasp of economics. The volume might serve an educational purpose; and if it suggested that nationalism was not much of an answer to the underlying problems of the economy, so much the better.

We spent a good part of 1952 and 1953 preparing a score of chapters by a dozen authors on different elements of the Scottish economy. I had hoped to write only the introductory chapter, but instead I found myself re-drafting one chapter in its entirety and re-writing large chunks of several others. I was pleased with the final volume, which moved Professor Brinley Thomas, my counterpart in Wales, to produce a parallel volume on "The Welsh Economy". The public impact of the book, however, was negligible: I was slow to learn that research has to be marketed as well as produced, and that if one wants publicity, one has to work hard for it. It is not enough to produce a good piece of work: one needs also to bring it to the attention of the media and point out the newsworthy features.

---

[1] The Scottish Economy: A Statistical Account of Scottish Life, by members of the staff of Glasgow University (ed. A.K. Cairncross), Cambridge University Press, 1954 "The Scottish Economy" formed the second in a series of seven social and economic studies, published for the Department by Cambridge University Press in the 1950s. The first was the volume on "The Crofting Problem" referred to below; and the others included Tom Paterson's "Glasgow Limited" and Donald Robertson's "Factory Wage Structure and National Agreements".

## Relations with local industry

One advantage I was able to offer my staff in the new department was ample contact with local industry, especially at the middle management level. No doubt my colleagues would have found ways of contacting local industries sooner or later. But the process was accelerated by the courses we began to offer in management studies. Few universities offered such courses at that time. After my first year or so, the professor of accountancy asked for my help in some form of management training. I had not thought much about the subject, and protested that economists were largely ignorant of what went on *inside* a firm. However, we agreed to begin a formal course of evening lectures on economics and accountancy, limiting the number admitted and charging a low fee.

We were deluged with applications. At the end of the first course, we were pressed to repeat it, and pressed also to put on a second-year course. That in turn led to a third-year course. We simply could not shake off the young managers who were desperately anxious for University contact. Almost all paid their fees out of their own pocket. They felt the need for a *Weltanschauung*, a philosophy of industry that showed them their true place and responsibilities in the scheme of things. They were also anxious to compare notes on the handling of situations for which their earlier education had not prepared them.

Meanwhile our whole style of lecturing in the management course changed. So did the subject matter and its treatment. We continued to work on the basis of one evening a week after dinner, but abandoned formal lectures for seminar-style discussions, giving more prominence to industrial relations. This subject rather than more technical matters was what mainly excited the managers. They were naturally also interested in public policy and the reasons (if any) for the apparent unpredictability of government. From an early stage we also organised an annual weekend conference for our management students, usually at St Andrews. This allowed students from different years to mix, and they were also attended in due course by those who no longer came to our evening sessions but had formed a Management Club of their own.

All this represented quite an addition to the load on those who ran the courses. We stuck to the rule that no special payments would be made for this work. But, although the fee was quite a small one, there was usually quite an appreciable profit on the operation. So far as I know this was the only educational operation in my time from which Glasgow University made a profit. It was therefore well disposed to support other claims from the department for University funds. More important, the courses brought into the University a large cross-section of Glasgow's middle management and gave us personal contact with men from nearly all the larger and many of the smaller firms.

The management studies courses turned out to be a more effective link with local industry than the department's research, relevant though it was. For example, the ship-building industry took no interest in Jack Parkinson's research. Some of the ship-builders insisted that their industry would flourish if only its foreign competitors ceased to receive subsidies from their governments. Others were absorbed in their difficulties with the labour force, especially demarcation disputes. These received the kind of publicity later accorded to similar disputes in the motor-car industry. But when we organised an afternoon lecture at the university on the problems of the industry, no one engaged in it attended.

This may have been partly the result of our inexperience in publicising our work. But I suspect that the major difficulty was that management in the industry was almost non-existent. In a large yard, employing more than 5,000 workers, the organisation of the work below board level was in the hands of the yard superintendent, who was distinguished from the other workmen by his bowler hat and not much else. But there was no planning staff of the kind customary in modern factories. That work was devolved to the foreman on the job, and he set about it like a foreman on any building site. Each ship was built as a one-off job, and the design kept as closely as possible to earlier designs for similar ships, with such modifications as the customer proposed or the foreman had discovered would be useful. With so slim a managerial structure — even at Board level one could find responsibility limited to two or three men — it was hardly surprising that no one could find time to talk about the economics of the industry.

What was disturbing was that the shipbuilding industry was fairly typical of the traditional structure on Clydeside. Management was still slimmer in the coal-mining industry, where it consisted effectively of the mine manager. In the engineering industry, the product was nearly always a one-off job, and design changes took place by progressive modification rather than after research and development. All over the area, jobs tended to be skill-intensive, with resulting high labour costs, unadventurous design and demarcation difficulties. In other parts of the country, particularly in the consumer-durable industries, skill had been economised by careful pre-planning and high management intensity. But on Clydeside, in spite of its extraordinary diversity and adaptability in the 19th century, consumer durables had not taken root; and since these were the one boom business of the inter-war years, the region had missed out on the techniques of management that were indispensable to expansion. It was only the coming of American firms, towards the end of the decade, that provided a seed-bed for these techniques.

In the second half of the decade, I became more directly involved in business affairs. After I returned from Washington, Mr Haynes, General Manager of the Scottish Amicable Life Assurance Society, approached me with the offer of a directorship, which I accepted; and about the same time, the other Glasgow-based insurance company, the Scottish Mutual, made a similar approach (which of course I had to reject). It was striking to me how much more lively and imaginative the management of Scottish financial services companies were than that of the older engineering businesses. The Amicable, at that time a mutual society, was well managed and building up a branch in Australia. It had a particularly good record as an investor. Then Alastair Watson, a director of J. and P. Coats, a Glasgow textile company (before the first world war, it had been the largest manufacturing company in the country), invited me to join the board of the Ailsa Investment Trust. He followed this up later with an invitation to join the smaller Alva Trust which was under the same management. I accepted both, but the appointments came when I had only a short time left in Glasgow and I had little influence on either. I was also elected to a directorship of the Chamber of Commerce, and attended meetings regularly.

## Scottish affairs

As time went by, I became more immersed in Scottish economic affairs. My understanding of Scotland's economy was extended by my contacts with three bodies: a small committee on local development which I chaired; a grander committee on Scotland's financial relations with England, to which I gave evidence; and a commission of inquiry into crofting, the special system of land tenure that prevails on many of the islands and parts of the mainland in the far north of Scotland.

The Scottish Council, a private body which promotes development in Scotland, persuaded me to chair a committee on local development which reported in 1952. The research we did into the growth of employment in different towns and areas brought out rather strikingly that the fastest growing areas were not necessarily those where new factories had been built, and that there was no necessary association with a high level of factory employment. Our report generated a great deal of interest, mainly because of its emphasis on what are now referred to as "growth points", areas which were likely to be the location of future industrial development.

About the same time I gave evidence to the Catto Committee on Scottish Financial and Trade Statistics. This was a high-powered group set up to defuse the controversy that Scottish Nationalists had fomented over the contribution Scotland was making to the British balance of payments, particularly through sales of whisky for dollars. The Nationalists also claimed that tax revenue raised in Scotland exceeded government spending in Scotland, allegedly creating a southward financial drain. The committee examined all this with great thoroughness, emphasised the complications and ambiguities of calculating the true picture, suggested a form of return on government revenue and expediture and discouraged any attempt to work out a Scottish balance of payments. But it was clear from the Report that Government spending was higher and the total tax take lower in Scotland than in the rest of the United Kingdom. Whether this learned dissection of the issues had much part in the comparative quiescence of the nationalists in the rest of the 1950s I am inclined to doubt.

Shortly after this I found myself the only economist on the Commission of Inquiry on Crofting, a form of agricultural tenure found only in the Highlands. I had first learned about crofting from Adam Collier, an outstanding young economist who had been killed in a mountaineering accident in the war, and had written a detailed study of the subject which formed the first of my Department's series of social and economic studies. Crofters were very different from farmers. They had little arable land, but more rough grazing, suited to sheep farming. They earned their living in a wide variety of ways, of which farming was only one. They rented their land, but with such security of tenure that it was virtually impossible to dispossess them.

The Commission assumed that what was wanted from it was a review of ways in which the economic basis of crofting could be made more secure — eg, through amalgamations into larger units, or by introducing new sources of employment. The Inquiry was an agreeable change from desk work in Glasgow, but it was not apparent what we could usefully recommend. Our chairman, Tom Taylor, the Principal of Aberdeen University, was obviously anxious to report in favour of the industrial development of the Highlands as a supplement to the limited possibilities offered by crofting. There was a small machine tool factory at Inverasdale run by a Mr Rollo from Coatbridge, near Glasgow, which featured frequently in the press as an example of what could be done. When we interviewed Mr Rollo, my reaction was that if he put into a business in England the energy and enthusiasm he showed for Inverasdale, he would end up a millionaire; and if it took a steady flow of millionaires to run factories in the Highlands, we might as well forget about industrial development. In any event, a visit to Inverasdale revealed only two workers in the factory that day. There might be twice or even thrice that number on other days, but it did not bear out the optimistic headlines we kept seeing in the press.

Each crofter I spoke to in the Shetlands appeared to feel his croft was too small, and when asked how much more land he needed, almost every one wanted as much land again as he already had. There seems to be a limit of vision, not confined to the land, that allows each man to aspire to twice what he has but leaves anything more beyond the horizon of ambition. But limited vision was not the only reason why crofters were dissatisfied with the size of their holdings. I recall a talk with a young crofter in the Shetlands, who wanted a croft to work. Yet he apparently already owned one. Then why didn't he work it? For the very good reason, he told me, that his tenant, as a crofter, had security of tenure and there was no way that he could resume possession.

As this incident showed, tenure in the Highlands was calculated to foster the general trend in Scotland towards the extinction of the landlord. This was particularly notable in Glasgow housing. A legal structure originally designed to offer tenants redress against extortion or arbitrary eviction had gradually come to bestow on the tenants virtually all the rights of ownership, subject to a small tax known as rent. On the other hand, landlords ran risks of heavy financial loss. One friend told me how he had come close to financial ruin because a well-meaning relative had left him some miners' cottages on which he could have been required by the local authority to spend large sums in improvements if he had not been able to pay somebody to take the property off his hands. In Glasgow any sensible owner of tenement property (blocks of apartments) either left the district without trace or found some tramp to whom he could convey his "property" rights gratis.

Most of the crofters lived in the northern and western isles and not on the mainland. This made it extremely difficult for them to carry on any work involving high freight costs or easy communications, and put pressure on them to move elsewhere, if only temporarily, in search of a cash income. The croft, in any event, usually ran only to a few acres and was often little more than a very large garden, more suited to retirement than farming. So most crofters had other sources of income: They might be primarily fishermen, as in the Shetland Islands; or foresters; or do work on the roads, or as postmen; or knit stockings and sweaters; or rely on government benefits or remittances from relatives who were working elsewhere.

The Orkneys and Shetlands made an interesting contrast. The Orkneys have good agricultural land on old red sandstone which affords the farmer a reasonable living. At one time, the crofters had more chickens per acre than any other county except Lancashire. But raising chickens in a perpetual hurricane has its difficulties; and the crofters relied mainly on cattle farming, taking advantage of the best agricultural advice and treating their beasts with care and skill. In the Shetlands, on the other hand, the land is not easily reclaimed from the bog and so in those days, fishing was the main activity. The Shetlander, we were told, might be off whaling in the South Atlantic for up to two years at a time, and had usually accumulated a fair amount of money before his return. What better use for it than improving his house? So in the Shetlands we found farming in a bad way and housing rather impressive, while in the Orkneys, what income the crofter could spare went into his byre, or cattle-shed, and not his house.

On the northern Hebridean isles such as Harris the prevailing mood seemed to be, "when the Lord made time, he made plenty o' it." But when one looked at such islands, the marvel was that anyone lived there at all. On the east side of the island, facing the mainland, there was no more than a line of rocks along the coast, with a thin tatter of soil in places, often in "lazy-beds" — rocks with soil spread over them by hand — in which to grow vegetables or other crops. On the western, Atlantic side, only a mile or two away, stretched magnificent sandy beaches that in the chill Hebrides brought none of the throng of tourists that would have covered them in a different climate.

We reported, as is the way of Government committees, in favour of a new authority to put new life into crofting. It did not amount to a great deal, but there was certainly scope to reorganise the crofts in some areas into a smaller number of viable holdings. Before much could come of it the prospects, particularly in the north, were completely transformed by the discovery of oil and gas under the North Sea.

### The Phillips Committee

In 1952–53 I served on a committee that dealt with a matter of much greater long-term importance and astonishingly little public debate: the implications for public policy of the rising proportion of old people in the population. The Committee on Old Age was chaired by Sir Thomas Phillips. He was not an imaginative chairman, and was more influenced by the views of the Treasury than of the committee. I found myself drafting a substantial part of the report.

Our report expressed concern at the prospect that a rise in expenditure on pensions, without a corresponding rise in National Insurance contributions, would lead to an increasing deficit in the National Insurance Fund. The deficit was expected to grow from £100m a year currently to £364m a year in 25 years' time. The scheme assumed payment of contributions from age 16 for nearly 50 years in the case of men, and nearly 45 years in the case of women, although no existing pensioner had made payments on anything like that scale, and it would be many years before any pensioner had done so. As a result, the state had assumed a capital liability of about £12,500m for retirement pensions, even after allowing for future contributions.

Our recommendations envisaged a progressive rise in the minimum pension age, to 68 for men and 63 for women, spread over 15 years. We recommended also that in future, when pension rates were increased, the parallel addition to contributions should be such as to cover the whole prospective cost of the increase, not merely what would be appropriate to someone joining the scheme at the age of 16.

In signing the report, I expressed a number of reservations. First of all, I thought that, in an inflationary world, increments in money benefits might be intended either to reflect a fall in the value of money or to correspond to a rising standard of living; and that our recommendations, in their reference to entrants aged 16, confused the two situations. If benefits were raised merely to reflect a fall in the value of money, it would be enough merely to raise contributions on the same scale. I also took exception to the "earnings rule", under which pensioners aged between 65 and 69 (but not pensioners of 70 and over) could draw their pensions only if they earned from work no more than £2 a week. In the event, my note on this second point was included in the main report and attracted much attention, although the government did nothing about it.

I wrote one chapter that the chairman excluded, on housing. I had pointed out that households covering different generations that had tended to live together in a single house at the beginning of the century were increasingly breaking into separate units with separate housing requirements. That added to the total pressure on the housing stock, and created a need for resources to improve housing for the aged. Sir Thomas, however, thought the subject was outside our inquiry's terms of reference and I reluctantly accepted his ruling.

The Phillips Report was in fact soon overtaken by events. We had proceeded on the basis of a flat rate of contributions to pensions and of benefits, which we had recognised as setting a minimum that people with higher incomes might supplement with private insurance or membership of an occupational pension scheme. But not long after we reported, the whole basis of the state pension scheme was changed to abandon the flat rate and to relate state pensions to a worker's earnings. These changes did not, however, resolve the basic problems of financing state pensions, and indeed the debate continues to this day in much the same vein as in the time of the Phillips Committee.

## Writings

My output during the decade included several articles I wrote in the aftermath of my time at the OEEC on Germany's economic recovery; on Scottish industrial development and prospects; on long-term trends in Europe's trade; and on the outlook for raw materials. But perhaps the most important piece I wrote during these early years at Glasgow was a paper on "The Place of Capital in Economic Progress" which I wrote in 1953. In it, I sought to debunk the idea that more investment of capital was automatically the key to faster economic growth. So far as it did contribute, it was more by creating new kinds of assets than by adding to the stock of assets of a type already in use. A large proportion of total investment went on housing, fuel and power, transport and stock-building, all of which were relatively capital-intensive, not in equipment for manufacturing industry, most of which was not nearly so capital-intensive. Capital might be a carrier of innovation, and by helping to enlarge the market, might facilitate a rise in productivity. But without technical change, economic progress would be much slower, whatever the level of capital investment.

In 1953 this view came near to heresy and in some quarters still is. But since 1953 many other economists have expressed somewhat similar views, so that what I argued then is no longer novel. The report of the conference at which I delivered my points was not published, however, until 1987. The one economist on whom I made an impression was Austin Robinson, who told me how much it made him rethink the whole process of economic growth.

Throughout this decade at Glasgow, my academic interests were being shaped and broadened. My time was devoted mostly to what were in those days unfashionable aspects of economics: questions of how labour markets worked, how innovation and economic growth occurred, how businesses were run, and what made cities thrive. All these issues are much more studied today than they were in the 1950s — a change which I welcome. To some extent, indeed, the research done at Glasgow during my time laid the foundations for some of what was to follow.

## 13

# *The Economic Devlopment Institute, Washington DC, 1955–56*

In the late spring of 1954 I was approached by Dick Demuth, whom I had first met in Berlin in 1945–46, to act as a consultant to the World Bank in Washington. He asked me to review a proposal that the Bank should provide some form of training for senior administrators from the less developed countries. This proposal had originally been put forward by Paul Rosenstein-Rodan, by now a professor at MIT. It had strong support from some of the Bank staff who were keenly aware that many of these countries lacked administrators with the skill and understanding to evaluate large capital projects. It was hoped that a form of management education aimed at key officials would make the task of Bank loan staff easier (and perhaps increase the flow of capital to credit-worthy countries).

The question was not so much whether there was something that needed doing as whether it could be done better by the Bank or by existing educational institutions. A further uncertainty was how such a proposal would be viewed in the countries concerned: would there be enough applications from sufficiently senior people? And might they not prove too heterogeneous in command of English, familiarity with economics, age, seniority and so on to form a teachable class?

I was intrigued by the proposal; all the more so because it came shortly after we had launched our experiment in management education in Glasgow and after I had visited the Administrative Staff College in Henley, which at that time was the only body in the country engaged in full-time management training. In addition, I had spent the previous summer at the first session of the Merrill Center, a kind of prolonged academic seminar on current problems in a large private house in Southampton, Long Island. It had seemed to me a kind of Elysium where gladioli grew by the acre and the lawns could swallow up a polo ground or two. Fascinating discussions with leading economists, government servants and politicians were combined with sumptuous meals at a local hotel where a "small steak" represented about a week's ration in Britain; and a large steak was something I got round to ordering only after more than a month's practice. I came back to Britain ten pounds heavier — putting on weight on a scale I have never experienced before or since. So the prospect of spending some more weeks in the United States in July and August was enticing. I was not as conscious then as I am now how uncomfortable the Washington climate can be in mid-summer.

Once more I left wife and family behind and this time headed west. I discussed the proposal with as many members of the Bank staff as possible and went in search of academic opinion to Harvard and elsewhere. I had a particularly interesting talk with Jacob Viner, who was professor of economics at Princeton and who put it to me that an administrator might gain far less from a course of study in Washington that from someone looking over his shoulder and commenting on successive problems as they landed on his desk. It seemed to me, however, that there was no immediate possibility of following this recipe, and that if the Bank meant to educate its customers, it had better put over its ideas and draw on its experience where its own staff were at work — i.e., in Washington. I had Henley in mind as a guide to what might be attempted; and for this reason thought first in terms of a country house in the vicinity of Washington but sufficiently removed from the Bank to force participants to concentrate on their studies, undisturbed by the diversions of a large city. The amenities of the Merrill Centre also coloured my initial thinking and even made me contemplate Southampton, Long Island, as a possible site in spite of its distance from Washington. I was anxious that the atmosphere should be soothing and restful. The irony of this hope became apparent to me later.

What I suggested in the end was a staff college to consider case studies drawn from the wealth of material which must exist in the Bank; a maximum of 25 participants; and a course lasting six months. These recommendations were accepted. The Bank's President, Eugene Black, needed little persuasion but the Vice President, Bob Garner, was more doubtful. It was the idea of a staff college that overcame his doubts; as he meditated on the proposal he grew increasingly enthusiastic at the prospect of a growing number of administrators throughout the world who had shared a common training at the Bank and would come to be a kind of *corps d'elite* in the world of economic development. It was a vision that was at least to some extent realised. When I visited South Korea in 1977, for example, I found that a large proportion of the top administrative jobs were filled by former participants, proud of their association with the Institute that the Bank created, and grateful for the training they had received there.

Other recommendations in my report created more difficulty. It was simply not possible to find accommodation of the kind I had suggested, and the Bank in the end settled for a mansion house in Belmont Street that had belonged to its first President, Eugene Meyer. To cut costs, I had also made no allowance for the transport and housing of wives and families. But, as the French executive director of the Bank was quick to point out, this Anglo-Saxon view of life was unrealistic and less than human. However, the scheme was approved and the Ford and Rockefeller Foundations offered to meet a substantial part of the cost, which worked out at $10,000 for each participant, excluding the cost to his government of releasing him.

The new institution was christened the Economic Development Institute and was scheduled to begin operations in January 1956. The first requirement was to find staff and the Bank inquired whether I was willing to be the first director. Since I had no wish to abandon my career at Glasgow after only four years as head of a new department, I suggested that I should ask for two years' leave of absence and see the first two courses at the Institute through to completion before turning the directorship over to someone else. This suggestion met with resistance from my Vice Chancellor. So I submitted a compromise that was acceptable to both the Bank and to the University: that I should go for 18 months, from July 1955 to December 1956, returning briefly to Glasgow halfway through to deal with any urgent matters affecting my department. The second course would start

Staff of Economic Development Institute, World Bank, Washington DC, 1956 Marquez (Mexico);
John H Alder, Alec Cairncross; Bill Diamond; M Hoffman; K S Krishnaswami.

earlier than foreseen, in October 1956, so that I could launch it during my term of office and leave only when it was well under way.

These practicalities were not my only concern. I knew very little about developing countries, having hardly ever set foot in one, and was equally ignorant of the literature. The developing countries were infatuated with the construction of development programmes. But, as far as I could make out, there was hardly any adequate theory of economic development. Most of what there was had nothing to do with developing countries or even with the fundamental problems of development in industrial countries: it took development for granted. So, in order to teach others, I would have to work out my own theory. But I had one great and unforeseen advantage. I had been an administrator and I had been a planner. I knew what went wrong with plans and I could imagine what went wrong with development programmes.

When I reached Washington, my first task was to find a house for the family; and on this I had great good luck, for I was able to rent a house in Cleveland Park. It was in a cul-de-sac, free of traffic, so that young children could play out-of-doors. I was even luckier in finding staff, since the Bank made available to me two very able men, John Adler and Bill Diamond, who combined administrative and teaching ability and undertook their duties with zest. Both spent the rest of their careers with the Bank, John Adler holding the post of Director of the Institute for a time and Bill Diamond becoming an expert on development banks. The Bank took charge of organising and sifting applications for the first course. This still left plenty of time-consuming administrative chores, among which the selection of the right shape of table for seminar discussions stands out in my memory (we settled in the end for a U-shaped table divisible into five sections that could be used separately when required).

Although 14 participants from as many countries were selected for the first course, only one had arrived by the beginning of 1956. As the days went by, we wondered how many would eventually show up. By January 4th, when two more arrived, I had my first experience of consumer resistance at the Institute. The Pakistani member of the course was in a great rage and demanding to see the President: there was no morning tea, no one polished his shoes, and he felt insulted by "the attic which has been assigned to me". From then on I had ample opportunity to observe how the living conditions that I had hoped would foster study bred grievances instead.

On the Monday when the course opened, I noted some of our housekeeping difficulties in my diary:

"The front door was repaired endlessly, keys cut three times, finally a new lock fixed; yet the handle came off at the first pull. Table not installed until yesterday. Only nine participants arrived in Washington by dinner time on Friday. Icy weather for today's inaugural address at 10am with practically no audience at the start. Fuses all the time. No cupboards in two of the rooms. No keys for any of the rooms. No maps for the front hall. No pigeonholes (my instructions countermanded). Notice board far too big and had to be taken down — in fact, no new board up yet. Mice. No light in the library except one that is badly placed. TV late. No chess, Scrabble or any other diversions even now."

Most of these difficulties were soon sorted out but others remained. The front door continued to give trouble. Two men had rooms at what we might call garden level, which to them was simply the basement; bathrooms had to be shared, and as they were often located between bedrooms, there were plenty of opportunities for absentmindedly locking the other fellow out. Nobody had their own car, or telephone, or personal servant. And so on, and so on. The trouble was that, while the house was a rather splendid 19th century mansion with more than 20 rooms, it was ill-adapted for use simultaneously as a dormitory, office and seminar centre.

The participants were a mixed bunch: mixed in age, in seniority, in command of English, in garrulousness, in educational achievements. We had a few PhDs, including one from Harvard, but that was no guarantee of intellectual depth. One or two were clearly accustomed to throwing their weight about, but the large majority were neither very assertive nor unduly demanding. They did not, however, take readily to what approximated to undergraduate life.

Many of the men felt cut off from their families and from female company. They might even feel some frustration because they knew that their wives suspected them of having a high old time while they were unable to justify the suspicion. The one young woman among them, Virginia Yaptinchay from the

Philippines, might be a dead loss from the training point of view — although she profited from her time in other ways: she took back 19 trunks full of clothes and other purchases — but she certainly worked her passage in helping to restore morale, and was an unfailing source of good humour and high spirits.

Virginia made no bones about how she had come on the course. She had diligently cultivated the President's wife and had prevailed on her to use her influence in the right quarters. She clearly had little to learn about public relations. She had accumulated a large dollar balance in New York while working in the import licensing department of her central bank, and not long after her return to the Philippines, she was arrested and imprisoned. However, she was subsequently released...

Other members of the course were at least as colourful. There was, for example, the Belgian who had some vague responsibility for the Congo but came from Brussels and once admitted to me that he had agreed to join the course because he understood that it was much easier to obtain in the United States the drugs his condition required. He drank large quantities of beer, and wastefully kept opening lots of cans from which he never drank. I was startled one day to hear a distinguished guest speaker exclaim, as he watched this performance, "Doesn't he know he's drinking poison?" I asked what he meant. "That fat chap", he said, "suffers from a disease I know only too well, and the last thing he should be drinking is beer. He's killing himself." Sure enough, within a week of two, we had to send the Belgian to hospital and he took no further part in the course.

I had imagined that the participants would want to exchange experiences and talk shop like old Whitehall hands. It hardly ever happened. One of the few occasions on this course when I heard one participant cite his experience for the benefit of another occurred in an exposition by the Egyptian member of the case for the Aswan High Dam. "I can tell you", said his Yugoslav colleague, "what the result will be. We have had very ambitious investment programmes too. And what is sure to happen is that you will have a rip-roaring inflation."

If one participant was asked to introduce a discussion of the problems of his country, the others would protest. "We don't want to know all about Ceylon, or Nigeria, or Mexico. Besides, it's all so boring. We came to listen to what *you* could tell us and hear how the Bank set about development." This created two difficulties. First, if they had no chance to expound their own views and undergo the criticism this would provoke, they might go back none the wiser; to listen and make occasional comments was no way to learn. We could put before them the most outstanding thinkers on North America, but if they merely listened, there was no guarantee that any new ideas would lodge and develop in their minds. Indeed, only too often it was evident that they had missed the nub of what was said.

The second difficulty was greater. Like them, I had conceived of the Bank as a storehouse of development experience readily available as teaching material. I had seen enough to know that the Bank's thinking was not always abreast of current economic theory and that in some respects it was decidedly obscurantist. But I assumed it could make up for this in case studies illustrating what was liable to go wrong and how to make a success of things. Instead, the last thing the Bank staff wanted to do was to dwell on what went wrong. We found ourselves having to dig up our own material and sometimes putting a totally different complexion on cases where the Bank's staff seemed to be emphasising quite the wrong things. As I should have known from past experience, most people know only part of the story, even when they have been working on it all along and understand only some of the implications of the policies they have implemented and decisions they have taken.

The construction of a suitable curriculum was not straightforward. I found it hard enough to find time to give the matter thought in the middle of pressing administrative duties (and those gin-soaked social evenings that sabotaged attempts to think things out in Washington in those days). But we ultimately devised a course that consisted of more than a dozen seminars, each on a different topic and spread over several weeks, some chaired by myself, some by John Adler or Bill Diamond or by Professor Prasad, the Indian Executive Director of the IMF or Ragnar Nurkse, who was professor of economics at the University of Columbia and came down from New York once a week to lend a hand. Before each session of any seminar we circulated an outline of the argument and a reading list; where the articles cited were difficult to procure we had them photocopied. At half or more of the sessions we had a guest speaker, sometimes from the

Bank, sometimes from business, government or academic life. Other speakers such as Simon Kuznets of Johns Hopkins, a leading analyst of economic growth, and Wallace Notestein, a world expert on population movements, came to give an evening talk. It was a rich diet and required a good intellectual digestion.

In order to give some respite from everlasting seminars, we went on field trips from time to time to see factories and other enterprises, mainly for a day or two at a time, although in the middle of the course we went for an entire week on a visit to that great example of pre-war American public works, the Tennessee Valley Authority (TVA). It was not always easy in those days for a group which included non-white participants to find hotel accommodation, especially in a southern state such as Tennessee, and there were some embarrassing moments even in a border state like Maryland. But we had no difficulty in gaining access to a wide variety of places of interest.

Many incidents on those trips come back to me. I assumed that the participants would want to see examples of American industry, and so took them to the Bethlehem Steel plant at Sparrows Point, the only plant of its kind within easy reach of Washington and one of the largest in the United States. At one point, just after I had been expanding on 28-foot hearths beside the blast furnaces, the Nigerian participant (a graduate of King's College, Cambridge, with first class honours in law) came up to me. "Mr Cairncross," he said, "they keep talking about 'iron or'. Iron or *what?*" Some of the participants on this trip were deeply suspicious of my choice and accused me of trying to discourage them from trying to build up their own steel industry by showing them something they could never copy. On the other hand, when they went round the railway workshops in Baltimore, they asked why they should spend time looking at such a plant when they had railway workshops in their own country.

Whatever the participants learned from these trips, I found them very illuminating. They gave me an insight into the flexibility of industrial organisation in the United States that was just as valuable as the earlier education in industrial technology I had acquired in my visit in 1936. I found, for example, that Safeway, a supermarket giant, had a separate company inside its large Washington warehouse which maintained and operated its forklift trucks. At Pittsburgh, when we saw over a nail-making plant; there turned out to be a small independent cooperage business in the middle of it, making containers. When we visited the TVA, we met a farmer who was already, in 1956, using linear programming to work out the formula for mixing his feeding stuffs. On this visit, too, we saw what was then the largest power station in the world at Kingston, Tennessee, in a building that looked no bigger than a moderate-sized warehouse.

I had visited the TVA in 1936 and was familiar with the claims made for it as a dazzling spectacle of multi-purpose planning. That was how the participants saw it. For me, it came as something of a shock to find that the dams had become a comparatively insignificant part of its activities and that, in terms of its financial operations at least, TVA was now largely a supplier of electric power, generated from coal shipped from further up the river, and supplied at Oakridge to make plutonium.

The Oakridge plant used enriched uranium as its fuel. I asked whether this was indispensable in the generation of nuclear energy and was assured that this was so. I had happened, on the way to Oakridge, to read in *The Times* of the opening that week of the magnox power station at Calderhall. I was therefore able to point out that, in Britain at least, we were able to produce power using raw uranium. The merits of other kinds of nuclear reactor, including Boiling Water Reactors and Pressurised Water Reactors, were already being canvassed by the World Bank — but the layman felt just as lost then as now in the debate between the experts.

As the first course drew to its end, I kept wondering how to judge its success. As an educator, I was used to the simple tests of examinations, but examinations were irrelevant to the objects of a course designed to make the participants better administrators. How could one tell whether they would do their jobs better on return? For that matter, how did a grown man learn and what contribution could a teacher make to his progress? We had not been trying to communicate lumps of information or tricks and techniques. Our purpose was to educate: to improve their judgment by increasing their understanding of the background to the judgments they had to make. What they had learned, whether through our efforts or otherwise, would show only over the years in their future careers.

When, at the end of the course, I invited frank criticisms, I was not prepared for the vehemence with which they were delivered. It was obvious that many were deeply disappointed, both with their living conditions and with the course itself. The seminars had gone on too long; the questions we had been discussing had been too elementary; the discussions had been too inconclusive; they had spent too much time looking round factories. On the other hand, they assured me that their criticisms were meant to be constructive and that they wanted to see the Institute continue. And some, at least, obviously intended to set up a similar course in their own country, much as schoolboys think of becoming teachers, and were taking back as much of our teaching material they could pack. I was tempted to conclude from their criticisms that they had not grasped the full significance of economics as a discipline.

Eugene Black, the Bank's president, was rather shocked and indignant when he heard of these reactions, but I saw no harm in some escape of steam. It was clear that we must provide separate living accommodation for all future courses and this was found initially at the Hotel 2400, where meals had been served to those on the first course. This change by itself worked wonders, and the atmosphere in October, when the second course began, was altogether different. There was also a question mark against the length of the course. We had picked on six months rather hesitantly, afraid it might seriously curtail the number and seniority of applicants, but recognising that it would be easier to contract than extend the initial period. I concluded that we should continue to offer a six-month course, and in the end we had no difficulty in attracting 25 good candidates to the second course — a more homogenous and less eccentric group as it happened. So far as the course itself was concerned, we made no radical changes, but tightened it up and revised our seminar outlines to take advantage of what we had learned. It was also agreed that we should add to our staff someone from a less developed country, and we were joined by K.S.Krishnaswami (later Deputy Governor of the Bank of India) who, like John Adler, served later for a time as Director of the Institute.

One of the great strengths of the Institute was the unstinting support we enjoyed from the staff of the Bank. Senior staff took part in many of the seminars; the Executive Directors showed a keen interest; the administrative arrangements were excellent. As

I had foreseen when I recommended setting up the Institute, contact with the Bank was for the participants perhaps the most fruitful part of the entire course. It gave them access to staff and knowledge of Bank procedures which could be extremely valuable in any future loan negotiations. For this reason alone, study at a university would have been a poor substitute.

I hoped that another development would grow from the Bank's entry into the educational business. I began to see the Institute as a link between the Bank and the academic community, from which it was largely cut off. I saw advantages to both sides if economists were attached to the Institute for a year or two, since this would bring the theory and practice of economic development closer together. The Bank might learn a thing or two from the economists and they in turn might form a more realistic view of the problems of development or of the practices of the Bank. For the same reason I was anxious that we should start to publish our teaching material. If the Bank had more experience of development than any other institution, then we ought to make that experience widely available. In the end, however, we were too pressed for time; and the one volume which did eventually appear — Bill Diamond's book on development banks — owed at least as much to reading and study of material already in print as to anything gleaned from the experience of the Bank[1].

I tried to build various other links with the academic community. The Institute acquired an academic advisory committee of distinguished economists. Some professional economists continued to take part as members of staff, rather than just as guest speakers, in subsequent courses at the Institute. I also agreed to give a public lecture at the Bank on the tenth anniversary of the opening of the Institute, in the hope (never fulfilled) that this might encourage the establishment of an annual lecture there on some aspect of development. But, with the exception of Krishnaswami, no academic from outside the Bank was invited to direct the work of the Institute.

So the bridge I had hoped to build never really came into existence. Nevertheless, the Institute itself grew and flourished.

---

[1] "Development Banks", by William Diamond, published by the World Bank in 1956, was the only book issued by the Institute in its first two years.

The number of courses multiplied; the courses were given in more languages and more countries; the modest professional staff of three grew to one of nearly 40. Watching these developments, Dick Demuth thought that they should be reviewed periodically from outside, and I was twice invited to report on them. My main concern, on these occasions, was with the scaling down of the general course with which EDI had started. There seemed an undue concentration on matters of technique in the numerous courses on project evaluation which came to dominate its work. When I was invited to the concluding session of one such course, which had spent much of its time on discounted cash-flow calculations, I asked the participants what rate of discount they would apply when they got back to their own countries. There was a long and embarrassing silence. It was finally broken by a young Mexican: "I would use Bank Rate," he said. This incident did nothing to dispel my doubts.

The founding of EDI had not only a deep personal interest for me — it might have been the beginning of a entirely different career — but it provided a case study in the creation of a new educational institution. At the final session of the first course, I pointed out that much could be learned about economic development from reflection on that case study. The establishment of the Institute had been itself an effort of development in which one could observe in microcosm the elements that made for success and failure. The theories that economists had devised to explain development could, I told participants, be tested against their own experience. If they imagined that it would be easier to develop their countries than to develop the Institute, they would be mistaken. To make a success of the Institute meant that everybody had to be emotionally involved in making it work; and, in the same way, successful development of a country called for a general feeling of participation in the process. That process, moreover, was essentially educational: development was fundamentally about the need to organise the transfer of knowledge and experience. This could be done in many different ways; and the best way to do it was the EDI's main concern. The experience of the EDI might therefore have lessons of much wider significance than its own future.

The longer I thought about economic development, the stronger grew my conviction that the same elements governed the process, but in different proportions, as went to the growth of an industrial country. The difference in proportions, the gaps, the lack of necessary knowledge, habits and institutions, were for some purposes critical; but there was a great deal that was common to the further development of an industrial economy and to the early development of a non-industrial country.

# 14

## *The Radcliffe Committee*

We returned to Glasgow early in January 1957, taking occupation of our house in Lenzie for the second time in the middle of winter. We found that living in America bred dissatisfaction with Scottish housing[1] that lasted like a fever while the householder sought to make one improvement after another. We felt as though we had been expelled from some domestic Eden, which we tried to recapture by remodelling our kitchen. But nothing we did was much of a substitute for American sunshine.

I resumed my duties at the university. A couple of months after our return, I had a letter from the Treasury, putting me on warning that I would shortly receive an important communication to which a reply should be sent at once. Since we were leaving for an Easter holiday on the Solway, I made arrangements that any envelope that seemed to contain an important personal message should be sent on to me. Some time later, an official-looking envelope with red seals reached me, and I opened it expecting to find an invitation to join some Treasury Committee: conceivably, although I hardly dared to expect it, the rumoured successor to the Macmillan Committee which reported in 1931 on the working of monetary policy. However, it was a Ministry of Labour seal, and the letter was from Iain MacLeod, asking me to join a committee on anthrax.

---

[1] The dissatisfaction extended to David, my youngest son, then aged 4. "We're not going to live in this rickety-tackety old house, are we?" he exclaimed when he saw it. "Can't you get a new house?" I explained that new houses cost money. "Money!" he said in astonishment. "You can get money." When I asked where, he suggested that banks had plenty of money. I pointed out that there might be some difficulty in persuading a bank to lend money to me. "But don't you work in a bank?" he persisted, for no-one had explained to him that the World Bank was not a real bank. His reaction was similar to that of many adults I was to meet over the next few years.

I didn't even know what anthrax was. I was tempted therefore
to reject the invitation out of hand. But, taking account of the
earlier letter from the Treasury and the importance which
Whitehall seemed to be attaching to the appointment, I sent a
more qualified response. "The subject", I said, "lacks sex appeal",
and I felt sure that others were much better equipped to
contribute to any investigation of it. If the Minister insisted,
however, I was willing to accept. Inevitably, the Minister did
insist, without troubling even to comment on my scruples. I was
therefore committed to an inquiry which, with ordinary efficiency,
might have occupied three months but in fact dragged on for
well over two years.

When we got back to Lenzie I found in the waiting
correspondence a familiar blue envelope (without seals) and
inside was an invitation to join what was to be known as the
Radcliffe Committee on the Working of the Monetary System.
There could be no question of rejecting such an invitation. Not
only was the committee the most important on which an
economist could hope to serve; it included among its members
such old friends as Sir John Henry Woods, who had been my
permanent secretary at the Board of Trade; Sir Oliver Franks,
who had been Professor of Moral Philosophy at Glasgow
University before the War, ambassador to the United States after
the War, and was now Chairman of Lloyds Bank; Lord Harcourt,
Chairman of Morgan Grenfell and the Legal and General; and
Richard Sayers, Professor of Economics at the London School of
Economics and the only other economist on the committee. The
only question I asked myself was whether membership was
compatible with all my other duties and whether I should
withdraw from my commitment to join the committee on
anthrax. I decided to let things take their course.

There followed two very busy but fascinating years. The
committee met more or less weekly, on Thursdays and Fridays,
and between meetings there was a mass of written evidence to be
read and digested as well as, towards the end, a good deal of
drafting to be done. It was nearly 30 years since the Macmillan
Committee had sat and there had been no public inquiry into the
working of monetary policy since then. There had been
disagreement inside and outside the government over how the
monetary system worked or should work, and the Bank of

England and the Treasury had not always seen eye to eye on these matters. So we were being asked to resolve controversial issues both in monetary theory and in practical affairs — issues on which we ourselves might be in as much disagreement as the monetary authorities. The precedent of the Macmillan Committee pointed in this direction: no two of its 14 members had found themselves in entire agreement with one another, and only the Chairman had abstained from signing a reservation, addendum or memorandum of dissent. There was therefore some surprise when we eventually arrived at unanimous conclusions, and some disposition to find in this unanimity an explanation for the alleged vagueness of our conclusions[2].

We had to decide more or less right away whether our hearings should be open to the public and the evidence released to the press. Oliver Franks was strongly in favour of open evidence, while George Woodcock, the General Secretary of the Trades Union Congress, was equally strongly against. This was the first of a number of occasions on which Franks came out for "openness" and Woodcock mocked him for political naiveté; these two tended to get across one another, although all our discussions were otherwise very amicable. After some hesitation we decided that our proceedings should be in private, but that at the end of our deliberations, all the evidence should be made public.

We started off with a meeting off the record with Humphrey Mynors, Deputy Governor of the Bank of England, to talk over our remit. There were differences in the committee on the interpretation of our terms of reference. The Chairman, for example, took a narrow view and identified "the monetary and credit system" with banking, while Richard Sayers and I thought it inconceivable that we could prepare a report without some examination of the capital market and the role of the banks alongside other institutions as investment intermediaries. It was not long before we found the scope of our inquiries expanding steadily as Sayers and I had predicted.

One of the pleasant features of the meetings was that we arranged to have lunch together at the United University Club,

[2] I tried to answer some of these comments on our Report in my Wicksell lectures which are included in my "Essays in Economic Management", Allen and Unwin 1971, pp64–105.

then in Suffolk Street, a few yards from Spring Gardens where the committee hearings took place. Our discussions over lunch ranged far and wide and prompted me to resume the practice of keeping a diary which I had followed during the war and occasionally thereafter[3]. Sometimes we would reflect on the evidence we had heard or on parallel events such as the evidence given to the Bank Rate Tribunal in 1957–58; at other times, my colleagues would reminisce about personalities they had known.

For example, Radcliffe recalled that John Anderson who had been Lord President of the Council had become steadily more pompous and had always looked ten years older than he was. That was an advantage when young but not at 60. Apparently, if Churchill and Eden had both died in the war it would have been Anderson (on Winston's recommendation) for whom the King would have sent to succeed them as Prime Minister. Anderson had escaped assassination in India: he had been kneeling on a carpet at the time, and when he tried to get up, he slipped and fell in a rather undignified way but escaped being hit. Radcliffe, who took a keen interest in the arts, thought it was a mistake for Anderson to let himself be drawn by his second wife into the arts where he was inexperienced and lacking in judgment.

It was usually Radcliffe who had the most interesting anecdotes and reflections. He had enjoyed the confidence of people in widely different walks of life; chaired so many committees; and taken part in so much of our post-war history that he had endless material for conversation. He had a lawyer's precision of language with a hatred of superfluous epithets and contrived phrases. He talked freely with a clipped, rather flat enunciation, but with admirable lucidity. Yet there was something aloof and inscrutable about him, so that we were often at a loss to know his mind on the issues on which we were asked to pronounce, and for a very long time without guidance from him on how and when our Report was to take shape.

There was no discussion by the Committee of drafting arrangements before the Secretary, Robert Armstrong (a future Head of the Civil Service), circulated a long section in 1959. We agreed to put this aside, just as a Secretarial draft prepared for the Macmillan Committee was not pursued. But even at that stage,

---

[3] My Treasury diary for 1964–69 was published by The Historians Press in 1997 as "The Wilson Years". My diary for the years 1958–64 is due to appear from the Institute of Contemporary British History in the course of 1998.

Radcliffe gave us no guidance as to the form our Report should take. The Committee might assume that Richard Sayers, as the senior economist on the committee, would be the draftsman, but neither he nor anybody else had any instructions. The months went by; Sayers went to America and came back having suffered a mild stroke which made it difficult for him to take part in the discussions, and there was a danger that he would be unable to undertake drafting. In consequence, at one stage I felt that I might have to take on the entire job myself.

The one issue that absorbed the Chairman was that of the relationship between the Bank and the Treasury. On this, he submitted a draft that was accepted almost without comment from the Committee, and this formed Chapter IX of the Report, written by Radcliffe personally in his large florid hand. It was the only part of the Report which he drafted; and once his proposals were accepted, he resumed his career on the Bench, ceasing to call daily at the offices of the Committee.

The proposal that attracted most attention in this chapter was for a Standing Committee on monetary policy of which the Chairman officially would be the Chancellor of the Exchequer and in practice the Economic Secretary to the Treasury. The members of the Committee would include the Governor, Deputy Governor, and two other representatives of the Bank, four Treasury officials and two from the Board of Trade. The recommendation, as Robert Armstrong predicted from the start, proved to be stillborn. It was thought inconceivable that anyone so junior as the Economic Secretary to the Treasury could preside over such a Committee and there may well have been objection, too, to a body on which the Governor was put on the same level as six government officials who outnumbered the representatives of the Bank.

The truth is that a formal arrangement of this kind was unlikely to do much good. What was really needed was provision for regular consultation between the technical experts of the Bank and the Treasury so that the Chancellor did not find himself between two sets of advisers, each ignorant of the basis of the advice (sometimes of the advice itself) tendered by the other. Contact in the 1950s between West End and East End advisers was restricted by the somewhat hierarchical structure of the Bank so that, for example, Robert Hall, the Economic

Adviser to the Government, used to complain that he did not know what went on between the Chancellor and the Governor, and the staff of the Economic Section had little direct contact with the economic staff of the Bank.

All this changed a good deal in the 1960s, and there were even proposals from time to time for an advisory council on credit policy, such as now exists in the form of the Monetary Policy Committee. The Radcliffe Committee marked a watershed in relations between the Bank and the central government: not only at the formal level, but in the wider area of responsibility for policy. After Radcliffe reported, there was no doubt that the Chancellor must take primary responsibility for setting the direction of monetary policy while the Bank continued to manage policy from day to day and to enjoy the standing in its formulation that inevitably corresponds with wielding the instruments that give effect to policy. This point has become all the more important as, over the years, governments have increasingly given priority to monetary policy over fiscal policy. In this situation, no government can surrender responsibility for the framing of monetary policy, however much ministers may devolve on the Bank of England the responsibility for putting the policy into effect.

Looking back on our Report, of which I drafted about a third and Sayers the rest, apart from the chapter by the Chairman, I recognise that large changes have since taken place in the freedom of individual countries to pursue their own monetary policy. But I do not find a great deal in the Report I should now want to unsay. I should still want to argue for the primacy of fiscal instruments and the subordinate role of monetary weapons in domestic policy. Exclusive reliance on monetary weapons in a country heavily dependent on international trade risks exposure to unwanted fluctuations in exchange rates, as high interest rates lead to an inflow of funds and a consequence concentration of deflationary forces on the export sector. Indeed, events in 1998 have provided a further demonstration of this point.

I should be more willing to concede the direct influence of interest rates on final demand, and accept that monetary conditions exercise a powerful, more indirect influence. I should want, as is now increasingly accepted, to lay emphasis not on the money supply narrowly defined, but on liquid assets and the

Our children Philip, Frances, Sandy, David and Elizabeth, 1963.

state of liquidity, however defined. I see little more reason now than then for supposing that control of the money supply is a sufficient (or even a particularly attractive) way of putting an end to inflation with a unionised labour market. There may be a so-called "stable demand for money" under stable conditions of employment; but that tells us nothing at all about what happens in the very conditions of instability in which monetary policy might be invoked.

There are two respects, however, in which I should now put things differently. First of all, I thought at the time and see more vividly now, that we did not bring out clearly enough the interconnection between the money supply and the Government's borrowing requirement. If the financial surplus or deficit of the public sector fluctuates widely, the fluctuations are almost certain to find an echo in the money supply because of the difficulty in procuring equal fluctuations in the sales of gilt-edged. This would not matter too much if the fluctuations were limited and around a recognisable trend, since the abnormal addition to the money supply in any one period would shortly give way to an equally abnormal reduction in the next. If the government were successfully stabilising employment by spending more heavily when private spending was easing off, there need be no special problem. But if debt management on the necessary scale proved awkward and the reactions in the gilt-edged market were "perverse", the outcome might be an expansion in the money supply that had undesirable side effects and generated fears of inflation. This would be particularly likely in the vicinity of full employment, under conditions in which wage claims were unrestrained by trade depression. Keynes himself had recognised these dangers; and we should have emphasised them in our Report.

Events have changed my view in a second respect. The money market in London has long been dominated by international influences. But, with the enormous growth in the Eurodollar market since the publication of the Radcliffe Report, these influences are not only dominant but compelling. Short-term rates of interest in London cannot diverge from rates in the Euro markets except to the extent that there is uncertainty about the future value of sterling. A distinct national monetary policy, unconstrained by the monetary policies of other countries, is now unthinkable. To an extent much greater than 40 years ago, monetary management has to be international; and so far as there is scope for national initiatives, these have to be made through fiscal rather than monetary policy.

My involvement in the Radcliffe Committee had one other unexpected consequence. Early in June 1958, Per Jacobsson, now the Managing Director of the International Monetary Fund, sounded me out over dinner on my willingness to join the IMF as Vice President. We had kept in touch since we worked together in Germany after the War, when he had clearly taken a fancy to me. I asked for time to consider the matter, and took the opportunity of consulting Robert Hall, who was head of the Economic Section. He was strongly in favour of my accepting the offer which, he said, would certainly be welcomed by the government and was likely to be urged on me by Cameron Cobbold, the Governor of the Bank of England. The IMF had now begun to play the part for which it was originally designed and in Robert's view it would continue to do so. But if I were to agree, I should insist on clear and precise conditions of appointment, all the more so because Per Jacobsson might not be in his current job for much longer.

A week later, the Governor asked me to call and converted this into an invitation to lunch. He came straight to the point: Jacobsson's offer had his wholehearted approval. What was wanted was not a monetary economist, so I should not be deterred by any inexperience in that area. There was a time, he said, when the IMF had done little or nothing and he, Cobbold, had been as much responsible for this as anyone. But now things were different, and the Fund would have an increasing part to play. This was where I could be most useful and I ought to go not later than the end of 1959. There had to be a Briton in one of the top posts: he didn't mind from what nationality the posts were filled, so long as the men appointed had the necessary ability. "In matters of this kind," he said with great emphasis, "we have to be international." There had to be someone who could take on the technical experts and speak direct to Finance Ministers; and there were few men of this calibre around. He went on to say that he had backed me strongly for membership of the Radcliffe Committee and that this should prove a quite adequate training for the job.

All this was very flattering and persuasive, but I remained hesitant. It became apparent, too, that there were difficulties at the Washington end and that Jacobsson did not have an entirely free hand. A year passed in which I had made clear my willingness to consider a formal offer, but none reached me. When our Report appeared, Jacobsson dropped the whole idea. "You don't really believe all this stuff, do you?" he asked when we met in the autumn of 1959; and with this expression of incredulity, he allowed me to conclude that he had now repented of any suggestion that I might join the IMF.

The key issue, as I write, is no longer how the monetary system works in any one country, but how there can be one monetary system and many governments. How can a single monetary policy make provision for wide differences in the pressure of demand, in areas under separate governments? And, if the answer lies in the use of fiscal policy, how can freedom in the use of fiscal policy be reconciled with its absence in monetary policy? If reconciliation is impossible, can much in economic policy be left to national governments? Is not the logic of one monetary policy a single government, as in the United States? These are issues that the Radcliffe Committee mercifully never had to address.

## 15

## *Assignments abroad 1957–60*

Throughout the 1950s, and especially after my return to Glasgow from a year and a half in Washington, DC, I kept being asked to lecture abroad, to take part in international conferences and to advise on a variety of current economic problems in one country or another. In countries as diverse as Yugoslavia, Turkey and Ethiopia, all of which had embarked on some form of economic planning, I was able to draw on my experience of planning in wartime Britain and during the subsequent transition to a peacetime economy, just as I had done during my earlier travels such as the visit to Moscow in 1952. Equally my time on the Radcliffe Committee provided me with material on monetary policy that I was able to use when I delivered the Wicksell lectures in Stockholm in 1960 and later when I was asked to advise on the scope for adapting monetary policy to regional needs in Eastern Canada — a subject not without relevance today, in an age of common currencies.

Each assignment was an opportunity to develop my own thoughts on issues as diverse as planning, monetary policy and innovation, and to broaden my understanding of the way different economies share similar problems. The problems I encountered or lectured on were ones that crop up again and again in economic policy: the relationship between investment and growth; the relationship between economic planning and the practical constraints on public spending; the problems created by a single monetary policy for a country with regions with widely differing patterns of demand. The 1950s were a period when the parallels in policy dilemmas in differing countries were particularly interesting: the West was recovering rapidly from the war; the Soviet block was also recovering, but with a completely different economic model; and many countries in the developing world were uncertain which economic system to adopt.

## Yugoslavia

My visit to Yugoslavia in 1957 came at the invitation of Vlady Perlot, who had been a fellow-student of economics at Cambridge in the early 1930s and was now head of the Foreign Trade Research Institute in Llubjana. He was at a loss to know on what principles the foreign trade of a Communist country should be planned when prices and costs were completely distorted by multiple exchange rates and controls. For example, there was one exchange rate for hens, another for eggs and a third for feathers. Would I be interested in coming to Yugoslavia to advise on the problem?

This was irresistible, although it took some time before confirmation reached me. The issue of a visa came at the very last moment: I was still telephoning Belgrade the day before I was due to leave and London an hour or two before my departure from Glasgow. I finally obtained my visa by calling that evening at the West Kensington home of the official in charge.

I had a delightful week, of which my most vivid memory is standing by a level crossing in the country, and watching the Orient Express go by on its way to Istanbul. Its imagined splendour vanished as two run-down passenger coaches drawn by a somewhat stunted locomotive chugged past us.

Vlady had arranged for me to give a public lecture and I spoke — rather rashly, I thought — on the problems of economic planning. I was a little taken aback to find my Yugoslav hosts in general agreement with my de-bunking approach, and still more surprised when Jan Tinbergen, a well-known Dutch economist, who turned out to be in the audience, rose to his feet to elaborate one of my less carefully considered ideas. The lecture was subsequently printed and circulated in other Eastern European countries, as I found when I met economists from these countries a year later in Turkey.

I did little to resolve my friend's problems, but I received some insight into the Yugoslav economic system, partly from Vlady's remarkable career. When war broke out, he had been in the National Bank of Yugoslavia. Arrested by the Germans, he survived life in a concentration camp; was transferred to work with the Todt Organisation which was responsible for the construction for the Germans of the Western defences in Normandy; escaped after being sentenced to death and hid in woods and ditches before surrendering to a British tank whose commander turned out to be a friend from his Cambridge days[1].

After the war he first held a key post in the licensing of imports. The director of a new factory approached him for a licence to import from the United States what Vlady called "mice (maize) brew", and is known to chemists as corn steep liquor. This is a chemical compound of a special kind supplied only in Kansas used for making penicillin,. Since there was an ample supply of maize from domestic agriculture, Vlady saw no need to grant an import licence. A year went by, the factory was built and a furious director then denounced Vlady to higher authority for sabotaging his production of penicillin. As a result, he was thrown into prison and his official career came to an abrupt end. It took many years before he was able to rehabilitate himself in an academic post.

## Turkey

A few months later, when the International Economic Association was for the first time organising a conference for economists from East and West, I was asked to give a paper on trade between countries with different social systems. The conference, at Bursa, in Turkey, nearly came to a premature end after Richard Gardner, an American economist who later became US Ambassador to Italy and to Spain, expressed himself with some forthrightness about Russian labour camps. It was also in some danger because of the absence of Turkish coffee — or indeed coffee of any other kind. This caused particular misery to Jacques

---

[1] These experiences left him with such dreadful arthritis that his doctor warned him that he had at most one year to live. Sent home from hospital, he took up bee-keeping. At the end of the year, still very much alive, he called on his puzzled doctor, who was unable to account for his survival until at the mention of bees he struck his head. "Of course! Why didn't I think of it? Bee stings were the one remedy for your arthritis that I completely overlooked." In gratitude to his preservers, Vlady was ever after an enthusiastic beekeeper and distributed to his friends cans of honey from the Julian Alps.

Rueff, an influential French economist who was close to General de Gaulle. Since my wife had insisted that I take some coffee with me, in spite of my protest that this was the equivalent of carrying coals to Newcastle, I was able to bring a little relief and revive the flagging interest of my continental colleagues.

Among the moments I remember from this conference, I treasure an intervention by Professor Haberler, then Professor of Economics at Harvard, when he asked his Soviet colleagues why the foreign trade of the Soviet Union was no greater than that of Switzerland. It was a nice illustration of the use of a single telling fact in place of a long and unconvincing piece of analysis. I remember too the *cri de coeur* of Jacques Rueff who wanted to have it explained "before I die" whether it was really true that the money supply was fixed by the monetary authorities "as the Anglo-Saxons maintain" or whether it could respond, as he himself believed, to influences on the side of demand.

Apart from the interest of meeting economists with a quite different outlook — sometimes too stridently insisted upon to carry conviction of so great a difference — the conference provided an opportunity of seeing a little of Turkey, and I had my first chance to see Athens on the way out and Rome on the way back. With Alec Nove, a fellow economist from Glasgow and an expert on Soviet affairs, I spent a long day in Athens, from shortly after dawn until the late afternoon. We wandered round the Parthenon, lunched with Governor Zolotas at the Bank of Greece, and gazed upon the golden mask of Agamemnon in the National Museum. Coming back through Rome on Easter Sunday I stood among the enormous crowd gathered to hear the Pope in the square outside St Peter's, and hurried from one church to another to take my fill of monuments.

Another journey took me to Nancy in April 1958 to lecture (in French) on British economic problems. I unintentionally mystified my audience by referring repeatedly to "le UK". My wife, sitting at the back, had to endure bewildered whispers of "Qu'est-ce que c'est que 'le UK'?"

Whenever I went to a conference abroad, I took the opportunity to extend my visit and see a little more of the country. On a visit to Berlin in 1959 I was struck by how much it had changed. It looked curiously "normal" because of the removal of the rubble and the tidying up of the buildings. The

Wall had not yet been built and a woman economist on whom I called took me by car without difficulty to and from her parents' home in East Berlin. We were also able to visit Siemenstadt, an industrial part of the city to which large numbers of workers employed there travelled daily from the Russian sector. We also saw some of the refugees from the Eastern zone at the reception centre in Marienfelde. A woman who had fled with her daughter explained that what had brought matters to a head was that it was not possible for her daughter to be married in church. It was the kind of reason for migration that one might have expected centuries ago rather than in 1959.

## Ethiopia

In November 1959 I had a cable out of the blue from Addis Ababa, sent by Mekki Abbas, Director of the Economic Commission for Africa, whom I had never met. He asked me to come for a week to discuss economic planning. The invitation seemed so absurd that I found it irresistible. As it was the middle of term, I had to rearrange some of my lectures, but I managed to extend the week to ten days, spending one day in Rome and another in Beirut on the way out, and working in a long evening in Cairo before catching my plane just after 3 a.m.

The evening in Cairo almost became longer still. When I arrived at the airport I looked for a bus to take me into town. The only one I could see was half-filled with (Syrian) airmen in full uniform and there was no indication of the destination on the front. I climbed aboard, trusting to luck. No one spoke and no one asked me for a fare. We bowled along in complete silence and in the dark. After about half an hour or so we pulled up in what I hoped would turn out to be the centre of Cairo. But even if it were, how was I to get back for my flight when it was already 9 p.m. on a Saturday night?

Fortunately, I saw not far off a TWA office and arranged to catch an airport bus about two hours later. Without a map I had no idea how to spend my time. But, as I walked around Ibrahim Pasha Square, I got into conversation with a young Egyptian who claimed to have spent ten years as a British spy. I thought I might as well chat to him as try to find monuments in the dark. It didn't seem to me that he could have been a very successful spy, since he said he had been swindled out of £700 by an Italian girl-friend and he clearly had not been hanged, as he claimed most of those serving British Intelligence had been. After denouncing Nasser and running down his compatriots, he was content to let me buy him some coffee and a cake, beg a piastre or two and take his leave. And so I returned to the airport for the early morning flight to Addis.

At that time, Addis Ababa was a city of few modern buildings — so few that the opening of a new petrol station was attended by the Emperor in person. There were no terraces or rows of shops or even huts fronting on the street, but a series of scattered offices, hotels and what looked like fragments of African villages, complete with animals, half-hidden in the background. From above, as we approached out of a warm blue sky, we could see a sprawl of flat, galvanised roofs, grouped here and there without pattern; straw huts in little circles; and a few more metropolitan areas with flat stone facades, never rising very high but standing out in knots of more solid building. There were also — somewhere — a large number of royal palaces; and a market, where I bought my second son a drum. Round the town grew eucalyptus in abundance, so that the air had an agreeable, if somewhat antiseptic, freshness.

The conference occupied us for most of the week, with a break half-way through when we went to see the Emperor. To enter the palace, we had to pass a couple of his lions, couched sleepily in front of it. We were shown into a waiting room where the bookcase contained bound volumes of *The Reader's Digest*; and the usual present from Queen Victoria, a grandfather clock, stood by the wall. We were then taken to a large audience chamber and lined up with the Cabinet facing us as if about to dance the Grand Old Duke of York until mead was brought in and the ranks were suddenly broken in a rush for this curious refreshment. The Emperor, on arrival, stood at the end of the two lines, and we were taken to be introduced to him one by one. The conversation, as I recall, was rather one-sided, since His Majesty seemed somewhat taciturn and insisted on the use of French. However, it isn't every day that one can carouse with a Cabinet, drinking mead out of golden vessels, and lecture an Emperor on the virtues of education.

Some of the young Ethiopians at the conference persuaded me to come back with them on the Friday evening when it ended and tell them what I could about planning. But somehow this was converted into a publicly announced address on "Planning in Africa" to be given in the National Library of Ethiopia. So, after five days of almost continuous debate and with an acute sense of ignorance about everything African, I was taken through a vast crowd, some of them sitting on tables or standing in the aisles, to my place on the platform. Another British economist who had come from Uganda was to speak after me, and the chair was taken by an enthusiastic young Ethiopian. The three of us shared a kind of pulpit, in front of which hung a microphone labelled "Voice of America". Judging (rightly) that it was not working and that nobody in the audience knew how to make it work, I decided there was nothing for it but to bawl loudly and continuously — as soon as the Chairman had finished his lengthy introduction — and this I proceeded to do.

In the course of my speech, I happened to introduce my customary warning against the unguarded use of statistics, citing the parallel that Ely Devons once drew between statisticians and witch doctors, and comparing the politician's response to statistics with the Roman habit of consulting the entrails. At question time, one of the audience rose at once to ask why I thought so poorly of the activities of witch doctors. "Who is this man?" I whispered to the Chairman. "He's the local witch doctor," he replied. "He used to work for a bank here, but since they got a Swedish manager, he's out of a job." I thought it prudent to indicate that my remarks had been misunderstood.

I have often wondered since how these alert and attractive young Ethiopians fared in the upheavals in their country. There was something a little dilettante and over-sophisticated about them, and yet it was clear that they were part of a new generation, eager to accelerate the development of their country. I gained some insight into their dilemmas when Alexander Desta, a grandson of the Emperor who was killed in the late 1970s, came and sat beside me in the aeroplane shortly after we left Addis Ababa. He had spent a year at Dollar Academy in Scotland before going to Wellington and later to the Royal Naval Academy. He spoke English fluently.

He told me that that about 20 young men who had returned from abroad over the previous five years with a training in economics had prepared a Plan with the help of Yugoslav advisers. But they had operated largely in isolation from the Council of Ministers, which viewed their activities with scepticism and was inclined to argue that they must be duplicating the work of the departments. These were already staffed with people who had experience of planning hospitals, schools, roads and so on. If the young men were going to tell these people what to do, they had better come and run their departments. A further difficulty was that, if the plan called for particular kinds of enterprise, somebody had to be recruited to run them and find a market for their output; this would be beyond the powers and competence of the planners. There was also the risk that projects might be held up and fail to win approval for several years because the Minister concerned was busy with day-to-day problems or other new projects.

Desta told me also that a Planning Board had been set up with the full backing of the Emperor, who initiated all major decisions. But there were problems with the way the Board operated. It was a cumbersome machine, with 26 members drawn from different departments and no separate Minister to report to. The Board was still operating on the basis of an older plan, and putting forward fresh projects at an accelerating pace. But spending cuts were plainly needed: the Minister of Finance was being asked to approve a rising total of departmental expenditures involving a rising outlay of scarce foreign exchange, just when export prices and proceeds were falling.

I found such administrative difficulties familiar enough[2]. I have always felt that the Minister of Finance should ideally be the Minister of Planning too and should certainly see eye to eye with him. There had to be a close personal link between the planning staff and the staff of the spending departments, and an explicit attempt to relate the general plan to the specific projects at its core. Without such co-ordination, there would simply be a muddle.

I was interested to know what Desta thought of the situation. He maintained that Parliament was freely elected and that

---

[2] I discussed some of them in my address to the World Bank in 1966 on "The Long Term and the Short Term in Economic Planning". Reprinted in my "Essays in Economic Management". (Allen and Unwin, 1971).

ministerial policies had to be explained and defended before parliamentary commissions; but he admitted that, in practice, the policies were never voted down. There were no parties and there was a lack of dominant personalities among the members. Parliament was beginning, however, to show more inclination to insist on further information about ministers' proposals or even at times to withhold approval of such proposals.

When, later on my journey home, I talked to Abdul Rahman, the Egyptian member of the conference, he took the view that some of the difficulty in Ethiopia had arisen because of the behaviour of the Yugoslav advisers. They had put forward plans and projects that came as bolts from the blue to the Departments; and they had tended to report first to their Ambassador before coming to any committee meeting. This did not endear them, or their conception of planning (which was one of carrying a whip in the hand), to their hosts.

From that day forth, I heard no more of my Ethiopian friends or of the Economic Commission for Africa. Once or twice I attended a reception at the Embassy and spoke briefly to the Ambassador, the unfortunate Mr Makonnen, who was killed shortly after the death of the Emperor. Mekki Abbas I saw years afterwards in Oxford when he had long since ceased to direct the ECA. But with the others, of whom I saw so much in those seven days in Addis Ababa, all contact was lost for ever.

### Sweden

At the end of April 1960 I visited Sweden with Mary to deliver the Wicksell Lectures.[3] Although only two lectures were required, I went to great pains in preparing them, choosing as my topic "Monetary Policy in a Mixed Economy" so as to be able to expound my own reflections on the issues debated in the Radcliffe Committee Report. I was, if anything, over-impressed by the importance of the occasion, and put into their composition as much effort as would have allowed me to draft an entire volume[3]. I was invited, too, to address the Political Economy Club, chaired by Bertil Ohlin who had been Professor of Economics at the Stockholm School of Economics and for many years leader of Sweden's main opposition party, although never

---

[3] Also included in my "Essays in Economic Management" (Allen and Unwin, 1971).

Prime Minister. I took the opportunity to outline my views on what has always seemed to me the rather loose relationship between technical innovation and investment. My view — although not very fully developed at the time — is that innovation responds to an expanding market. This is likely to be accompanied by high investment, which in turn is likely to involve more advanced technology, but it is a mistake to assume that high investment *of itself* guarantees a faster rate of innovation. In any event, most investment takes place outside industry and tends to be concentrated in housing and power and transport, so that a high rate of *aggregate* investment has very little causal connection with industrial innovation.

I was interested to find that my Swedish friends readily took the point that innovation was primarily a learning process which manifested itself in rising productivity even when little or no investment took place. They cited a study of productivity in the Swedish steel industry which corroborated this: it found that productivity had risen year by year with little or no capital investment.

The Swedes were wonderful hosts. At the dinner parties which they gave for us, my wife and I were the only English-speaking guests, but everyone spoke English as if it were the most natural thing in the world — so much so that, when we had to ask the way one evening in a Stockholm street, it did not occur to us that we might have difficulty finding anyone who could understand us.

## Canada

Later in 1960, at the request of the governments of the Atlantic Provinces of Canada (APEC), I went out to Halifax, Nova Scotia, to look at monetary policy in a regional context. I concentrated on the way the 1959–60 countrywide credit squeeze affected the eastern provinces when the pressure of demand there was comparatively low. What I undertook was, in other words, a kind of sequel to the Radcliffe Committee, pursuing issues that had been debated since the Committee reported and which arose in the different context of regional development.

I spent five quite fascinating weeks, visiting each of the four provinces and conducting a long series of interviews with bankers, officials, lawyers, farmers and businessmen. Because my terms of reference were not confined to monetary matters, I was able to take the opportunity to analyse the economic development of the Atlantic Provinces, migration flows, changes in industrial structure, the prospective level of employment and the measures that might be taken to raise it. I was the more interested in the analysis since the Atlantic Provinces in relation to the rest of Canada and of Canada in relation to the United States provided a close parallel to the situation in Scotland in relation to the rest of the United Kingdom and of the United Kingdom in relation to Western Europe. My report was therefore simultaneously an attempt to anatomise a credit squeeze and to form a view of the possibilities of regional development[4].

Apart from everything else, my assignment provided me with an unusual opportunity of seeing Eastern Canada, meeting the leading personalities in the region and entering into the struggle to establish its identity and destiny. I heard a great deal of history, learned much about the forces behind industrial development and became familiar with the ideas and outlook of hundreds of people. I moved between sharply contrasting environments, physical and social. If Halifax was far removed in atmosphere from Ottawa, Newfoundland was both literally and metaphorically a thousand miles away. It had only recently been made part of the Dominion of Canada and the sudden inflow of family allowances, paid to mothers, had transformed the sociology of the fishing villages, elevating the mothers and grandmothers into the ruling figures in the average underemployed household.

When I visited the island, the prime minister, Joey Smallwood, was in the middle of a Cabinet meeting when I was due to see him. So it was arranged that I should stay to lunch. The lunch was attended by the entire Cabinet, not with any view to hearing anything I had to say but because pressure of business made it necessary to continue discussion over lunch. So I found myself in the middle of an informal Cabinet meeting in which Quebec and Newfoundland were behaving as though they were two independent states, rather than parts of a single country. The spirit of the Heptarchy — the division of Anglo-Saxon England into seven separate kingdoms — was very much in the ascendant.

---

[4] My report, issued in 1961, was entitled "Economic Development and the Atlantic Provinces".

Joey Smallwood was keenly interested in expanding employment in Labrador, which borders Quebec but is constitutionally part of Newfoundland, hundreds of miles away, and was putting pressure on Brinco (a large power company in which Newfoundland had a stake) to employ more citizens from the state at the expense of citizens of Quebec.

As to my main task, it turned out to be remarkably difficult to assemble clear-cut evidence that the credit squeeze alone had done serious damage to local businesses. Curiously enough I came across a rare exception on the day of my departure when I went to return the dictating machine which I had hired. The proprietor of the business, after hearing what I had been doing, told me that he was having to close down a thriving and quite profitable new business because the bank which financed his machines now found it impossible to maintain its line of credit. In general, though, such instances were rare.

A key conclusion of my final report ran:

"It was not too hard to find examples of businesses that had fairly evidently been the victims of a change of credit policy in 1959–60 and would normally have been able to get the credit they wanted; but...at the same time, it was rare to find that the only difficulty facing such businesses had been to obtain credit, or that failure to obtain more bank credit had had a marked effect on the scale of their operations."

A year or so later, when I had moved from Glasgow to the Treasury, I was faced with the identical problem of devising a regional monetary policy — but in a British context. The same question was being asked: why should Scotland be obliged to suffer heavier unemployment in order to cure overheating in London and the south-east? The answer was also the same: that while the full impact on Scotland could be eased to some extent (for instance, by exempting Scottish banks from credit ceilings), monetary policy could not be used to bring about a more even pressure of demand between regions. If the pressure had to be reduced by monetary means in one major region, it would be reduced in other areas as well. All that could be done was to use *non*-monetary instruments such as public expenditure to discriminate in favour of the less prosperous regions, and even this might do little more than help check the outflow of workers in search of jobs elsewhere. Members of the European Monetary Union may yet experience the same problem in a European context.

With my Canadian visit, my days as a travelling academic were drawing to a close. I made a visit to Prague in December 1960. I had thought I was going to speak at a conference about international trade which might lead to a change of policy, but it turned out to be the usual propaganda affair and I quickly lost interest. I chiefly remember the discovery that the street cars had mahogany seats and had been in use since before the First World War. I was due to go to Mexico the following July for a conference of agricultural economists. In preparation for it I wrote a lengthy paper on "The Contribution of Foreign and Domestic Capital to Economic Development"[5]. But alas! long before my departure I had been persuaded to rejoin the Treasury and by July 1961 I was deeply involved in an economic crisis of the usual type and could not be spared for frivolous academic pursuits in Mexico. Instead of being involved, at one remove, in discussing appropriate policy for many differing countries, I found myself directly involved in helping to make it for one — the United Kingdom.

[5] Included in my "Factors in Economic Development (1962)".

Alec Cairncross and Sir Denis Rickett (HM Treasury) with Lucius Thompson-McCausland (Bank of England) at Working Party No.3 of OECD, Paris 1964.

## 16

## *Whitehall once more: The Treasury, 1961–69*

Just before Christmas 1960 a letter arrived from Sir Frank Lee, Joint Permanent Secretary of the Treasury, offering me the post of Economic Adviser to the government. I had some qualms about my fitness for such an appointment, but it was not an offer that I could have borne to reject. Some of my hesitations must have surfaced when I had lunch with Frank in February, for I learned later that he began to wonder whether I was the man for the job. I recall also that I asked Sir Robert Hall, who was retiring from the job, "What do I say when I don't know?" and he replied that I should let it show in the tone of voice. I had had no such doubts when I was asked to serve under Stafford Cripps and Harold Wilson as economic adviser to the Board of Trade in the 1940s, partly because I felt more at home with industrial problems than in the macro-economic world of the Treasury. But, to tell the truth, as soon as I got to work, all doubts disappeared.

I was due to take up my appointment in June. As Economic Adviser, my responsibilities would be to give economic advice — to the Treasury rather than to ministers; to provide regular assessments of the economic outlook; to comment on policy issues; and recruit an increasing number of economic specialists to Whitehall posts. I was also Director of the Economic Section, a group of about a dozen economists in the Treasury. I was to stay at the Treasury for the following eight years, years which saw not only the election in 1964 of the first Labour government since the 1940s, but also an increasingly desperate battle to defend the sterling exchange rate, culminating in the 1967 devaluation. Under the Conservative government which I advised for my first three years at the Treasury, I was involved in a number of battles over policy issues. Under the Labour government that succeeded them, I initially found myself fighting for the future role of the Economic Section in the Treasury.

I called on the first Chancellor I was to work with, Selwyn Lloyd, in February, when he was wrestling with his first budget. As I discovered later, Selwyn had expected to go to the Foreign Office, not the Treasury. He was not at home as Chancellor. In matters of economic policy, he was somewhat out of his depth, although he shared the traditional Tory ambition to cut public expenditure and improve business incentives. He was, however, capable of introducing entirely new instruments of policy, such as the two tax regulators[1], as part of demand management; and he was sufficiently bold to become the first Chancellor to adopt an incomes policy (as distinct from a wage freeze). Unfortunately, he had no rapport with the trade union leaders, and his encounters with them resembled what might have occurred between creatures in quite different environments, such as a whale and a herd of elephants.

At our first meeting in February, he was chiefly anxious to secure approval for giving greater incentives to business executives in the form of lower rates of "surtax", as the higher rates of income tax were then called. As I noted in my diary, "I recall no distinct impression made on me beyond one of a rather shy, hesitant personality, with no command of words or ideas, uncertain of the whole profession of economists, lacking in humour and exuberance, but with a force and pertinacity which his political record bears out."

## The July measures

When I next saw Selwyn Lloyd, on my first morning in the Treasury on June 5th, a foreign-exchange crisis was already boiling up. The deutschmark and the Dutch guilder had both been revalued in March, and this had aroused the markets to the possibility of further changes in exchange rates. The Chancellor,

---

[1] The two tax regulators, introduced in the 1961 Budget, empowered the Government to change the rates of indirect taxation at any time without prior recourse to Parliament. Regulator No. 1 allowed a 5% or 10% increase or decrease in the rate of indirect taxes such as purchase tax; Regulator No.2, which was never used, allowed for the introduction of a kind of payroll tax, to be paid by employers.

who had his jacket off and was chain-smoking Turkish cigarettes, was confident of riding out the crisis; listed the various sources from which he could meet pressure on the pound; and pointed with approval to the support he was offered by the National Institute of Economic and Social Research, *The Economist*, and other commentators. My sympathy with his point of view did not survive a talk with my new colleagues, who were all of one mind. They maintained that demand was excessive and likely to become more excessive in 1962, so that measures to cut demand should be taken as soon as possible.

On the basis of a new set of economic forecasts just becoming available, I submitted a paper to the Budget Committee, which was the Treasury body that dealt with all issues of taxation. It had been drafted by Bryan Hopkin who was the most senior economist in the Economic Section, and whom I had known at Cambridge 25 years previously. The paper called for additional taxation of £300m (or 1% of GDP in 1961) through the use of the regulator. This was only half what was originally proposed, but as much as I judged to be politically acceptable; it was also, as I discovered later, double what Robert Hall had thought a big enough dose of deflation in the 1950s. Thus in my first week I set on foot what came to be called "the July measures", denounced by *The Economist* as "probably.....the biggest immediate cut in demand that has been deliberately imposed by a British government on any single afternoon in British history."

A day or two after my submission to the Budget Committee, the Bank of England warned the Treasury of a rapid loss of reserves which could not be allowed to continue. In the first six months of 1961, £164m was drawn from the reserves, and in addition it was necessary to borrow $910m under an agreement made with other central banks at Basle in the spring. However, the government took no immediate action — not even raising Bank rate — and no new taxes could be raised until the Finance Bill had passed into law — i.e., until July 25th. So, for over six weeks, the Government held back, waiting until it could take the stringent measures it now knew were required.

The measures differed from what we originally proposed. No use was made of "Regulator No.2", a kind of payroll tax that we thought could bring in £100m; on the other hand, I successfully urged an increase in Bank rate which neither the Chancellor nor the Governor of the Bank of England had initially contemplated. I was unable to hear the exposition of the measures by the Chancellor in the House of Commons because I was by then on the way to Washington, to negotiate a standby loan of $2,000m with the IMF. But I learned later that he confined himself to a short summary that made a poor impression. He had promised, while we wrangled over Regulator No.2, that "there would be plenty of time to find the words," but he never did. Nor did Harold Macmillan, the Prime Minister, carry out the promise he made to me at Chequers, before the announcement of the measures, when I had asked him what I was to tell the IMF in my forthcoming negotiations: to cut public expenditure by £100m.

The July measures were successful in stopping the drain from the reserves, but less effective in improving the balance of payments. The basic balance of current and long-term capital transactions moved briefly into surplus in the winter of 1961–62, but it was soon back in deficit. Unemployment began a climb that took it in 20 months from 1.3% to 2.4% — levels which may seem trivial by today's standards, but which caused great shock at the time. The measures had got rid of excessive pressure of demand at the cost of some loss of production, but they had not brought the balance of payments into surplus.

After his second budget, in the spring of 1962, Selwyn Lloyd was conscious that some of his colleagues were gunning for him. Macmillan also developed doubts when the economy lost momentum early in the summer of 1962, and felt that the burden of making incomes policy work would fall on him, rather than on the Chancellor. As the debate on pay policy in 1962 (described below) continued, the Prime Minister reached the conclusion that a new Chancellor was needed.

So, after I completed my first year in the Treasury, there was a general change at the top. In mid-July, Selwyn Lloyd was dismissed. Having left the Treasury, he proved to be a successful Speaker of the House of Commons; instead of being tense and prone to stammering, as he had been as Chancellor, he became relaxed and amusing. He was succeeded by Reginald Maudling; and not long after, Sir Frank Lee retired and was succeeded by William Armstrong. It was a striking promotion: he had been two grades below Lee, but was by common consent the ablest administrator available.

Maudling was a very different man from Selwyn Lloyd. He had a rather shambling gait and off-hand manner, as if he never took anything very seriously. Frank Lee, who knew him well, was dismissive: "He's the rich man's Harold Wilson," he told me, "with no principles at all." This seemed to me rather a harsh judgment. At least he was at home with economic problems and weighed his risks carefully. He rarely consulted me, as Selwyn had done, and held himself more aloof from the Department than seemed to me desirable. Officials, for their part, did not take to his liking for gimmicks and for putting his individual mark on things. He was also fairly free in rejecting advice and in indicating distrust, so there was a certain coolness in his relations with civil servants.

Maudling could count on the backing of the Prime Minister, shared his enthusiasm for economic expansion, and knew how to play up to him. He had no lack of ideas, but not all of them were adequately worked out, and he was liable to go further in his speeches than was prudent. In his 1963 budget — his major act of policy — he increased public expenditure too much, when the balance of payments was already weak and deteriorating. When, as a result, the balance of payments moved into heavy deficit in 1964, he did little to check the boom and restore balance to Britain's international accounts.

As for William Armstrong, whose parents had been members of the Salvation Army, no previous permanent secretary had sprung from origins anywhere near as humble. He had been private secretary to successive Chancellors after the war. He often gave the impression of being either bored or exhausted, but he was always capable of interventions that went to the heart of the matter with a phrase or a question. He seemed to have read everything, and to have heard all the gossip, as if he had been up all night. Having worked in conjunction with the Economic Section, he had become familiar with the main outlines of economic theory. He could dominate a meeting with an occasional intervention, but was never aggressive or rude. He would make a Budget submission that did full justice to the views of the Budget Committee and add something of his own; and in negotiations with the International Monetary Fund, of which we were to have our fill, he would draft at great speed the Letters of Intent inserting conditions that he knew would be acceptable to the IMF but for which, I suspect, he had no specific authority. Although I did not get the feeling that he was deliberately withholding anything from me, I was rarely sure that I knew what he really thought, especially on the dominant issue of the first half of the 1960s, the question of devaluation. Did he ever make up his mind whether we ought to devalue, and if so, when? On this controversial issue, I never heard him give his point of view.

## Planning and floating

The course of events in the early 1960s was much influenced by two conflicting elements in public opinion. One was a faith in planning as a means to faster economic growth; the other was a belief in floating exchange rates, or at least in a greater readiness to devalue, as a means of preserving full employment. The prototype for planning was France, but hardly anybody knew *how* the French planned, and even members of my own staff thought that they did it independently of the French government. This seemed to me so patently mistaken — after all, we had had plenty of experience of planning during and after the war — that I sent Bryan Hopkin to Paris to make inquiries. He told me on his return that the draft plan was prepared in the French Treasury and that the head of the Plan Organisation also sat in the French Cabinet. It was also apparent that France grew no faster than other continental countries which had little enthusiasm for planning; and that rapid growth had become manifest in France and elsewhere before planning could have done much to accelerate it.

The Chancellor, however, wanted a growth target for his new National Economic Development Council (the NEDC, generally dubbed "Neddy" at the time) to aim at, and contemplated a rate of 5% per annum. Since the growth rate in Britain was not appreciably above 3% — although there were claims that it was accelerating — this was too big a jump, even if one was satisfied that planning would of itself yield faster growth. With some difficulty, I persuaded the Chancellor at the last moment to come down to 4%; and at 4%, the planning target remained, until it was all too apparent that long-term growth was nowhere near achieving it.

The case for floating the pound had a different origin. It derived from Britain's balance of payments difficulties and the "stops" that this enforced every few years with a loss of production and underemployment of resources. Opinion was strongly against "stop-go", without appreciating that fluctuations in activity were no greater in Britain than elsewhere. Some economists — notably Nicholas Kaldor— argued that "stops" could be avoided if the exchange rate was allowed to float and (as he put it) "take the strain". Several ministers in the 1952 Conservative government, including Rab Butler, the Chancellor of the Exchequer, and Oliver Lyttleton, the Colonial Secretary, had supported the idea of a floating pound when it looked as if reserves were running out.

In the early 1960s Harold Macmillan as Prime Minister toyed with the idea as a way of prolonging expansion if an exchange crisis threatened to put an end to it. Before the expansionary Budget of 1963, Macmillan set out his views in a long memorandum[2], warning the Chancellor (by that time, Selwyn Lloyd had been replaced by Reginald Maudling) that, with a fixed rate of exchange, his budget would be "snookered by a balance of payments crisis, a run on the pound, and all that". A fall in the exchange rate offered "the only effective and immediate form of import control", and the initial fall might in due course reverse itself. Macmillan was alive to some of the arguments against a float, including the danger of "a wild wage inflation if people felt free from the discipline of a fixed exchange rate", and concluded rather weakly that "the idea should not be lightly set aside". Maudling had similar hesitations. He told me that if the pressure on the exchanges became too great, "we could always float". But the policy alternatives that we in the Treasury were asked to examine were not floating, which was not mentioned, but quota restrictions on manufactured imports and an import surcharge such had been used in Canada.

I relate the two ideas of planning and floating because of an inconsistency between the two. The more precise and rigorous a plan, the more necessary it is to know on what terms (and so at what exchange rate) trade will be conducted. The National Plan of 1965 was prepared when there was an imminent danger of devaluation — i.e., an uncertainty that the Plan could not resolve. Much of the Plan rested on the (concealed) assumption

[2] Memo by Prime Minister to Chancellor, 21 February 1963, in PREM 11/4202, in Public Record Office.

of eventual devaluation; and when the government took measures in 1966 to avoid devaluation, the Plan foundered. Plans should be directed not to abolishing uncertainty by fixing rigid targets but to handling uncertainty by making appropriate dispositions which inevitably change through time.

## Restraining pay

In the winter of 1961–62, we were chiefly occupied with working out the principles of a long-term incomes policy to take the place of the "pay pause" which Selwyn Lloyd had included in the July measures. Treasury officials sat round Frank Lee's office table, cobbling together what was issued in February as the first White Paper on Incomes Policy, and came down in favour of a "guiding light" — a 2%-2$^1/_2$% annual increase in wages which would allow the cost of living to remain more or less constant except in unusual circumstances. We also argued in favour of adjusting increases in wages in particular occupations to the degree of labour shortage. Both propositions were attacked: the first because the figures were too low to stand any chance of acceptance, and the second because changes in relative wages were said not to be an important element in adapting the supply of labour to the demand in particular industries.

Later in the year, Macmillan became impatient, because it was taking so long to set up the institutions needed to give effect to the policy set out in the White Paper. He organised discussions at Chequers on machinery for an incomes policy which took the form of a National Incomes Commission (NIC). This body was not a success. It contributed to the dismissal of Selwyn Lloyd, because of his failure to take the lead in bringing it into existence. It was boycotted by the trade unions, and George Woodcock, the General Secretary of the Trades Union Congress, dismissed it as an "impertinence". I was familiar with his views as I had gone to see him after the July measures and he had told me then that we ought to have consulted the "experts" in industrial relations (i.e., the TUC). Efforts to check wage inflation, he told me, might hold for about six months, given backing from the TUC, but if the labour market became overheated, there was little that even the TUC could do. Whether this was so obviously depended on how overheated the labour market became.

In the absence of co-operation from the trade unions, the NIC was doomed from the start. It heard evidence on four cases only before it was abolished by the incoming Labour Government in 1964. I gave evidence for the government, in the first case before the NIC, arguing for a $2^1/2$% limit to wage increases sought by the Scottish plumbers' trade union. The National Institute of Economic and Social Research then suggested that a $3^1/2$% "guiding light" was much more likely to win acceptance, without much danger of serious inflation. The Chancellor, who was now Reginald Maudling, accepted the suggestion, and linked it with his 4% growth target in the 1963 Budget. But the TUC was unpersuaded.

Personally, I was more impressed by the marked way in which inflation slowed down in 1962 when unemployment was on the increase, and by the renewed acceleration in 1964 as the labour market tightened. I took the view that, if we tried to run the economy with unemployment well below 1% in large tracts of the labour market, as we did in the mid 1950s and again in the second half of 1964 and for much of 1965–66, it was hard to see how we could avoid wage settlements in excess of $3^1/2$%. The Economic Section regarded an unemployment rate of about 1.8% as the lowest that could be sustained without accelerating inflation, but we never quite decided whether that was an average for the whole country, or related only to the Midlands and South-East which usually made the running in wage settlements.

At the begining of 1963, the situation deteriorated. The year began with General de Gaulle's veto of Britain's entry into the European Community. The negotiations had been far advanced and looked likely to be successful. Indeed, according to Eric Roll, then a senior civil servant who was a leading figure in the negotiations, Olivier Wormser, the leader of the French team, had admitted to him that Britain was nearer than its government knew to a favourable outcome.

I had taken no part in the negotiations, although in an informal chat with Edward Boyle, the Financial Secretary to the Treasury, I had indicated that I was not particularly enthusiastic about membership. Indeed, the Economic Section was by-passed completely. Maurice Allen, the Chief Economist at the Bank of England, had warned me that if Britain's application was rejected, we would have to go over to a floating exchange rate, and I had earlier written a note giving a warning of my own along somewhat similar lines.

The government was in an awkward dilemma. In the appalling weather at the beginning of 1963 — the worst of the century — unemployment had mounted to 933,000 and the index of production had dropped by 4%. Even if the "temporarily stopped" were not included, unemployment was at 2.4%, which in those days was thought much too high. To reduce it, some stimulus was clearly required in the Budget on top of what had already been done in the closing months of 1962. But what of the danger to the balance of payments, which had been in deficit throughout the second half of 1962? In the first quarter of 1963 it was again necessary to borrow from other central banks, and the outlook for the rest of the year — and still more for 1964 — was not very reassuring.

In late 1962, I had already recommended to the Budget Committee that tax policy be used to provide a broad measure of reflation. That suggestion had been turned down: Maudling had preferred a more limited tax reduction on motor cars. In February 1963, I recommended tax cuts of £250m. Cuts on this scale were included in the Budget.

There was a great spurt of output in 1963. The margin of slack in the economy contracted rapidly and each successive balance of payments forecast showed a bigger and bigger deficit. Something had to be done to slow down the expansion; but the utmost we in the Treasury could persuade the government to include in the 1964 Budget was an extra £100m in taxation. Maudling promised us action in July — it would not have amounted to much. In any case, by that point it was not clear what was happening to the expansion: the figures for production appeared to show that it was remaining flat month after month, although there was considerable doubt whether they could be relied on. In the event, he did nothing.

The truth was that 1964 was an election year, and the Cabinet deliberately chose an autumn election, against the advice of the Chancellor, because the longer the economy expanded, the more the polls swung back towards the Tories. Unfortunately, they put off the election just a little too long. The recovery in employment over the summer was small, but the evidence of a collapse in the balance of payments became startlingly clear, with some forecasters predicting a deficit of £800m. It did not add to the standing of the government that, in the six months since the Budget, it had taken no further action of any kind to moderate the pressure in the labour market and on the foreign exchanges.

## Life in the Treasury

What was it like to work in the Treasury? When I first met my colleagues in the Economic Section in 1961, I told them that I was the salesman for the Section, and they the producers: I would do my best to market what they provided. And so it proved. I might see comparatively little of them and even less of the Chancellor. But I was for much of the time a middleman, sending forward their forecasts, approving their minutes, and relying heavily on what they told me.

I usually got to the Treasury a little before 10am and left between 6pm and 7pm. I regularly took work home, and often dictated on tape minutes and memoranda to be typed next day. In my seven and a half years in the department, I must have written or dictated at least 4,500 minutes of varying length, amounting at a guess to about 2m words. So I kept a highly efficient secretary and her assistant very busy. On top of that were all the papers to be read and the meetings to be attended. When photocopying arrived, my in-tray filled much more quickly. I had no staff to act as a filter and so I could establish what I ought to read only by reading it first. It was therefore largely a matter of chance whether I read my papers in the right order and with the right degree of care.

After the Labour government brought in more economists in 1964, meetings also tended to multiply. The economists Labour brought in were reluctant to divide responsibilities among themselves, and spent a good deal of time arguing and discussing with one another matters that had previously been left to me.

The job also required a great amount of travel. There were regular meetings to be attended in Paris of two OECD committees of senior finance-department officials, Working Party Three and the Economic Policy Committee. For these, I received enormous briefs, usually at the last minute, and dictated afterwards some account of the proceedings for the benefit of the Chancellor. Sometimes, especially before 1964, I went to the annual meetings of the IMF and the World Bank, and to meetings of the

American Bankers' Association. Then there were meetings of various bilateral economic committees — Anglo-German, Anglo-Italian, Anglo-Canadian and so on — at which I had to expound the economic situation and outlook in the United Kingdom. From time to time I was invited on a goodwill visit to a country such as Hungary or Yugoslavia; and there were occasional trips to Washington to maintain contact with opinion there.

Within the Treasury, my main responsibility as Economic Adviser was to supervise and interpret the economic forecast. The three official forecasts were prepared during the year mainly by officials in the Economic Section, under the guidance of Wynne Godley, who had a particular gift for this work. I kept a close eye on trends in the labour market and in trade, and would add a commentary and suggest lines of action. At times, these forecasts were pooh-poohed or reviled. Yet, in 1961, they were the outcome of the only systematic review of all the evidence of what was happening in the economy (although the NIESR was, with Treasury help, rapidly acquiring the technique). I found them helpful (if carefully interpreted) and less likely to lead to serious error than snap judgments based on more limited information.

The forecasts, however, were not themselves advice: they were simply guidance to the Chancellor on the balance of risks that he faced. Interpreting them called for insight and familiarity with the way the economy worked. So did my broader responsibility of giving advice on issues of macro-economic policy. Decisions had to be taken relatively infrequently during the year, but they were of cardinal importance and required much thought and preparation. In the case of fiscal policy, I took part in the work of the Budget Committee in advising on the changes to be made in the annual budget. I was expected to give advice on the "budget judgment" — i.e., the extent to which taxes should be altered so as to withdraw or supplement consumers' purchasing power. I kept in touch on banking policy with the Bank of England (which was also represented on the Budget Committee), either through the Governor or Deputy Governor, or in discussion with Maurice Allen. But I saw relatively little of the Home Finance Division of the Treasury, which dealt with monetary policy and tended to operate in isolation. Inevitably, the balance of payments was a matter of constant concern, although I was not much involved in changes in exchange control. From the pay "pause" of 1961 onwards, I was asked to advise on the principles of incomes policy, and continued to brief the Chancellor on the subject even after responsibility had been taken over by the Labour Government's new Department of Economic Affairs.

During my previous spells in government (and subsequently in academic life) I had concentrated on micro-economic issues, and I felt some frustration in the Treasury that these were rarely referred to me. I would have liked to have had more opportunity to comment on all the problems of improving industrial efficiency and competitivity. For both, the state had a major responsibility: the government still owned a large part of British industry, and it financed nearly half the fixed capital investment undertaken each year. Could the nationalised industries not be more enterprising and less wasteful? In transport and energy, which absorbed vast amounts of resources, change was badly needed. We ran coal mines and railways at a loss; yet, on the other hand, in an effort to outstrip other countries in technology, we were pouring money into ultra-modern junk: Concordes that would never pay and Advanced Gas-cooled Reactors that had not been properly developed. Our anxiety to grow faster thus perversely slowed us down.

I thought it perhaps the greatest weakness of British industry that economists and engineers rarely came together, and that so small a fraction of the greatest talent in the country chose to study engineering or, if it did, found no scope for its abilities in British industry. I tried to arrange for students of engineering to be offered higher university grants as a indication of national priorities, but I was thwarted by the Ministry of Education (which opposed discrimination) and subsequently by the Department of Trade and Industry (which maintained, to my astonishment, that engineering students themselves would oppose discrimination).

There were, of course, a great many other policy issues in which I became involved, together with the Economic Section, from the reform of the budget accounts, to the financial targets to be set for the nationalised industries, to agricultural subsidies. But a great deal of my time was spent on many things that had little to do with macro-economic policy. In particular, I had to recruit staff, first to the Economic Section and after 1964 to the Government Economic Service. Since most recruits were for two, or at most five, years, there was a high rate of turnover, and I felt it necessary to select economists who met exacting standards. This resulted in innumerable letters and interviews. In all, the business of recruiting took up about one third of my time.

I also had to recruit for other departments in need of economists and for occasional posts elsewhere. Only a few of the Section's staff were "established" — i.e., permanently employed; several were on five-year appointments; and an increasing number came on two-year appointments from the universities, an arrangement begun by Robert Hall which I did my best to develop. From this group, there were secondments to be made: to the embassy in Washington, to the National Institute of Economic and Social Research, and to various government departments. One department after another asked for an economic adviser, and the more important of these appointments had to be made on a personal basis. There was thus a good deal of coming and going, and a correspondingly extensive correspondence. Senior economists were particularly hard to find. Staff could not be politically committed and, more important, had to be both rather outstanding and of a practical turn of mind. Above all, in a small group like the Economic Section, there had to be an enthusiasm, a compatibility and an *esprit de corps.*

In addition, there were problems of pay and pensions (problems of which I had personal experience). I was apt to be negotiating with a well-established academic, unable to offer more than a principal's salary, which was at that time roughly the pay of a junior university lecturer. When I joined Whitehall, Bryan Hopkin had just been made an undersecretary, but there were no others in the Section at that level, which meant that they had relatively low rates of pay. To make matters worse, the demand for economists was rapidly increasing. In 1962, Neddy was in the market for a substantial number; and private industry was increasingly recruiting them.

In 1963 another new body, the Centre for Administrative Studies, also needed economists. This organisation was a brainchild of the Economic Section, suggested by Bryan Hopkin, accepted by Frank Lee, and floated by Desmond Keeling, a civil servant who subsequently became its first director. It was designed to give to all Treasury Assistant Principals (the main entry rank for university graduates) six months training in economics and public administration before promotion to Principal. The quality of the students was exceptionally high. In its first year, no less than nine of those taking part already had degrees in economics (including Peter Jay, a future ambassador to the United States, and David Hancock, who would one day be head of the Department of Education); but the tutors thought other members of the course equally adept at grasping economic problems. I recruited Kit McMahon from the Bank of England as chief instructor in economics, he returned to become eventually Deputy Governor.

I made several attempts to get agreement to an expansion of the staff of the Centre so as to allow it to undertake research, to form a reserve of economic administrators for special purposes, and to provide a base to which officials might be seconded for a spell of study leave. But I had no success. The cachet attached to the Centre was thus thrown away. Instead of being broadened and enlarged, it was absorbed into the Civil Service college — an admirable institution, but with a quite different character.

The shortage of economists led me to suggest a desperate remedy which, rather to my surprise, was accepted. My proposal was that we should recruit to the Economic Section candidates who had no degree in economics but who had taken a first-class degree in some other subject. Such candidates would then be allowed to study for a Master's degree in economics over a two-year period and would only then enter on a career in the Treasury or some other department. I was encouraged in this idea by reflection on the number of prominent economists who had come to the subject from other disciplines. When asked what was to be done if, after two years' training, candidates preferred employment outside government, I replied that the need was not confined to government, and that there would be a dividend to the nation if we trained a few more first-class economists.

## The Labour Government

By the autumn of 1963 the possibility of a change of government within the next year was widely canvassed. Such a change would have repercussions in the Treasury if the Labour Party gave effect to its plans — then still rather vague — for a Ministry of Planning or Economics. George Brown, who was a very influential figure in the Opposition, was visualising a Treasury that confined itself to control of public expenditure. Whatever the division between the two departments, it was important that it should be clear-cut, and that we should know who was in charge of economic policy. What, in particular, was to happen to the Economic Section? Would the new department have first pick of the limited supply of trained economists in government service? Would it be likely to acquiesce in the recruitment and management of Government economists by the head of the Economic Section of the Treasury? I asked myself — and William Armstrong — these questions, but received no answer to such questions until after the election in October 1964. I pointed out to him in a memorandum that, so long as the Chancellor retained control of the Budget, bank rate, the rate of exchange, the use of the Regulator and all the other instruments of economic control from day to day, it was "inconceivable that any other Minister could imagine himself to be in charge of economic policy.... The only satisfactory division I can imagine is between decisions calculated to regulate the economy within its existing structure and decisions calculated to change that structure."

But even once the election had occurred and Labour was victorious, many issues remained unresolved. One was the division of duties between the Treasury and the Department of Economic Affairs. Even after a concordat between the two departments, the division was obscure. The new Prime Minister, Harold Wilson, talked of "creative tension" in relation to the new department's impact on other departments, particularly the Treasury. There seemed to be a presumption in Whitehall that the new Department of Economic Affairs (DEA) would deal with long-term issues and the Treasury with short-term ones. My own view, which I set out in an address to the World Bank in January 1966, without explicit reference to the situation in Britain, was that a division into long-term and short is simply not sustainable in matters of policy. Indeed, my experience in those years was that the DEA's attention wandered irresistibly towards the short end of the spectrum, while the Treasury economists became frustrated because they could not give enough time to long-range problems.

My own position also presented problems. My post as Economic Adviser to the government was an established one —

Lord Callaghan with Sir Alec Cairncross at 80th birthday conference, Glasgow University, 1991.

ie, one that by custom could be assumed to survive any change of government. Instead, it had been abolished without any forewarning and no indication of what was to happen to the Economic Section. When I asked Sir Laurence Helsby, the Head of the Civil Service, what I was to do, he pressed me to go to Washington and take over from Eric Roll, who was then Treasury Representative at the British embassy, and was being recalled to become Permanent Secretary of the Department of Economic Affairs. I imagine that this was a well-meaning sop, thought up by William Armstrong. In fact, I had no lack of alternative jobs: after the *Guardian* reported that I was being thrown out, an assortment of academic and other appointments reached me, including one from the World Bank to become a Vice President in charge of the economic staff.

But it was not for such duties that I had left my chair in Glasgow, and whatever I did, I was anxious to ensure the continued existence of the Economic Section. My main concern was that the Section should not become the staff of a political appointee, and it seemed likely that, if I left, the job would go to Robert Neild, a Cambridge economist who was a known supporter of the Labour Government and whom I knew would be unacceptable to senior members of the Section as my successor.

In the middle of negotiations with William Armstrong and the new Chancellor, I took to my bed with pleurisy. Fortunately, William Armstrong took the view — and Neild agreed — that there was no question of Neild taking over the staff of the Section. Instead, he became Economic Adviser to the Treasury. I was still Director of the Economic Section, and in practice, my duties remained almost unchanged. As I had visualised in my memorandum to William in June, the Department that retained the instruments for economic management was the Treasury; and as long as it did, it would of necessity manage the economy, whatever the new DEA pretended.

I ended up with the title, "Head of the Government Economic Service". Ironically, the Economic Service has survived to this day, while the Economic Section vanished in the 1980s. The Service was to cover economists employed in all government departments, while the Economic Section was based in the Treasury alone. But, initially, my new title carried little meaning. For instance, it did not mean that I was able to take undisputed charge of the recruitment and management of government economists. Instead, ministers made a practice of appointing their own economists, usually without a word to me, and a series of private armies, over which I had little or no control, came into existence in a number of departments. In particular, Thomas Balogh, a Hungarian who was one of the new arrivals, felt free to recruit, to jobs that might or might not exist, without consulting me. He was also given to denouncing in extravagant terms the appointment to government agencies or committees of economists such as Harry Johnson, a distinguished Canadian, or my old friend Ely Devons. The Government Economic Service was therefore at first largely a fantasy.

Robert Neild and Thomas Balogh were not the only new arrivals. Donald MacDougall joined the DEA with a staff from the National Economic Development Office where he had been Chief Economist; and Nicholas Kaldor was nominally an adviser on taxation and spent most of his time in the Treasury. Instead of a shortage of senior economists, we now had a plethora, all wanting a say in the important decisions, extending and prolonging the already elaborate system of consultation among officials.

Of the four economists I have listed — there were, of course, many others elsewhere — Robert Neild and Donald MacDougall were old Whitehall hands: Robert had been a member of the Economic Section for some years in the 1950s, and Donald had served under Lord Cherwell, Churchill's adviser, in wartime and in the early 1950s. From my point of view, Robert was a decided asset, acting as a kind of personal assistant to the Chancellor; and Donald was an old friend with whom I might disagree but never quarrelled. Nicky Kaldor was a distinguished and extremely ingenious economist who came to fit remarkably well into the Treasury, much to his surprise — and ours. He could quote a wide range of statistics on almost any subject and proposed a new tax at the drop of a hat. He was a firm believer in market forces and financial rather than administrative instruments of control. It was this that made him such a dedicated believer in floating exchange rates, and that attracted him to taxation as the ideal way of adjusting market signals to the needs of a socialist society.

Nicky had two weaknesses. The first was an inability to be brief. When he appeared as a witness before the Radcliffe

Committee, I recall that his answer to the first question put to him seemed to continue for at least 15 minutes. His prolixity might reflect an abundance of ideas; but it did not make for a balanced discussion. His second weakness was an excessive reliance on logic. A good example was the Selective Employment Tax, a tax that he dreamt up and the Labour Government introduced, which was levied on service industries and rebated to manufacturers. Nicky offered the most ingenious proofs that the effect of a tax on services would be to release labour without a rise in prices. But he never asked how people would react to such a tax . When corporation tax was introduced, he had expected it to reduce the incentive to invest abroad, but it turned out to do just the opposite.

Tommy Balogh was of a very different colour. He was an ally of some ministers, including Harold Wilson and Richard Crossman, with whom he was particularly close, but was not much liked in Whitehall. Many officials regarded him, with some justification, as the Prime Minister's spy. He would come into a meeting when it was already under way, make remarks, and leave early, pretending he was called away to telephone the Prime Minister. He would walk round the office at No 10, picking out papers at will to read unchecked. He attempted to hector Permanent Secretaries and to gain access to the papers of the previous administration. And so one could go on. From any point of view in the management of the economic service, he was an unmitigated nuisance. Yet he had many admirers who credited him with remarkable powers of intuition, and an ability to see further and deeper than others into politics.

It was to this group of new arrivals that the Labour Government looked for advice in its first two years, from 1964 to 1966. Within the government itself, economic policy was driven mainly by an inner circle which consisted of the Prime Minister, Harold Wilson; George Brown (who was First Secretary and head of the newly created Department of Economic Affairs); and the Chancellor, James Callaghan.

Inevitably, I saw a great deal more of Callaghan than of the other two. He had done his best to prepare himself for his new duties by taking some instruction in economics at Nuffield College, Oxford. He was a man of attractive personality, good-humoured and relaxed, considerate to his officials and on good terms with them. On one occasion he returned from a City lunch after delighting his hosts with song. I found him courteous, entertaining, a good listener and sensible in his comments on most things. But on the one issue that really mattered — devaluation — he was not open to persuasion. He neither weighed up until too late the costs of failing to devalue nor had the power to obtain from his Cabinet colleagues acceptance of the measures that were required if devaluation was to be avoided. My own view was that the government was right to put up a fight, but that tough measures would be needed if devaluation was to be avoided later.

Callaghan was not left to frame economic policy as he thought fit, and he could not count on Wilson's support in Cabinet. He also had to contend with George Brown and the DEA. In that sense, the situation resembled that at the end of the war under the post-war Labour Government, when Hugh Dalton was Chancellor of the Exchequer, but Herbert Morrison, as Lord President of the Council, was nominally in charge of economic policy. Neither Wilson nor Brown was willing to leave economic management to the Chancellor; the triumvirate of Ministers, although far from seeing eye to eye, composed their differences as best they could, often without reference to the Cabinet.

**Devaluation**
In the winter of 1964–65, there was a series of meetings at No 10 after dinner, or at Chequers during the weekend, which I attended regularly, and which discussed economic problems or proposals. They were attended by the triumvirate and sometimes, especially at Chequers, one or two other Ministers. The officials invariably included the new economic advisers, with the addition of a few permanent secretaries (William Armstrong, Eric Roll and Richard Powell, the permanent secretary at the Board of Trade) but never the professional civil servants with responsibility for the matters under discussion, and never any representative of the Bank of England, even when matters of finance were talked about. It was an unusual group, meeting in an unreal atmosphere to conduct a rather childish discussion. There were no formal papers, no set agenda, no minutes. Harold Wilson conducted the discussion, which was informal and usually random, moving

from one subject to another at Harold's discretion. No attempt was made to reach any firm conclusion, except when a poll was taken of those present. George Brown, whose sobriety in the evening was always in doubts, would ask questions such as: "Does anyone in this room think business is expanding?" when there could be no doubt that it was. A discussion of employment would be punctuated by assertions that the least whiff of deflation would raise unemployment to 2m.

At the early meetings, there was much discussion of exchange control and the handling of the forward foreign-exchange market. Ministers complained — as all ministers tend to do, in my experience — that the statistics were inadequate to show what was really happening. It was a topic Wilson enjoyed, perhaps because it recalled the inquiry he had conducted in 1947 into the collapse of the short-lived spell of convertibility. But there seemed little point in assembling such a group to pursue a discussion of forward markets, investment allowances, the promotion of science and technology and so on.

What I found particularly piquant was that the four new economic advisers, who had been admitted to the inner circle at No.10 to the exclusion of nearly all established civil servants, were ranged unanimously against the government on the issue that took precedence in economic policy over everything else for the next three years: devaluation. Almost as soon as the government took office, a decision was taken — in keeping with Treasury advice — not to devalue, not to float, but to introduce a surcharge on imports. When a run on the pound developed in November 1964, the four advisers recommended devaluation, while the Economic Section suggested a dose of deflation. The same day, the Bank of England, managed to raise $3 billion from other central banks on a short-term loan. Both sets of recommendations were then removed from circulation and destroyed, and officials were told that the subject of devaluation was from now on "unmentionable".

The story of the next three years is of a struggle to maintain the exchange rate, using all manner of devices. One deflationary package after another had to be thrown to the pursuing furies: far more than would have been needed, had it all been done at once in 1964. The deflationary measures that the government was initially so determined to avoid had eventually to be taken: in a mild form in 1965; in a formidable package in 1966; and, when yet another crisis broke in the autumn of 1967 and there was no escape from devaluation, in a massive effort to bring the current account into surplus[3]. As it happens, in 1965 and 1966 the current account actually *was* in surplus, but that did not prevent the government from getting deeper and deeper into debt with creditors abroad, including the International Monetary Fund. Roughly speaking, in 1964–66, it was necessary to find £1,650m in foreign exchange to support the pound, when the whole of Britain's reserves at the beginning of 1964 had amounted to about £1,000m. By 1967, the limits of foreign borrowing appeared to have been reached, and the economy was highly vulnerable to the accident of strikes at home and a downturn in world trade abroad. Long before it occurred in November that year, the chances of avoiding devaluation had virtually disappeared.

For nearly two years after the crisis in the autumn of 1964, though, the issue of devaluation was never brought to Cabinet; and after the crisis of July 1966, when it was at last debated and rejected, Cabinet was again not consulted until it was almost too late. Nor was the Treasury, at any time after November 1964, asked to express its opinion. Because devaluation was regarded as unmentionable, Ministers were debarred from considering the balance of argument for and against. Worse than that: there was not, until the beginning of 1967, any attempt to formulate a strategy to maintain a parity we were debarred from changing deliberately. The Government was reluctant to admit that a price would have to be paid if devaluation was to be avoided, and to consider what price would be necessary. Over the years, despite the ban on discussion, a Treasury committee prepared a war book for devaluation — but it was purely procedural and was silent on the burning issues of when, why, how much, and with what accompanying measures.

Events in the first half of 1967 did not alert us to what was to come. The trade deficit in the first half of the year was negligible compared with what happened later in the year, when it reached

---

[3] I have traced the events of 1965–68 at length in my Treasury Diary, "The Wilson Years" (The Historian's Press, 1997) and in "Managing the British Economy in the 1960s" (Macmillan, 1996).

£330m at a quarterly — unsustainable — rate in October. In the first quarter of the year, we took more than £500m into the foreign exchange reserves, and even in the second quarter, the flow of foreign exchange was more or less in balance. But changes were already under way, disturbing foreign holders of sterling. Some of these were financial. Thus the government's borrowing requirement had risen year by year, and turned out to be nearly three times higher in 1967–68 than it had been in 1965–66; the central government's financial surplus in 1967–68 was half that of the previous year, the ceiling on bank advances was removed in the April budget. At the same time, investment, both public and private, was expanding much faster than current savings. The trade balance reflected the strain, and sank from surplus in the second half of 1966 to deficit in the first half of 1967.

Early in May 1967 I warned Callaghan that he had had all the good news. The Government, with poor timing, was making a fresh attempt to gain entry to the European Community. Instead of taking restraining action, the Government began to reflate. Against Treasury advice, it made a small cut in income tax that month, relaxed hire purchase restrictions on motor cars on June 7th — the day when the Suez Canal was closed in the Arab-Israeli War, an event that should have signalled to it that the world economy might become less buoyant; and relaxed hire purchase restrictions further across-the-board at the end of August. Investment remained high and rose slightly. Unemployment began to fall. Consumer spending rose throughout the year faster than at any time in the 1960s.

When I returned from holiday in mid-September, I asked myself what Ministers could say next spring, if asked why they had taken no action in the face of large prospective deficits and growing pressure on the pound. Inaction throughout the winter would be indefensible. They could hold off acting for a time, but I saw no likelihood of further deflation; and quota restrictions, even if acceptable to the international community, would do no more than buy time. If there were no option, the sooner we devalued the better. Indeed, for some time I had been of the view that devaluation would sooner or later be forced on us, because the Government was simply not prepared to do what was necessary if it were to be avoided.

Before I could put this to the Chancellor, he had left for the annual meetings of the World Bank and the International

Monetary Fund in Washington. I delayed on his return, because in the interim I had found that some of my colleagues thought my conclusion a little premature. By the end of October, however, we were all in agreement. I waited no longer. When I spoke to William Armstrong on the 30th, he told me of a meeting on October 25th that had just occurred between the Prime Minister, the Chancellor, the Governor of the Bank of England and himself, at which the Chancellor had come down strongly in favour of waiting until the spring before deciding whether to devalue, when the economic trends might be more favourable. He and the Prime Minister were confident that it would be possible to count on help from the United States, which feared the impact on the dollar of the failure to hold the sterling rate. The upshot was thus exactly what I had expected in mid-September: Ministers proposed to do nothing. But, since September, the reserves had begun to melt away, and there would soon be little left in the till, and not much chance of borrowing on the scale required either.

In December 1948, while I was at the Board of Trade, I had written a letter to my Minister, urged devaluation (see pp. 146–7). Now, on William Armstrong's advice, I prepared the following short memo, and sent it under cover of a personal note to the Chancellor on November 2nd. In fact, I doubt whether it did more than slightly weaken the Chancellor's stand against devaluation.

Dear Chancellor,

As you know, I have not in the past been an advocate of devaluation and I am well aware of the arguments against it. I am also very conscious of the strong personal commitment which you feel and the public stand which you have taken on this issue. This alone would make me hesitate very much before adding to your worries by a note explaining why I have changed my mind. But I think that in this respect I am probably typical of quite a large body of expert opinion which started out from a conviction that we ought to try hard to solve our problems without resort to devaluation. The choice now seems to be between doing just that and doing something that would be worse either in the short run (like further deflation) or in the rather long run (like quantitative restrictions on imports). I don't believe that we can just sit back and do nothing except borrow: that smacks too much of 1964. I also believe that world opinion would now be highly sympathetic and that British opinion would not hold it against you or treat it as anything but an act of courage (although no doubt there would be an effort to reap party advantage). The line to take would be that devaluation is highly unpleasant, as you have always said, and calls for accompanying measures that must also be highly unpleasant. But the government has now tried every other way open to it of giving strength to the balance of payments, and they have proved insufficient. If it is to be sure of accomplishing this object, there is now only one remaining recognised method and, given what is left in the till, little alternative but to act soon.

I have consulted William before sending this memorandum to you and I do not propose to send copies to anyone except him. I also appreciate that in this as in other matters it is a lot easier to advise than to decide, but in offering advice, I have tried my best to put myself in your shoes and see how the alternatives looked.

When I saw the Chancellor next afternoon in his room, the lights were blazing (in broad daylight) and the walls were newly painted white. It was, I think, my first chance to have a talk with him alone since he came to office in 1964. He thanked me for sending my note and said he saw the force of my arguments. He had been conscious that my view of devaluation was changing and supposed it was the economic forecasts (which had just appeared) that had completed this change. Did I think it irresponsible of him not to devalue? Why shouldn't he borrow? What if there were a big inflow of capital from abroad? It would be wrong, he argued, to devalue when the future was so obscure and everything at its worst. Why not wait till the spring? I must not think that it would be possible to hold incomes and prices at their current levels or that he would be there to do it. He didn't complain of the forecasts we had made, but we had, after all, shown a handsome surplus for 1968 in our February forecast and now showed a large deficit.

I agreed that the government had been out of luck. World industrial production had fallen since the beginning of the year — something almost without precedent since the Second World War — and world trade in manufactures had been flat or falling. This was worse than we could safely have predicted, although we had implied, in the draft of the Budget speech, that British exports would be flat. I went on to remind him that we had already had to borrow more than £1,500m from abroad; the Bank of England had an enormous total of over £1,100m in forward contracts, entered into to support the exchange rate; and we were in danger of seeing our lines of credit run out by the end of the month. It would need a *lot* of fresh borrowing if we aimed to wait to the spring.

He gave no sign in our conversation of worry or perturbation. His demeanour was that of a man who had thought it through, come to a firm conclusion, and was incapable of being ruffled. But his autobiography makes it clear that he was at least a little shaken by my démarche, and that it set on foot the Ministerial discussions that ended a fortnight later with devaluation. The pity is that it came so late. Had the decision been taken even a fortnight earlier — immediately after our conversation — without all the intervening discussion and preparations, the country could have saved more than half the £356m lost by the Bank of England in interventions to support the exchange rate.

As I had always emphasised, in all the Treasury's discussions before devaluation, what mattered was not simply the decision to devalue. If the new exchange rate was to stick, the decision had to be backed by measures that would allow devaluation to re-allocate resources between domestic and foreign markets. I had long feared that the measures to which Ministers could be brought to agree would be inadequate, and that they would end in a renewal of the imbalance that devaluation was intended to cure. As it turned out, the Chancellor refused to accompany devaluation with a large enough package of measures to make sure it was effective. Having struggled for three years with the spending departments over reining in public expenditure, he was influenced by a fear that the Cabinet would give inadequate backing to fresh cuts.

There was much discussion in the Treasury afterwards as to when it would have been best to devalue. Many felt it should have been done earlier. It may be that, after the deflationary measures of July 1966, it made relatively little difference to the balance of payments — except in terms of exchange losses — what date was chosen. But the most striking point is how unprepared for devaluation the government was, right up to the last moment. A long trail of budgetary cuts, and a long period of time, were needed to make devaluation work.

## Making devaluation work

In conformity with his pledge, Callaghan resigned as Chancellor after devaluation. His place was taken by Roy Jenkins who was, in my judgment, the ablest of the four Chancellors I served. He listened to advice, but made up his own mind, explaining to his advisers the grounds for his decision. He was at times able to foresee contingencies of which his staff had not warned him, such as the possible devaluation of the French franc, and was judicious in assessing such contingencies and deciding what measures were appropriate to the circumstances. He was not afraid to take extreme measures to overcome major dangers, adding more to taxation and cutting more from public expenditure than his advisers suggested and showing a sound judgment of what was at stake. This resoluteness in the circumstances in which he took office enabled him to carry the Cabinet with him after three years in which they had shrunk from much milder action.

He needed his courage for many months after the passage of the measures themselves: for a long time it seemed as if the measures were ineffective, and it was nearly two years before the visible balance of trade moved into surplus. Indeed, 1968 was a year of constant anxiety and repeated crises. The drain from the reserves in four successive quarters, from the middle of 1967 to the middle of 1968 was never less than £500m. Even in the final quarter of 1968 it was not much less. By the end of 1968, our external debts (two-thirds to central banks, one-third to the IMF) had mounted to over $8 billion — about double our debts at devaluation.

We spent a large part of that year coping with crises: crises approaching, crises in progress, crises subsiding. In the spring, there was the "gold rush": the price of gold in London, the main market, went through the roof, setting off currency speculation once again. As the dollar's value was at this time pegged to gold, central banks were forced to feed the market with gold to hold the price at $35 an ounce. A solution was found — for the time being — by separating transactions between central banks at the fixed price from private transactions at the market price. Then came a fresh upset in the currency markets: speculation against the French franc began in April and intensified in May with the student riots. Pressure developed against sterling as funds were transferred into the comparatively safe deutschmark and, when they flowed out again, they tended to be reinvested in Eurodollars, for which American banks were bidding strongly. On top of this, the May trade figures showed an unexpectedly large deficit.

What were we to do? I suggested a 5% surcharge on imports for six months, but Douglas Allen, who had by now succeeded William Armstrong as permanent secretary at the Treasury, thought it would be insufficient if the news about the trade balance in July were bad and unnecessary if it were good. Ministers preferred the use of import deposits — obligations on importers to deposit with the banks a certain sum related to the value of what they were importing. These were open to the same objection. In any event, we were in the midst of negotiating with other central banks in Basle for exchange-rate guarantees for the countries that held sterling balances, and with the IMF for a standby loan of $1,400m. So long as these negotiations were in progress, we could use neither import deposits nor import surcharges. Indeed, when the Chancellor asked us, "what were we to do if the French devalued at the weekend?", we agreed that there would be no alternative to allowing the currency to float. Fortunately, when the June trade figures appeared, they showed a drop in the deficit of over £100m, and we could breathe again.

Some of the gloom in 1968 was exaggerated. In July, for instance, the London and Cambridge Economic Service forecast a surplus of no more than £100m in 1969. However when, a week or two later, I spoke at the OECD in Paris, I ventured to predict that the current account surplus would be running at an annual rate of £500m before the end of 1969 — a forecast that was laughed at when I repeated it at a London dining club in October. The Treasury's own forecast was a good deal less optimistic. In fact, it proved to be an underestimate. Even the IMF, which, it was heartening to find, thought the Treasury too cautious, underestimated the outturn: it suggested that the current account surplus might reach £350m for the year of 1969.

In the final quarter of 1968 we were again in crisis. Like the crisis in March, it originated in events that had nothing to do with the British economy. Indeed, one might say that it originated in non-events, since it arose from the expectation of a devaluation of the franc and a revaluation of the deutschmark, neither of which took place that year, in spite of a great meeting in Bonn, ostensibly for those purposes. The mere expectation of these changes was enough to provoke a flight to the deutschmark and heavy losses from the British reserves. Again, the question was what to do to stop the drain. We went over a long list of measures: a 5% devaluation, a rise in Bank rate, the Regulator, import deposits and so on. The first two were rejected, the last two accepted. Treasury officials opposed the use of import deposits, but the Chancellor was satisfied that it would not be politically acceptable if he tried to deflate without some form of direct action on the balance of payments.

Towards the end of 1967, I had decided to leave, for reasons described in the next chapter. Right up to my last month in the Treasury, sporadic crises continued. In early December, rumours spread that the Chancellor had resigned, and then that the Prime Minister's resignation had followed. There was no truth in either rumour, but they were enough to cause an outflow of $100m from the reserves, while the gilt-edged market plunged. All through the weekend, the press was full of gloom. Even on the Tuesday, another $200m was lost in the morning. This time, however, the crisis was relatively short-lived: in the afternoon, the mood of the market changed and the outflow ceased. The next morning, the Bank launched an attack on speculators who sold sterling, and $100m flowed back into the reserves.

By the time I left at the end of 1968, I was already fairly confident that devaluation was working: indeed, I remember saying so emphatically at a farewell party. In fact, it was long after I had gone, to become head of an Oxford college, that the danger of a second devaluation was removed: sterling did not return to parity (the official rate of exchange) until the end of 1969. But, just as I had left the Board of Trade after the devaluation of the pound in 1949 with an easy mind, confident that things would now go well, in 1968 I left the Treasury equally reassured.

For all the annoyances and tensions I experienced there, the Treasury seemed a happy and confident department in my time. Life there was stimulating and friendly, and morale was high (even during 1964–66). In particular, I enjoyed working with the Economic Section. It was only a fraction of the Treasury: in terms of staff, about a tenth. But it was a most competent group. Whenever one of them went off— to the National Institute, to another Whitehall department, or (on one occasion) to Mauritius — I felt diminished.

Moreover, the Treasury had become more receptive to economic analysis than in the previous decade. Earlier members of the Economic Section had returned to academic life complaining that Treasury officials had difficulty in grappling with economic concepts. There were some in the 1950s who even recounted horror stories about such inadequacies in academic journals. I found the Treasury still conspicuously weak in economics and technology. By my time, most senior officials were familiar at least with the patter of economics. But I doubted whether the smattering that officials had acquired would be adequate in a new kind of world, full of conflicting views of wage and price inflation.

In the years after I left, the number of economists in the Treasury greatly increased, as it has done, too, in other parts of Whitehall. In the Government Service, more than 400 economists now work; many other civil servants are also economists and a Permanent Secretary of the Treasury, Sir Terence Burns, has for the first time been a professional economist, recruited as such.

But an opportunity was lost when the Economic Section disappeared. For with it went the system that Sir Robert Hall had introduced, of recruiting academic economists for a two-year spell. This was a useful way of keeping the Economic Service up-to-date with economic theory and at the same time giving academics a chance of observing the handling of economic problems in government and often of developing new interests in the process. Above all, by creating a link between economists in the universities and those in government departments, it brought together economic theorists and policymakers. These links, now beginning to be rebuilt in the late 1990s, are the best guarantee of sound economic advice and of useful academic research. The Treasury, as the key department in Whitehall, is not only best placed to revive them; it is the department that has most to gain.

## 17

*Back to Academic Life. Oxford University 1969–78*

By 1967 I had come to feel increasingly that there was little point in my continuing in the Treasury. Where in 1961 all the Treasury economists were in a single group under my direction, there were now a number of senior economists at large, with no division of labour and few specific assignments to keep them busy. The result was an over-concentration on a few major issues and endless meetings to resolve differences and revise drafts. One group that seemed particularly unnecessary dealt with issues of methodology, debating, for example, how much employment would result from different forms of public expenditure. An able young economist would have done the job quickly and without fuss.

At some point during the year I was approached by Professor Walter Hagenbuch, an old colleague from MAP, with an invitation to come to the new University of Kent as Master of Keynes College. I accepted the invitation verbally on condition that I could delay moving for a year or so. I did not, however, convey this to the Treasury, and there was no public announcement. Then, in late autumn, I had a letter from St Peter's College, Oxford, asking whether I would be willing to be considered for an appointment as Master of the College.

I had never previously heard of St Peter's (although one of my sons, as I subsequently discovered, applied for admission before electing to go to Cambridge). What I learned about it made it appear more my kind of college than the grander ones in Oxford. I travelled to meet my sponsors, the tutors in politics, philosophy and economics (PPE) and mathematics, choosing in error a train that took about two hours and must have tried their patience. It became clear to me that my name must have been put forward by John Corina, the Economics tutor, although we had never met. I agreed to let my name go forward, and wrote to Walter Hagenbuch to apologise for my change of mind. Only long afterwards did I discover that the election was a contested one.

I dined in October at High Table and was, in a sense, interviewed by the Governing Body just when the devaluation was about to be precipitated. The election took place early in December 1967 when Mary and I were at the Paris Embassy, but it was not until January 1969 that I took up my new duties. Even then, the Master's Lodgings were not yet ready for occupation, and Mary and the family were equally unable to move to Oxford because my two youngest children, David and Elizabeth, were still at school. So, for my first two terms. I occupied a small bedroom in the entrance to the College (now part of the library) and motored to London and back again at weekends.

When I had been at the College for a week or two, people asked how I liked academic life after the Treasury. I felt it was the other way round: nowhere had been so academic as the Treasury, and College life for me was largely administration. My principal duty was to take the chair at meetings of the Governing Body once a fortnight. But of course I was also expected to undertake some other College duties and to do what I could as a fund-raiser. That still left plenty of time for personal interests and, after talking things over with Robert Hall, who had also left the Treasury to become Master of an Oxford College, I accepted his advice that a Master should spend half his time on College affairs and feel free to use the other half for private or public purposes.

I was an unusual creature among the heads of Oxford colleges. First of all, I was not an Oxford man, as nearly all my colleagues were. I had much to learn about Oxford; while Oxford felt no need to tell me what I needed to know. It was an Oxford habit to assume that you already knew. To take a trifling example: when, in my first few days as Master, I was invited to dine at Oriel and arrived at the College, my hosts looked at me and asked, "Where's your gown?" Did I need a gown? Yes, I was told, of course I must wear a gown. So I had to go back for one. The following night I was due to dine at Keble, and took what I now knew to be the necessary precautions. My hosts looked at me and asked, "Where's your black tie?" Did I need a black tie? Yes, of

Sir Alec (wearing a Trinity College blazer from 1933) and Lady Mary in the Master's garden, St Peter's College, Oxford.

course: it was a feast and black ties were *de rigeur*. It was too late to go back, so I had to walk to High Table down the longest hall in Oxford, improperly dressed and in the company of a phalanx of penguins.

My appointment was also unusual in that I was an economist. One or two economists had been elected to head Oxford Colleges in the past: Sir Hubert Henderson at All Souls, Sir Robert Hall at Hertford and Sir Noel Hall at Brasenose. Such appointments, once very rare, are now increasingly common. In the 1990s at least three economists are now Heads of Houses. It was also highly unusual that I visited Iran, Mauritius, Rio de Janeiro and North America in the course of my period as Master; and that I took unpaid leave of absence for a term to undertake research at the Brookings Institution in 1972.

### Academic duties

Almost as soon as I left the Treasury I was catapulted into a new range of academic duties that I had not foreseen. I became President of one organisation after another, and spent a good deal of time writing Presidential Addresses. In 1969 I was elected President of the Scottish Economic Society, which I had helped to bring back to life in the 1950s. I had already been elected President of the Royal Economic Society. I was also, in 1969, President of Section F of the British Association, and two years after, President of the Association at its meeting in Swansea, the first professional economist to fill that post although Lord Stamp, who was among other things an economist, had preceded me. Then in 1972 I became President of the Girls' Public Day School Trust (GPDST) after serving for a couple of years on the Council, and I remained President for the next 20 years of one of the most successful organisations with which I have ever been associated.

In the autumn of 1971 I was also asked by Sydney Checkland, professor of economic history, if I would be willing to stand for the Chancellorship of the University of Glasgow. It seemed to me a rather preposterous suggestion, given the eminence of the other half dozen candidates, but I took heart from the recollection that an Alexander Cairncross, later Archbishop of Armagh, had held the office until driven from it in 1687 by James II of England (and VII of Scotland) as part of his Catholicising activities. If one with that name could be Chancellor, why not another three centuries later? I let my name go forward and more or less forgot about it until on Burns Night 1972 the news reached me that I had been elected. I promptly gave instructions that all undergraduates dining in Hall should have a beer at my expense to celebrate — although few of them, as I learned later, had the least idea what they were celebrating.

I doubt whether I ever had a prouder moment. To be head of my old University, elected by the graduates and free to continue in office indefinitely, gave me enormous pleasure. But when I learned that Sir Isaac Wolfson, head of the GUS mail-order empire, had come second, I had a rather guilty feeling that the University might have deprived itself of favours it could ill afford to lose. I am glad to say that Isaac sent me a most generous note of congratulation, and that the Wolfson family continued to offer invaluable support to the University.

My other spells as president of learned bodies were more fleeting. When my turn came to deliver the presidential address to the British Association at the Swansea meeting in 1971[1], I thought of the speech that Harold Wilson had made there in 1964, promising the white heat of technological revolution, and of the muddled thinking underlying it. I decided to dwell on the fundamental differences between science and technology, of which few people seemed conscious; to indicate my distrust of science if it became white hot; and to emphasise that innovation in technology was a commercial operation, more than a matter of scientific achievement. Since science was public knowledge, it was freely available to all countries and all producers; while improvements in technology, though they might draw on scientific knowledge, were almost always undertaken with an eye on the market and involved commercial risks such as scientists could ignore. If Britain had been less successful in absorbing modern technology than continental countries, it was for two main reasons: British companies failed to take advantage of the market opportunities that modern technology provided; and the government, in particular, misjudged the commercial risks, seeking to outdo America in things like Concorde, computers

---

[1] At Exeter, the previous year, the then President of the British Association, Sir Peter Medawar, after delivering a remarkable address on Saturday, had had a stroke in the Cathedral next day and never completely recovered.

and nuclear power, where America had all the advantages, and neglecting developments more appropriate to British circumstances.

My speech was not a success: the scientific correspondents, unused to dwelling on the links between technology and economics, took umbrage at what they regarded as a disparagement of science. There was, however, one fruitful outcome. It set John Bradfield, the Bursar of Trinity College, Cambridge, thinking of ways of encouraging industrial innovation, and led to the establishment by the College of a hugely successful Science Park, probably the first in Britain and in some ways the modern equivalent of a pre-war trading estate.

After my address, the economists at the meeting had a little dinner at which Nicky Kaldor, my former colleague in the Treasury, was in the chair and made a short speech. He had enjoyed being President of Section F and declared, "Everybody should be a President!"

For my Presidential Address to the Royal Economic Society, I chose a difference subject. There appeared to be very little literature on economic forecasting; yet the key responsibility of economists in economic management seemed to be to provide Ministers with the most reliable possible view of the future. Curiously enough, most writing on forecasts tended to concentrate on the extent to which past forecasts were right or wrong, and had little to say about the gap between what goes into a forecast and the decisions taken on the basis of its predictions. So I decided to speak on economic forecasting. Although I had little experience of constructing forecasts, I at least knew something of their uses and of the way a Minister should interpret a forecast in deciding what risks to take.

For my inaugural address as Chancellor at Glasgow I chose a more general topic, entitling it "Learning to Learn", which is one way of describing higher education. I spent the better part of my first month at the Brookings Institution in the spring of 1972 developing my theme. I pointed out that the universities absorb on their staff a high proportion of the most talented men and women of their generation. If this cuts them off completely from the business of the country, there is likely to be a lowering of the efficiency with which it is conducted. The country would gain, and more provision could be made for higher education and advanced study, if there were closer links between university staffs and productive industry.

I spoke also of the alienation of many undergraduates from modern business, whether publicly owned or in private hands. Those who feel "drafted by the Welfare State" are liable to experience some of the reactions of conscripts and develop novel discontents. They may either seek to repudiate the values of an affluent society in dress, physical appearance or style of life, or actively attack it. They have had before them all through their school and university the example of teachers motivated by ideals of service, rather than of profit, and they have experienced few of the compulsions that any well organised advanced society imposes on its members once they enter the labour market.

When I left the Treasury, I was offered various directorships and declined them, preferring to join Urwick Orr, a firm of consultants, first as director and later as trustee, in the hope of learning what consultants did. As trustee, I worked alongside two distinguished economists: James Meade and later Robin Matthews. I did indeed learn something of the work of consultants, but what I learned was not about "work study" (reviewing work practices), the bread and butter of consultancy at the time. I learned more about a special kind of economic advising in the course of making repeated visits to Saudi Arabia to provide advice on the impact on the West of the enormous increase in oil prices that took place in the mid 1970s, the likely impact on future demand for oil. More commonly the role of the trustees was to compose internal differences between the partners of a highly centrifugal organisation.

I had many other interests. I joined the London board of the Scottish Amicable Life Assurance company, on whose main board I had served in the 1950s in Glasgow. I took part with Lord Cromer, a former governor of the Bank of England, in an inquiry into Lloyd's in the early 1970s. The committee was asked by Lloyd's to look at, among other things, its loss of world market share. We became more interested in the structure of Lloyd's, and particularly in the potential conflict of interest that arose when brokers acquired the underwriting agents. These agents supposedly acted on behalf of the "names", the investors who took the risk, and there was a danger that they would take a disproportionate share of profits in good years, leaving names with a disproportionate share of losses in bad ones. The committee, with hindsight, accurately spotted the structural weaknesses which nearly caused the collapse of Lloyd's a quarter of a century later; but Lloyd's refused to publish our report in full.

At about the same time, I served on a committee of inquiry into some problems of the brewing industry. I continued to serve on the Houblon-Norman Committee, which kept me in touch with the Bank of England and with some of the research that was being undertaken in economic history. There were also, during the 1970s, a number of government assignments: a report, with Sir Charles Villiers, who was at that time chairman of Guinness Mahon, on financial problems in Northern Ireland and membership of a standing committee on government contracts under Sir William Slimmings, a senior partner in the accountancy firm of Thompson McLintock.

My professional interest in economics continued. I took part, early on, in launching the Institute for Fiscal Studies which was founded by a small group of accountants and others to promote economic analysis of taxation and public expenditure. I also wrote a good deal, but nothing of book length except a short discussion of long-term capital movements and their control that I began at Brookings in 1972[2]. In 1976 I published a short book of essays, which had already appeared elsewhere[3]. But I seemed to give more time to editing the works of friends: a collection of Hans Singer's articles[4] and later a Festschrift for him[5]; and, for Sir Richard (Otto) Clarke, a volume on the control of public expenditure based on his experience in the Treasury[6] and a half-completed study, interrupted by his death, of Anglo-American relations in the formation of British economic policy during and after the war[7]. Otto had been the source of many of

[2] "Control of Long-term International Capital Movements", Sir Alec Cairncross: The Brookings Institution, 1973

[3] "Inflation, Growth and International Finance", Sir Alec Cairncross, George Allen and Unwin, 1975

[4] "The Strategy of International Development, Essays in the Economics of Backwardness" by H.W.Singer: Macmillan Press, 1975

[5] "Employment, Income Distribution and Development Strategy, Essays in Honour of H.W.Singer", ed. by Sir Alec Cairncross and Mohindur Puri, Macmillan Press 1976

[6] "Public Expenditure, Management and Control" by Sir R.W.B.Clarke, edited by Sir Alec Cairncross, Oxford University Press, 1978

[7] "Anglo-American Collaboration in War and Peace" , by Sir R.W.B.Clarke, edited by Sir Alec Cairncross, Macmillan Press, 1982.

the Treasury's new ideas in post-war years. It was when I realised that I was being kept busy editing other people's books that I was galvanised into writing a long series of my own.

During this time, I was also involved in three projects that are worth describing in more detail. I took part in a group discussing appropriate economic policies for the European Community; I rejoined the London and Cambridge Economic Service; and in 1974 I served as joint chairman with Lionel Robbins, Chairman of the Court of Governors of the London School of Economics, of a committee on the affairs of the Royal Economic Society.

In 1974 I joined a small group under Herbert Giersch, professor of economics at the World Economic Institute at Kiel in Germany, to review the economic policies that the European Community should pursue. The group had many enjoyable sessions in Rome and Sicily. Eventually we published a volume[8] to which I contributed a chapter on monetary and fiscal integration. This dealt in some detail with the proposal for a common currency which had been endorsed by the Werner Report in October 1970 and agreed to by the Community in July 1972, only to be flouted almost at once when two members of the Community allowed their currencies to float. Monetary union, as envisaged by the Werner Report, presupposed (as our book put it) "a subordination of national economic management to the collective will of the Community and the decay of important instruments of national economic policy" without substituting adequate instruments of international economic policy. The Giersch group advocated a new European currency — the Europa — to circulate alongside national currencies and eventually replace them. But we also warned against premature monetary integration without complementary policies and powers and common institutions to give effect to Community-wide policies. We laid emphasis on the central importance of fiscal policy and the need for a "sizeable common budget". Listening to the debate on European Monetary Union in the 1990s, these conclusions seem to me still to have considerable validity.

When I left the Treasury, I rejoined the London and Cambridge Economic Service (LCES) of which I had been a member in the 1950s. In the 1970s the group, a panel of

[8] "Economic Policy for the European Community. The Way Forward" Sir Alec Cairncross et al, Macmillan Press 1974.

economists, now including some representation from Oxford and elsewhere as well, took it in turns to write twice yearly assessments of the current economic situation for publication in *The Times*. The idea was that one person wrote the piece, along lines discussed with the others.

In July 1974, it fell to me to write the articles. I found myself in the unusual situation of disagreeing with Wynne Godley, my former colleague in the Treasury, who now occupied a chair at Cambridge, on our interpretation of the state of the economy, but receiving emphatic support from Nicky Kaldor. Our disagreement sprang from Wynne's anxiety to maintain a high level of employment in the face of a an enormous external deficit that simply could not be allowed to continue. I made some amendments to my draft and as a result, Wynne disagreed less with what I eventually published. In December, however, without prior warning or consultation, he issued an ultimatum announcing the end of the LCES. I had not until then appreciated that he alone had the power to decide the future of the Service. Wynne justified his decision on the grounds that he could find nobody to write an article for the December issue, but I had not been asked, and I found it hard to believe that I was the only member in that position. The real problem was two-fold: Wynne intended to publish a medium-term economic assessment in his own Cambridge publication; and, when Peter Jay, the economics editor of *The Times*, discovered this, he broke off the association, telling Wynne that he would not take articles that he could write himself.

In the event, we were able to find an alternative publisher. The LCES was soon reborn as the Clare Group under the guidance of Robin Matthews, Master of Clare. The Group's contributions appeared first in the Midland Bank Review with the co-operation of Richard Sargent, the bank's economist, and subsequently in the review of the National Institute of Economic and Social Research.

I was involved in another rumpus in 1974, this time involving the Royal Economic Society, in a remarkable row that put an end to the domination of the Society by Cambridge economists. I had been President in 1969–70. During that period, Austin Robinson retired from his role combining the jobs of secretary-general, treasurer and publications secretary, and it had fallen to me as

President to make arrangements for finding a new editor for the *Economic Journal* and for the management of the Society's affairs. Brian Reddaway, my old Cambridge friend, became editor-in-chief and Charles Carter, a former Cambridge economist who had become vice chancellor of Lancaster University, secretary general.

But it became clear that there was some deep antipathy between these two, and on top of that, distrust of Nicky Kaldor, when he became President in 1974. Just before a Council meeting in November 1974, Charles Carter and Alan Prest, who was then Treasurer, suddenly resigned, in protest at an escalation in the stock of publications (mainly Keynes's "Collected Writings") just when the Society's assets were falling alarmingly with the collapse of share prices on the Stock Exchange. At the same time, Nicky was trying to bring a young, mathematically trained economist on to the editorial board of the Journal. David Champernowne, the Journal's associate editor, handled the more mathematical articles, and he had found his editorial responsibilities too heavy. But because the suggestion that he accept the help of a younger man came not from him but from Nicky, it roused suspicion that Nicky wanted eventually to put his protegé into the editorship.

In an effort to resolve the crisis, I was approached to take on the job of secretary general. I declined, as did Robin Matthews, who was offered both that post and the editorship of the journal, but was just moving to Cambridge to be Master of Clare. When the Council met again at the end of November, Nicky Kaldor was in the Chair as President for the first time. There was a long debate. David Worswick, Director of the National Institute, moved that Carter and Prest be asked to withdraw their resignations. The motion was defeated, all but two of the Oxford members and all the Cambridge members voting against. Then, a committee proposed by Donald MacDougall (an Oxford man), and with terms of reference drafted by him, was agreed, to decide how the Society should be run in future. No Cambridge representative — not even the President — was included among the members. Carter and Prest, when told what had been decided, agreed to continue in office. I had thought that Nicky should have been included on the Committee; but in truth, the Council could have reached this point much faster had it not been for Nicky's chairmanship which was clumsy, partisan, ineffective and very time-consuming.

Lionel Robbins and I were appointed joint chairmen of the committee to review the Society's future. In the course of our work, it became clear to me that the arrangements I had made while I was President had failed for one very simply reason: I had taken no account of the imperative need for co-ordination when the undivided authority that Austin Robinson had exercised gave way to decentralised management. I had failed to lay down how the multiple jobs that Austin had done should be shared among the various officers of the Society. The officers were given no clear terms of reference, and no steps were taken to ensure adequate co-ordination between them. The finance committee met only episodically; another committee, to make proposals for future arrangements, met once only; and publications arrangements were not handled by any committee. There was no steering committee below the Council, and it was too large to provide effective co-ordination. Undoubtedly, there was a need for a standing committee to meet regularly and ensure reliable communication of information and effective financial control.

Our proposal for what by this time was called an executive committee provoked a fresh resignation by Carter and Prest, who thought that there should be five meetings a year of the officers of the Society and complained that we were altering arrangements for which they were responsible: all we had done was to add a few members of the Council to those meetings and call the result an executive committee. But when Council met in March, it accepted our recommendations without an explosion. We were left free to make new appointments to all the main offices of the Society, for which we drew not merely on Cambridge, but on the whole range of British universities. The new regime started in 1975 and was an undoubted success. The Society has never again faced the difficulties that arose in the early 1970s.

## University life

I also had plenty to occupy me in unversity affairs at Oxford. For example, Norman Chester, the Warden of Nuffield, persuaded me to join the council of the Oxford Centre for Management Studies (later Templeton College). This was the beginning of the university's involvement in management training — a a development that later bore fruit in the Oxford Business School.

I also sat on the Conference of Colleges, the main body on which Oxford Colleges seek to come to a common view.

The 1970s were a period when college finances were much discussed. One of the university committees on which I sat was the Committee on College Finance which undertook a major study of the financial position and prospects of various colleges, one of a succession of attempts by Oxford to review the finances of the university. Another was the College Contributions Committee, which taxed the richer colleges in order to help the poorer ones such as St Peter's. On a third, the fees committee, a small group of college bursars, jointly with a similar group from Cambridge, negotiated with the Department of Education on the level of college fees. There were rumours at the time that the Colleges would not enjoy for much longer the freedom to decide independently the level of fees paid by undergraduates, and there were also proposals that all colleges should charge a uniform fee. There was a further dispute about the fees payable by post-graduate students to the colleges; it was argued by some that there was no reason for science students to pay such fees, since they were too busy in their laboratories to spend much time in the college to which they were attached.

It also fell to me, as chairman of the Conference of Colleges, along with Dennis Nineham, the Warden of Keble, to deal with the question of the sale of alcohol within college precincts, which the Oxford police raised with us. At first, it seemed as if the police intended to insist on a licence for every occasion when alcohol was supplied, whether to members or non-members of the college, with meals or separately. Rather unexpectedly, the police accepted my suggestion that we should consider only sales to non-members. That was less damaging but would still have been very awkward, since it would have implied licensing discos, conferences and balls. After several further meetings, the police dropped the whole idea. This, too, is an issue that still surfaces from time to time in Oxford.

Shortly after I arrived at St Peter's, I was surprised to discover that there was no University swimming pool. I therefore set about interesting others in raising funds for one. Five of the richer colleges pledged themselves to make a large enough annual contribution to meet the cost as it stood at the time. But the University then took so long to settle on a site and obtain planning permission that prices escalated with the boom of 1973, and it became apparent that I had raised only half of what was now required and would have to start all over again. In the end I had to abandon the project. Watching the difficulties of the backers of the proposed Oxford Business School in the early 1990s, I felt that little had changed at the University.

### College affairs

St Peter's had around 240 undergraduates, and I made contact with them by interviewing each of them briefly when I first arrived at the college. They were a much travelled lot: a few had never been abroad, but there were also one or two who had been round the world and many who had been well beyond Europe. In my youth, "going abroad" meant going to France or some adjacent country, but the aeroplane changed all that; and even with a motor car, undergraduates got as far as Iran, or further.

Quite a high proportion of the undergraduates came from the North: Liverpool, Manchester, Newcastle, even Glasgow. Many also came from state schools, but probably not appreciably more than in other Colleges, where the average was under 50%. All students in my time were male, the first women entering just after I retired. My children were great enthusiasts for mixed colleges, and I would have been happy to introduce women to St Peter's earlier, but it required a vote in favour in the governing body by three-quarters of those present, which meant that any five Fellows of the College's 20 or so Fellows might be able to veto the admission of women. I was able eventually to take a vote when only four opponents were present, after which women were admitted — although the first came just after I left.

We discussed with our children, four of whom by now had experience of university life, how to entertain our undergraduates, and decided on offering them breakfast on Sunday mornings at 10. The hour was important because chapel service was over by then and it gave us time to get ready (we had no domestic help). We reckoned to give every undergraduate a chance to come to breakfast during the year and to bring with him his girl friend if he had one. This meant inviting ten or a dozen undergraduates every Sunday morning, and an average attendance of 15–20. Mary took the precaution of inviting a number of girls from other colleges, including some from schools run by the

GPDST, and we also included any guests who were staying with us over the weekend. Graduate students were not included (we invited them to a sherry party in the Lodgings before their termly Middle Common Room dinners in Hall).

We played somewhat exotic music on the gramophone to mitigate the inevitable constraint and provided buffet-style breakfasts at several small tables in our sitting room. The menu included one course of stewed apples and cornflakes, and one of sausages and bacon, with coffee in abundance. Sometimes, on a cold morning, we would offer porridge, and once, when St Andrew's Day fell on a Sunday, we had haggis and whisky, with the whisky *following* the haggis, rather than poured over it, in the usual Scottish way. Naturally we took part in the breakfasts, moving around and trying to get the undergraduates to do the same.

The breakfasts were only part of Mary's college activities. She ran a party for the wives of graduate students, another at Christmas for the children of staff and, near the end of our time, brought together for the first time the secretaries of the various colleges at a party so that they were actually able to see what their counterparts looked like. She made it a condition, which I am glad to say has been fulfilled, that they should make it an annual event in one college or another. Yet another initiative was prompted by the discovery that the girls who sang in the College choir at the evening service — and splendid singers they were — were not provided with a meal and were too late for dinner when they got back to their own college. She arranged to provide them with supper, and if she was dining with me in Hall, would leave a bowl of soup in our kitchen for the choir to heat up.

My first impressions of the College were distinctly favourable. It had been founded by public subscription in 1928 in memory of Bishop Chavasse, Bishop of Liverpool, a highly popular leader of the Evangelicals and could be regarded in a sense as an evangelical response to Keble. The first Master had been the Bishop's son, Christopher. Another son, Noel, had not only won the Victoria Cross, but had won it twice, and a glass case full of his medals hung halfway up the stairs to the dining hall. The college had been governed by a council for the first 30 years of its existence and had been given its charter as a self-governing College only in 1961. It was the only new undergraduate college for men to have been founded in Oxford this century (if one rules out St Catherine's as not entirely new). I was the first lay Master — a fact with which Harold Wilson made some play when he told me, "All your predecessors have been bishops but I can't make you a bishop." In fact, only Christopher Chavasse had been a bishop: my other two predecessors had been canons.

There were just over 20 Fellows, and two professors (in Statistics and Geography) were attached to the college. Nearly all the Fellows seemed remarkably young — just under 40 or just over. They included some distinguished scholars, three of whom soon went off to chairs elsewhere. Above all, they were clearly keen to see the College succeed. In academic terms, when I arrived, it was at the bottom of Oxford's Norrington league table which compared the results of final exams.

But, while some of the Fellows hoped I would change this, they were disappointed. I had little control over the College's academic performance. I took no part in the selection of entrants: many of the dons felt that if they were to spend many hours for three years with those who were chosen, they ought to be left to do the choosing. I also had no hand in the teaching: for a term, I was allowed to tutor some economists before finals, but this was never repeated. When I lectured, it was almost always elsewhere than Oxford; and when I did lecture in Oxford, it was usually a chance replacement of a lecturer who was ill, so that the students had no knowledge in advance nor contact afterwards. After one lecture, in which I touched on devaluation, a young lady approached me. "Could you advise me?" she said. "I've just arrived from the United States and haven't changed my dollars yet. Do you think this would be a good time?" My lecture might have attracted more interest if I had started with that question.

One way in which I might have influenced academic performance was through the ceremony known as "collections". This practice seemed to consist of parading undergraduates before the Master one morning before the end of term to receive a commendation or rebuke. Supervisors were meant to give me a written report on each student in advance, but none ever did; instead, I had to rely on the few words spoken hurriedly by the tutor by my side. As a result, I was quite unable to praise or blame, and had to content myself with wishing each undergraduate a enjoyable holiday. Just after I had shaken hands with one young man, the mathematics tutor remarked: "He'll get a first all right." I remember my outrage that he had given me no inkling of the student's abilities earlier. Eventually I decided to scrap the whole arrangement, on condition that supervisors sent to me those undergraduates who were particularly in need of rebuke or who had done a particularly good term's work. This, too, failed to work. No student was selected for praise and hardly any were ever sent to me for rebuke.

One of the Master's duties was to maintain discipline; and my years at St Peter's were turbulent ones. The Paris riots had occurred just a few months before I arrived at the college in 1969; the LSE rioted shortly after, following the example of American universities such as Berkeley; and, apart from disorder, there was a growing drug problem. When I returned from London one Sunday evening in February 1969, I found the Dean much agitated because he had interrupted a party that had been smoking cannabis, nearly all of those taking part being visitors from London. The man in whose rooms the party was held was lying asleep in bed, dead drunk. The promoter of the party was a very self-confident English student, thought to be a drug pusher, who had had previous warnings and was well aware that he was in breach of at least three college rules. Other Masters would have sent him down — in other words, expelled him permanently — but I judged a suspension for a term severe enough. I also had to deal with the drunkard. Naturally, he protested that he had not smoked pot and was therefore guiltless. "How would it look", I asked, "to the reader of a morning paper if the outcome of the party in your room was that the guests were punished and the host exonerated by reason of his over-indulgence in alcohol?" After all, alcohol was a drug, too, and some might think his offence as host worse than that of the guests.

Coming from a non-residential university like Glasgow, where the staff had very few disciplinary powers, I had some scruples about expelling students, and can remember only one instance. A young man, whom I found entertaining at the college bar another student I had banned from college premises for repeated misconduct, refused (twice) point-blank to show him out when I asked him to do so.

Fortunately student misdemeanours at St Peter's were rare and never violent. One drug case in 1972 led to two arrests and, to my mind, rather harsh sentences: imprisonment for six months in Oxford prison just across the road from the college. The two students concerned had been allowed to take rooms some way out of Oxford on strict conditions about drug-taking and had nevertheless tried to cultivate cannabis in their attic. Some itinerant pusher, denied a sale, had given them away to the police, and although the hemp had yielded no seed, they were charged and sentenced without any opportunity for the college to give evidence. The two appealed and had their sentences curtailed. In the meantime I arranged with the Governor of the prison and the students' tutors that they should continue to be tutored in their cells. This proved successful. One student took a first and became a University lecturer, confessing to me that he had had a useful lesson and would not wish ever again to cause so much trouble to so many people. The other qualified in medicine and, when I last heard of him, was on the staff at Harvard.

A different kind of incident occurred when it was reported to me that a young American student had had a girl in his room overnight. He was a little surprised to be fined, but I assured him that I was charging no more than the current hotel rate.

A more serious incident occurred when the students, in the middle of a rent strike, took all the mail from the College pigeon holes. I got hold of the President of the Junior Common Room (the student body) at once, warned him that tampering with the mail was a criminal offence, and told him that if the mail was not returned to its pigeon holes within the next hour I would have no alternative but to expel him and the rest of his committee. I made clear that this was no bluff, although privately I had some qualms. The mail was put back, and my friendly relations with the JCR president were resumed.

## Fund-raising

One of the main jobs of the Master of an Oxford college, I soon discovered, is to raise money. St Peter's was one of the poorest colleges; but it also had, during my time there, some of the most ambitious fund-raising plans. I will come, in a moment, to the saga of the underground theatre; but our most pressing problem was a need for student lodgings. We had very little accommodation of our own in 1969, and were glad to supplement it with rooms lent to us by Brasenose in New Inn Hall Street. In the 1970s we were also allowed the use of property in Wellington Square that the University had owned and proposed to demolish. Building our own accommodation had financial drawbacks: because the rent we could ask from undergraduates for College rooms was not enough to cover our maintenance costs, much less interest and depreciation, any building we did would add not to our assets but to our liabilities. But, to attract good students, we required enough new accommodation to offer them two out of three years in college, and we were far short of that.

What I had to find, therefore, were benefactors who would finance new accommodation. Before I arrived, the College had already decided to construct one large block to house about 50 undergraduates and a second that would hide the first (which was rather unprepossessing) and complete one of our two main quadrangles. In the event, we were doubly fortunate: first, in finding benefactors to help finance both buildings; second and equally important, in setting about construction in 1970 before the steep rise in building costs of the following decade. Indeed, for my first three or four years we always seemed to have some new building in hand. Architecture was a subject of the deepest interest to the Fellows, and the details of each new building or revamping of an existing building were debated at length by the Governing Body.

Our first benefactor was Pat Matthews who had built up First National Finance, one of the fringe banks that flourished at that time, and had made a fair amount of money. He took to the College, and had his luck held, would have continued to help us: as indeed he did by financing a College quartet for about a year. But the financial upsets of 1973–74 came near to ruining First National and put an end to his career as a banker. A Canadian friend put me in touch with a second benefactor, Albert Latner, who was a partner in a construction firm in Toronto and had an impressive art collection. Both he and Pat Matthews had that compulsive generosity and interest in art and culture typical of Jewish people.

The money we received from benefactors was supplemented by large grants from the University. Under a system which operated from the late 1960s, the richer colleges paid a tax on their endowment income to the University from which payments

Sir Alec Cairncross with Deng-Xiao-Ping in Beijing, September 1979.

were made to the half dozen poorest colleges to bring their endowments up to what was judged to be an operational minimum. The amounts were not small: St Peter's received at least £1m through the College Contributions Committee while I was Master.

The College's fund-raising activities were greatly assisted by the more colourful efforts of Francis Warner, our don in English literature and a poet and dramatist, with a wide range of connections in the artistic world. Warner wanted the College to construct an experimental theatre to seat about 150, and he also kept urging us to buy works of art before they went through the roof. As a result, the company I kept at St Peter's (apart from the dons) was often very different from the people with whom the Treasury had brought me into touch. I was no longer in a world of bankers, accountants and company chairmen, but in constant touch with the arts and their backers. There seemed to be sculptors, musicians, film producers, actors, architects and artists of all kinds coming and going all the time — in the College and indeed in the Master's Lodging — and with them or independently an exotic selection of rich enthusiasts willing to sponsor artistic achievement if it appealed to them.

Warner had remarkable success in finding potential backers for the theatre scheme. On a visit to Canada, he interested Sam and Ayala Zacks, Sam being a former student of a distinguished Harvard economist, Allyn Young. Sam had subsequently made a fortune on the Stock Exchange. His wife Ayala was — astonishingly — a former major in the French army. Sam made a donation of £200,000 towards the construction of a theatre, and in recognition of this was made an Honorary Fellow. Francis Warner also obtained, at a festival in Budapest, a signed undertaking from Richard Burton, the actor, to contribute £100,000 towards the theatre. He too was elected to an Honorary Fellowship.

What seemed to have excited interest in the theatre was not just that it would be attached to an Oxford College, but that it would be built underground, below the College quadrangle. It was to be designed by Buckminster Fuller, the architect of the geodesic dome and guru of the young, or at least he was to advise on the plans. Norman Foster, another architect of world distinction, was also eager to take on the job of designing an underground theatre, surrounded by large college buildings (the chapel, the senior common room and Dining Hall and several blocks of student rooms standing round the perimeter of the quadrangle) and probably resting on water, since the water level was not far from the surface. Foster assured me that there was no danger to the buildings from excavating the quadrangle, but I still felt some hesitation.

Sam and Ayala Zacks, when they came for dinner at the college, brought with them a distinguished group for whom preparations had been made like those for the Marquis of Calabar, with hundreds of potted plants imported for the occasion and planted around the quadrangles. They included, if my memory serves me right, the propriatrix of the *Washington Post*; the lady owner of a well-known Toronto department store; and the head of a large museum in New York. It was an enjoyable evening.

Buckminster Fuller paid us more than one visit and he, too, brought others with him: Herbert Marshall, an authority on Eisenstein and a colleague of Buckie at the University of Southern Illinois; his wife, Fredda Brillant, who was a well-known sculptor and presented us later with a bust of Carl Albert, an old boy of the College and speaker of the American House of Representatives; Sorel Etrog, a young sculptor who also presented us with a piece of his work. On one occasion, a double-decker bus, was parked on a Saturday night in the College car park with the entire wedding party of Buckie's great-nephew on board; and next morning the entire party, which slept in the converted bus, joined our usual Sunday breakfast. On another visit, Buckie interrupted a journey to Delhi where he was to deliver a named lecture in a day's time, and spoke to a crowded assembly of our undergraduates after Hall, with such momentum that I feared a second hour would go by before he finished and had to find a way of stopping him.

The most memorable of our visits in support of the theatre was one from that remarkable pair, Jean-Louis Barrault and Madeleine Renault. They arrived separately: Madeleine Renault had a stage appearance in Paris on a Saturday night and came over on Sunday afternoon for a gruelling one-woman performance of Samuel Beckett's "Happy Days". On arrival, she naturally wanted a short rest, but when Mary offered her tea and cake, she could not resist, exclaiming, "J'adore le cak." Jean-Louis Barrault, arriving earlier, had quite a lengthy discussion with us, first about dogs (we had a mongrel) and from that, about how he became an actor. As a young man not yet a member of a theatre company, he had been in the habit of rehearsing speeches in front of his dog. He declared himself a devoted dog-lover. He put it very succinctly: "Moi, je suis chien." I was deeply impressed by his complete naturalness and the way in which he was so entirely at ease in discussion with a complete stranger in a foreign country. When I was living in Paris in 1950 I had seen the two put on an improvised show with the same ease and informality, but never thought I would one day entertain them and find them such understanding guests.

In the end, plans for the theatre were never drawn and it was never built. We did get as far as drawing up a trust to provide financial support for the theatre. But when it became clear that no other Fellow of the college would wish to take on the job of directing the theatre project, and that Francis stood no chance of being entrusted with the responsibility, I decided to call the whole thing off. I returned the donation from Sam Zacks but I was unable to return anything to Richard Burton for the simple reason that, in spite of threats to deprive him of his Honorary Fellowship, nothing had ever been received from him.

I can't say that I felt any great sense of disappointment over the theatre. It had served a useful purpose in bringing St Peter's to public attention and putting us in touch with possible benefactors. From my point of view it was essentially a dream, with the ease of meeting celebrities that dreams afford. I had dined with Samuel Beckett in Paris and travelled there in the company of Harold Pinter (mistaking him for one of Francis's students!). I had mixed with artists such as Sorel Etrog and Fredda Brillant. I had dined with Elizabeth Frink, another sculptor whom Francis Warner had brought to the College. She came for a magnificent dinner that Francis could ill afford and made us a vague promise of a statue to go with our new, puny fountain that never worked for long. In this case, too, nothing came of the promise — but since it was to be a statue of a naked man and we were a little apprehensive of its likely reception by the undergraduates, perhaps it was just as well.

Looking back at my years as Master, I find it easier to think of projects that I backed that came to nothing than of projects that succeeded. True, the College prospered. But the proposal to build an underground theatre died. I raised money for a University swimming pool that was never built. My years as a Director and Trustee for Urwick Orr ended with it being taken over. But I suspect that my experience echoed that of many others in those years. The 1970s were a dispiriting decade that did not breed many successes. The strains in the world economy and the worldwide loss of buoyancy made themselves felt in many unlikely places: even Oxford.

## 18

## Retirement: the Chunnel and China

On one of those railways journeys I made to Bradford on Sunday evenings in 1946 with other independent members of the Wool Working Party, I remember Sir Richard Hopkins, our chairman and a former head of the Treasury, saying to me with great emphasis, "Cairncross, take my advice: never retire. Never retire — you'll be busier than you were." He went on to illustrate how, in his case, retirement had exposed him to an endless series of pressing invitations to help good causes or assume public duties which he had been unable to resist.

It may have been good advice — it was advice I often heard repeated in later years — but at least, once retired, you can choose what invitations to accept or reject. No doubt if I had taken the advice that an Archbishop is said to have given to a mother who asked him for a word of wisdom for her son ("Teach him to say no," said the cleric), I could have had a quiet retirement. But I would have felt ill at ease with too much leisure; and I was easily tempted into new responsibilities. I became involved with the Channel Tunnel; with relations with China; and, increasingly, with my duties as chancellor of Glasgow University. Above all, I wrote.

### The Channel Tunnel
My involvement with the Channel Tunnel goes back a long way: to the summer of 1949, when I was asked to minute Harold Wilson, then President of the Board of Trade, on the merits of a tunnel at a time when my mind was full of the case for devaluing the pound. Nothing came then of the idea. The subject came up again in the 1960s when I was in the Treasury. Otto Clarke, who

dealt with the issue, was mildly in favour of the project at the time. When I discussed it again with him in August 1974, shortly before his death, he told me that the likely return on investment was "no more than adequate".

By that time I had been invited by Anthony Crosland, then Minister for the Environment, to chair a small advisory group on the Tunnel. I agreed rather reluctantly: as I pointed out, I tended to get caught up in discussions on the Channel Tunnel just ahead of a major economic crisis, and I took the invitation as a bad omen for the United Kingdom. It was difficult to find other economists to serve on the group, especially as those I suggested first were either already consultants on the Tunnel or not available. I thought we should also have someone with experience of assessing capital projects and so Sir Arthur Knight, who was finance director (and later chairman) of Courtaulds, and had spent three years on the inquiry into the new London airport, joined us in November.

Immediately my appointment was announced, letters began to flow in. I had telephone calls and invitations to see interested parties. I was in the midst of a particularly hectic time with obligations at Oxford, on various committees and abroad, and I had no secretary even to acknowledge the letters. A Mr L.E.Detwiler, who claimed to have been responsible for one or more of America's turnpikes and to have $3m in his pocket for the construction of a Channel bridge, came to see me the day after I took up my appointment, complete with a mass of papers and an architect. In his view, tunnels were out of date. He strewed the carpet of my room with papers and talked for an hour almost without interruption about the superior virtues of a bridge, while I tried to convey to him that he was wasting his time. My terms of reference, I told him, were confined to the project of a tunnel. If he wanted to promote a bridge he should go to No.10 Downing Street and convince the prime minister. But it was no good; he took no notice and talked on.

We had hardly started our inquiries when British Rail revised their estimate of the cost of a high-speed rail link from London to the Tunnel from £120m to £333m (i.e., nearly as much as the tunnel itself was expected to cost), largely because of the need to compensate landowners and householders along the route. This was a setback for Crosland who had insisted in opposition on the need to give the project a more "rail-oriented" bias. He announced on November 26th that the government was unable to proceed with the link because it was too expensive. It appeared also that the government was hoping to cut out something big and symbolic in the forthcoming Budget and might well pick on the Tunnel. When I saw Crosland at the House of Commons on November 12th, as Denis Healey, the Chancellor of the Exchequer, was delivering his Budget speech, he told me that opinion on the Tunnel in the Cabinet was divided, and that he was trying to keep open the option of building it until we reported. But it was only if we came down very firmly in favour that it stood any chance at all. Fred Mulley, Minister of Transport and one of his closest colleagues, had once been a supporter, but was advising him to "chop it now".

This conversation broadened our instructions very markedly. Earlier, there had been no question of making a recommendation one way or another. Our original job, I understood, had been to pass judgment on the work of Coopers & Lybrand, the consultancy firm which had previously studied the project, and on the way they had assessed the likely return on it. Now we were being asked to produce a report by April designed to persuade the public one way or another whether the Tunnel should go ahead.

Meanwhile, the arrangements for ratifying the Channel Tunnel Treaty by January 1st 1975 had been seriously disrupted by two general elections in 1974; and the government was asking the French government and the Channel tunnel companies to agree to a set-back in the timetable. The companies, however, rejected the proposal of a standstill and served notices of abandonment on January 2nd, citing the inability of the government to ratify the Treaty by the agreed date. Subsequent talks failed to yield any proposition that could be put to the Secretary of State, and the companies demanded a settlement on January 20th.

Thus the scheme was already dead before we could report. Nonetheless we carried on and submitted a report in the expectation that, sooner or later, the proposal would be revived. We were inclined to think that next time it would be a mistake to have four parties to the agreement — two governments and two companies — and that governments might be wiser to finance the project themselves.

The fact was that the Stock Exchange had fallen a great deal further than most people had expected and reached its nadir at the end of 1974. Against that background, the companies felt particularly reluctant to take on such a large risk. They distrusted the British government, which would give no assurance that the Tunnel would eventually go ahead, and they felt that, if they agreed to a delay, something would be cooked up that would make them worse off.

The collapse of the project aroused tremendous interest. I kept being asked why it had been decided not to proceed. I pointed out that there had been no decision — only indecision; no conscious effort to kill off a project that both the companies and the two governments probably wanted to keep alive. The French (who, I gathered, had offered to meet half the cost of the high-speed rail link) were particularly disappointed. Britain's "unilateral abandonment", said President Giscard d'Estaing, would result in a "substantial loss" for the Northern region of France. According to Le Monde, it showed that Britain wanted to remain an island.

In fact, plenty of people in Britain opposed the Tunnel on precisely those grounds, or feared that rats would arrive carrying disease, or argued for or against because they were rail enthusiasts or road enthusiasts. Few approached the decision in terms of the prospective return. My own provisional conclusion was that the return was likely to be marginal at best, and probably near the borderline between worthwhile and not worthwhile.

I had no doubt that the project of a Channel Tunnel would eventually be revived. Within a few years British Rail, which had shown little enthusiasm for the Tunnel in 1974, came up with the idea of a single-track tunnel through which trains would run first in one direction, then in another. There would be no high-speed rail link at the British end. Sir Peter Parker, then Chairman of British Rail, gave the scheme his backing, and I urged William Rodgers, Minister of Transport in the last days of the Labour Government, to arrange for it to be considered.

In October 1979, by which time the Conservatives were in power and Norman Fowler had become Minister of Transport, I was appointed without specific terms of reference to advise him on what had now become known as the "mousehole". I was free to consult my former colleagues on the 1974 committee as I thought fit, but we were not formally reconstituted as a group. Since my duties were essentially advisory, no report was originally envisaged. But, as material accumulated, I was asked to widen the scope of my inquiries in March 1980 to cover all fixed-link schemes. I decided in 1981 as I was winding up my study that I ought to draw together all my conclusions and the material on which they rested. My report was published early in 1982 in the rather curious form of an appendix to a four-page submission by the Minister that made no mention of it.

In drafting my report, I had to take a view of the wide variety of plans that were being put forward, rather than simply evaluate a single, preferred project. One option was to have no fixed link after all, and to continue to rely on ferries and air travel. Another possibility was a single-track tunnel of six or seven metres in diameter; yet another, a twin-track tunnel such as had been proposed in the 1960s. In 1980-81, several proposals were made for a Channel bridge, an idea that had first been proposed and rejected in 1963. It would have involved a risk of collision in what was the busiest shipping lane in the world, with about 300 daily ship movements through the Channel and another 300 (mainly of ferries) across it. There were also various schemes for immersed tubes carrying a two-lane motorway or a dual track for both road and rail traffic.

On grounds of navigational safety on the one hand and higher cost on the other, I judged that it would be unwise to embark on the construction of a bridge or an immersed tube. Instead, I concluded that, if a fixed link was to be built, it should take the form of a twin tunnel. In the event, that is what we now have. But I took the view that, while there was a case for constructing a fixed link, it was not an overwhelming one. It was, I said, "not yet entirely clear that the return would be adequate in financial terms" and more doubtful that, with the further development of ferries, such a link would represent a saving in productive resources.

I also felt that there were many unresolved uncertainties. One was the cost. Building the Tunnel would require burrowing through chalk, and might thus give rise to unpredictable expenditure. In fact, the unpredictability might be greater still: even at the outset, the French had found, not chalk but an unstable overburden (or covering) of gravel, that suggested even higher costs. In practice, when the Tunnel was eventually built, the original cost estimates were exceeded by a very large margin.

Large as were the uncertainties about cost, much greater uncertainty seemed to attach to estimates of the likely traffic. The ferries had greatly increased their carrying capacity and lowered their unit costs; they would compete vigorously and had attractions that the Tunnel might find it hard to match, such as easier access to duty-free goods and a more comfortable break for drivers of cars and lorries in the middle of a long journey.

There were other unanswered questions. Would the Customs and Immigration officers hold up passengers and vehicles at the entrance or exit to the Tunnel to make their customary inquiries, or would they be able to save time by doing so during the journey through the Tunnel? What railway terminus in London would be used, and would the choice speed up the journey to the coast? Would British Rail take full advantage of the opportunity to run through trains between places in Britain and places on the Continent? Most of these questions remained unanswered for more than a decade after my report in 1982. Indeed, when I look at the rows that accompanied the building of the Tunnel and the losses suffered by the shareholders, I feel that my early caution was more than justified.

## China

Between 1979 and 1992 I made five journeys to China, travelling to all parts of the country and taking part in one conference after another. I decided early in my retirement that the most useful thing I could do was to contribute what I could to the development of a peaceful and prosperous China, given the dominant position in world affairs that the country seemed destined to occupy and its potential for good or ill. The Chinese were more than willing to listen to what a foreign economist had to say and were remarkably quick to learn.

My association with China began by accident in September 1979. I was already chairman of the China panel of the British Academy, promoting scholarly exchanges between Britain and China, when the Chinese Academy of Social Sciences issued an invitation to the Academy to send a mission to China as their guests. A mission headed by Sir Isaiah Berlin was duly appointed. I was initially reluctant to be included, thinking it improper for the chairman of the Academy's panel to put himself forward, but was eventually persuaded by Sir Isaiah to do so. As he found it necessary to withdraw before the Mission left, I eventually went as leader of the group.

Our trip took us to many parts of China: the Forbidden City, the Great Wall and the Ming Tombs (in a splendour that had gone when I next saw them, because the exhibits inside the tombs had been moved elsewhere); Sian, and the Army of Dead Warriors; Hangchow, Shanghai and Soochow. It was an extraordinary period to be visiting China. Memories of the Cultural Revolution were still fresh, and dominated the conversation of our hosts at many of the places we visited. The mischief it did was described with great candour — at Fudan University, for instance, where whole faculties had been closed down and the campus ploughed up for use as a vegetable patch.

At Sun Yat Sen University the same was true. I was given a sketch of the curriculum in economics. When I asked whether the students read any works by Western economists, the answer was that it simply was not possible: very few of them had sufficient command of English to read in the original, even if — as was rarely the case — the books were available. At the time, virtually no works by foreign economists had been translated into Chinese, apart from Keynes's "General Theory", which had been translated in the mid 1950s. A number of other texts — Paul Samuelson's "Economics", for instance — were in course of translation.

When I asked about the employment of economists, citing my experience in Moscow, it became clear that the situation in China was not very different. Teachers concentrated on theory, and presumably expounded the "true faith", but lacked the knowledge of current institutions to analyse how things worked in the world economy at that time. They had no monthly statistical bulletin to give quantitative shape to their understanding of the Chinese economy, and had to rest at a very general level of analysis. This was most apparent when we came to talk about management and comparative economic systems. They accepted the need to study economic management, but had read none of the literature on the subject, and made no reference to specific problems of management although they all put stress on the need to find a more flexible model than the Russian. I found, on this and on subsequent visits, that several aspects of my own experience as an economist were more relevant to the Chinese than the experience of a younger British economist might have been. I had, after all, seen at close quarters the period after the Second World War, when a highly regulated economy gradually gave way to one in which regulations were lighter and the market played a bigger role. This was precisely the process that China was going through at the time. In addition, at a time when Britain was turning its back on planning, China was discovering how to apply it more effectively. When we visited Sian, I was called upon to deliver an impromptu lecture and found myself on a Saturday afternoon addressing a large crowd, mustered from town and country, on the subject of planning. I was delighted and amused to be told afterwards that they were repeating with approval my remark that, in a changing world, the essence of good planning was re-planning.

The Mission was also taken to meet Deng Xiao-Ping, at that time the key figure in China, and I had a discussion with him lasting half an hour or so. The British Ambassador, who accompanied us, urged me to ask a series of political questions, but I did not think this appropriate. It was at a time when citizens were able to display their views freely on a wall in Beijing, but Deng made clear to us that he was not in favour of unlimited free speech. He illustrated its dangers by pointing to the folly of shouting "Fire" in a crowded cinema. Instead of the Ambassador's inappropriate questions, I tried him with a subject suggested by Sandy, my second son, who is a water engineer specialising in developing countries. Sandy had asked me to find out how China dealt with the invasive plant known as water hyacinths. Deng was intrigued, and asked his staff to pursue the question.

It was six years before my next visit, in September 1985. I was invited by Ed Lim, of the World Bank, a brother of Cyril Lin, the head of the Department of Chinese Studies in Oxford, to join an international group of economists, including Otmar Emminger, a former president of the Bundesbank, and James Tobin, Professor of Economics at Yale University, in a kind of seminar on economic policy. It was to be held on board the Bashan, a specially equipped tourist boat, as it sailed down the Yangtze. The seminar covered an extraordinarily wide range of economic policies and lasted for several days. It was an unprecedented event, and became known all over China.

While in Beijing, we were taken to see Zhao Zhiyang, the prime minister, who discussed policy problems with us for an hour and a half. It was a remarkable experience to find the prime minister of the largest country in the world seeking advice from abroad and promising to study the report of our seminar with attention (as, apparently, he subsequently did).

An important by-product of this visit was the launching of a scheme to bring young Chinese economists (mostly officials) to Oxford for training in Western economic analysis. Ed Lim and I each conceived the idea separately of starting with Guo Shu-qing, a young Mongolian who had been an assistant in the prime minister's office, and bringing him to Oxford for a year. If this proved successful (and, in the event, Guo Shu-quing went on to become head of China's planning staff), the scheme could be enlarged and four or five able young Chinese might come every year. The World Bank backed the idea, and funds were provided by the United Nations Development Programme and the Ford Foundation. Ed's brother, Cyril Lin, took charge in Oxford, and found individual tutors for each student. If they showed sufficient ability as economists, they could also be supported by the World Bank to study for a doctorate. It seemed to me that, even if no more than a score of young scholars and officials were able to profit from the scheme, the impact on China would be cumulative, provided they all returned to China, as virtually all of them did. In a sense, the scheme was thus a Chinese version of the Economic Development Institute that I had launched in Washington all those years ago: a way to try to accelerate economic development by creating a cadre of economists in influential positions, trained in Western ideas. It was, however, very much less trouble than the EDI had been.

I made three more trips: one in September 1986 with the Great Britain-China Association; one to discuss financial policy in Beijing in December 1988; and a third visit with Mary to join a Chinese conference in Hangchow in March 1992, three years after the poignant events in Tiananman Square. Of these, the last was particularly interesting, since the conference was attended almost exclusively by Chinese officials. I was thus privileged to hear them debate most of the major issues of economic policy among themselves.

The years over which I visited China saw extraordinary change. When I first went, the country had just embarked on policies opening the economy to market forces and to foreign trade and investment. In the course of the next 20 years China changed enormously. Where its exports in the early 1970s amounted to $2 billion-3 billion, by 1996 they were rising fast and had reached $150 billion, so that China had become the world's tenth largest exporter. By the time of my last visit, in 1992, newly formed village enterprises and joint ventures with foreign companies were becoming important exporters. By then, eastern China no longer felt underdeveloped, even if western China still did.

Even by the time of my second visit, in 1985, the pace of change had accelerated. The economy was in the course of rapid development, visible to the naked eye. This was most obvious in urban transport, with a multitude of buses, mini-buses, motor cars and trucks on the roads, and diesel engines on the railways. Roads were being widened, and new roads constructed. There was a corresponding decline in horse-drawn traffic, although one could still see every variety of handcart and merchandise drawn by, or mounted on, bicycles or on the human frame. The look of the towns had changed: there were piles of bricks everywhere, and skyscrapers going up.

Clothing had been transformed. The sea of blue denim had almost vanished; instead, women took pride in colourful dresses, and it was more difficult to be sure who was Chinese and who from abroad. The hotels were becoming grander and more expensive, with colour televisions in every room and push-button telephones. But the past kept breaking in: for example, in the coffee room at Hangchow, where they served Western food, I was asked repeatedly for a meal coupon and invited to pay the excess over 25 yen a day, although my hosts had telephoned three times in an effort to prevent such requests.

One of the greatest pleasures of these visits to China was discovering the humour, intelligence and generosity of individual Chinese. I relished their pleasure in good company and entertainment: I remember, for instance, a magnificent banquet in Soochow on my first visit, where it was explained to us that food should appeal to all the senses, not just the taste and smell but the eye and ear as well (this as a crackling joint of pork was brought in). On another visit, I set out from the Peking Hotel to discover the times of our flights home, but went in the wrong direction along Chang-an. Walking faster and faster, I eventually tumbled over, breaking my spectacle frame and sprawling on the ground. I was soon surrounded by a crowd, anxious to be of help and offering to take me to hospital. I insisted, however, that I was due to lunch with the Ambassador and what I most needed was a bank, since I had no money. I was taken to a bank; and when that proved unable to cash a cheque, one of the Chinese ladies, who turned out to be a waitress, escorted me to a taxi and came with me to my hotel, paying the driver herself. Someone recovered my glasses and brought me a new pair of spectacles. I finally arrived at the Embassy only a few minutes late, and impressed by the kindness of ordinary Chinese.

## Chancellor of the University of Glasgow

When I was elected Chancellor in January 1972, my first impression was that it was like being elected Santa Claus, since my main duty was to give things away — in the form of honorary degrees — once a year. Many of the tasks I undertook for the University involved more pure pleasure than duty.

Of course, I was called upon from time to time to help the University in several ways. One was to represent it on various grand occasions, such as offering congratulations to the Queen in Holyrood House on the betrothal of the Prince of Wales in 1981, or receiving a royal award to the University at Buckingham Palace in 1994, or taking part in the celebrations of the quincentenary of Aberdeen University — as the representative of an even older Scottish University!

Another duty was fund raising. After the University had incurred heavy expenditure on a new art gallery at the end of the 1970s, it first sought to reduce the financial burden by selling off 11 duplicates of the collection of Whistler paintings that had been given to it by Miss Birnie Phillips earlier in this century. The University was authorised to do so in the deed of gift, but the proposal gave rise to extensive press criticism, and so a general appeal was launched to raise funds to make the sale unnecessary. To this I gave all the support I could. By September 1981 a total of £85,000 had been raised, attracting a matching grant from the

National Heritage Memorial Fund and allowing the University to recall from London the canvases it had intended to sell.

Perhaps one of the most important of a Chancellor's duties — and the main service he can render — is to provide a willing ear to the Principal (who, in Scotland, performs the executive role that is played south of the border by the Vice Chancellor), allowing him to unburden himself to someone not immediately involved in the University's affairs, to pose problems in confidence and to test how the possibilities might look to someone else. I was fortunate in my Principals, Sir Charles Wilson, Sir Alwyn Williams and Sir Kerr Fraser. Indeed, when I retired from being Chancellor — the first person ever to do so, which says much for the attractions of the job — I timed my departure partly so that the graduates of the University might have the opportunity of electing Kerr as my successor, which they duly did.

## Modern Economic History

Of all my interests in retirement, the one that has continued longest is studying and writing about modern economic history. I am fortunate not only to have done my early economic research into an issue of economic history and to have played so many roles in a period offering ideal material to the economic historian, but to have lived to see a revival of academic interest in the subject.

When I gave up the Mastership of St Peter's, I was approached to lend a hand in the development of European Studies at St Antony's College. I started off by organising a seminar on current problems of economic integration and ran it for two or three years. By 1982, though, I had come to the conclusion that I ought to move over to recent economic history — largely a discussion of problems of economic management as I recalled them from my own career from 1939 onwards. I started a series of weekly seminars, beginning with Margaret Gowing, a historian of the development of the atomic bomb, who spoke on a theme dear to my heart: "Wartime Planning". The seminar series continued for the next 11 years, and about 80 different speakers took part, many of them participants in the events under discussion. The seminars helped to encourage an interest in sustained analysis of the recent past, an activity of the utmost value in the formulation and assessment of current economic policy.

On another occasion, in 1991, Glasgow University kindly allowed me to hold a conference to celebrate my 80th birthday and discuss the economic legacy of the 1960s. It seemed an appropriate way to bring together my friends and former colleagues, to talk about a decade we had helped to shape. The participants included several key figures in that period, including Lord Callaghan, who presided, and Lord Jenkins, whom I had also advised when he succeeded Lord Callaghan as Chancellor of the Exchequer.[1]

My career as an author of modern economic histories began — or rather, revived — as a consequence of an account of the 1949 devaluation that I wrote for a volume in honour of Walt Rostow. I discovered that Barry Eichengreen, a Harvard economic historian, was in Oxford studying the 1931 devaluation, and suggested to him that, if we joined forces, we could publish an account of successive devaluations of sterling in 1931, 1949 and 1967. I would leave 1931 to him, revise my treatment of the 1949 devaluation, and prepare a history of the 1967 devaluation that used my inside knowledge without disclosing that I was doing so (and so not infringing the Official Secrets Act), by piecing together those parts of published accounts that I knew to be accurate. The outcome was "Sterling in Decline".[2]

This was the first of a steady flow of publications. In 1985 came "Years of Recovery", a study of economic policy in the post-war period under the Attlee Government. Once started, I found myself keeping up an average of about one volume a year, each volume calculated to occupy me for a year or so, since it seemed rash at my age to tackle subjects requiring a longer period. This schedule was made easier to fulfil because several of the books dealt with episodes of which I had personal experience. For example, "The Price of War" (1986) and "A Country to Play With" (1987) both dealt with the arguments in Berlin in 1945-46 over the future of the German economy and the Allied demands for reparations; "The Economic Section 1931-61" (in collaboration with Nita Watts, 1989), drew on my recollections of work in the War Cabinet Offices when the Economic Section was taking shape in 1940-41; "Planning in Wartime" (1991)

---

[1] The proceedings of the conference were subsequently published as "The Legacy of the Golden Age: the 1960s and their economic consequences". Routledge 1992.
[2] "Sterling in Decline" (with Barry Eichengreen), Basil Blackwell, 1983.

described how aircraft production was planned during my time in the Ministry of Aircraft Production in 1941-45 and outlined also how the job was done in Germany and the United States. Most recently, I published "Managing the British Economy in the 1960s" (1996), which drew on my memories of my time in Whitehall, as did my diary of my Treasury years, which came out the following year as "The Wilson Years" (1997).

I have also written broader histories, such as an account of the IMF crisis in Britain in 1976, written with Kathleen Burk and published as "Goodbye Great Britain" ; or an account of Britain's recent economic history, published in 1992 as "The British Economy Since the War". As I finish this book, I am preparing another: a history of post-war world trade. Writing has turned out to be the ideal indulgence for old age, requiring little physical effort, giving the pleasures of retrospect, and generating a modest income. I strongly recommend it.

# 19

## *Retrospect*

I have had a full life and a happy one. I chose a profession that suited me, and I have lived in the right century for an economist. I have not lacked for opportunities, and I have nearly always had great good luck.

In no respect is this more true than in my married life. It seems to me little short of miraculous that I should have met and married the one person on whom I had set my whole heart, and that throughout the most active years of my life I should have had her constant love and support. She has been the perfect companion: generous, interesting, surprising. And yet — it escapes me how she could have borne it — for days and months at a time she was for ever being left alone when I went on my travels or shut myself up to study and write. When, in 1943, I first brought Mary to the Ministry of Aircraft Production where I was working at the time we married, Sheila Mobbs, one of my colleagues, burst out in astonishment: "Where *did* you find her?" It is an astonishment I have never lost[1].

In our children and in abundance of friends I have been equally blessed. All our five children have grown up successfully, taken university degrees, embarked on widely different careers in all of which we can take pride, and presented us with a total of 11 grandchildren. As for my friendships, most arose out of common interests in my working life, and of course they multiplied as I moved from one job to another and one country to the next. Curiously enough, few of them go back beyond Cambridge days in the early 1930s, and those that are firmest are often furthest

---

[1] Mary died on June 26th, 1998, just as this book was going through the press.

away. Many of my greatest friends have been foreigners, or naturalised Englishmen: I relish an international atmosphere. In addition, I felt, especially in the years before my marriage, a greater kinship with those who came from outside English society.

My enjoyment of life has been increased by its variety. I have alternated between academic work and the public service, between jobs in Britain and jobs abroad, between official committees, governing bodies, faculty meetings, boards of companies and private huddles. I am conscious of the same variety *within* each day, which has nearly always been filled with the most curious antitheses. Life has seemed so often like a novel that one of my regrets is my inability to transmute everyday reality into fiction.

All my life it has been my good fortune to be pressed to do things of which I had no previous experience, and to write or talk about things of which I knew nothing. At the time, it rarely seemed like fortune. Yet it was in this way that I came to spend years in planning the production of aircraft components which I had hardly ever seen; in examining how to form central-bank policy without having set foot in a central bank; in training administrators from underdeveloped countries without having spent more than a month in any part of the developing world. When I served as an adviser, the subjects on which my advice was sought most assiduously were sure to be on matters to which I had given little attention. The articles I was asked to write were usually on subjects outside my normal range of interests, and the lectures I was invited to deliver involved me only too often in mugging up fresh material when I was ready to speak without effort on a whole range of more familiar topics. People seemed to lie in wait for me to find some new abyss of ignorance into which to tempt me. Again and again, I fell into the temptations spread before me.

Indeed, nothing was more calculated to build up self-confidence than these repeated encounters with the unknown. There was strength in the discovery that what saw you through one crisis was what you learned in a previous one. Equally important, one thing led to another: the opportunities that came my way came in part because I was willing to move sideways and add new knowledge and new experience. To rest content with the familiar is a way of remaining underdeveloped.

At one time or another I have been offered almost every job or appointment an economist could wish for. Some I have forgotten altogether. Some I dimly remember: co-ordinating post-war supplies in Malaysia, advising the government of Greece, sorting out the problems of Arab refugees. Twice I was asked to take on the directorship of the National Economic Development Office, once by Selwyn Lloyd and once by George Brown; earlier, I might have been Director of the National Institute. I nearly became a vice president of the IMF, and turned down an offer of a similar post at the World Bank. None of these were jobs I applied for: in fact, I can think of only two occasions on which I actually applied for a post, and in neither case was I successful. The first was long ago in 1936, when I was put on the short list for a Fellowship at Queen's College, Oxford, along with three others, all Oxford men; the second was in 1945 when the Jeffrey Chair at the University of Aberdeen was ultimately filled by the most senior member of the staff, after the selection committee had been unable to make up its mind between the candidates interviewed.

It follows, of course, that the opportunities that came to me were not of my seeking, and reflected someone's good opinion of me. I owe a good deal, therefore, to people who thought they saw in me potentialities of which I was not myself conscious. Since I usually ended up doing most of the jobs I was invited to do to their satisfaction, I think with gratitude and wonder of those who showed such percipience. I am not ambitious, and would cheerfully have carried on in almost any of the succession of jobs I undertook, once I had overcome the initial sense of inadequacy in them. It usually took a considerable effort of persuasion to induce me to move to a new job — again and again I have written, but not always posted, letters of refusal. Yet when I took the plunge, and entered on duties for which I felt no special talent, I gradually found that, in a sense, one job was much like another, and that success in one was the first recipe for self-confidence in the next. And self-confidence was more than half the battle.

It took a long time for me to perceive this. I was one of those who is easily impressed by people who seem to know what they are about, and come quickly to plausible conclusions as to what should be done. What I had not grasped was that decisiveness comes with decision-taking, and if one has experience of the matter to be decided, reasonable common sense and the assurance that one's judgement is final, it is easy to pronounce with confidence and by that confidence to silence objection. After a time, however, if some of the decisions are plainly wrong, one may begin to sigh for a little less self-confidence.

I remember an encounter in 1956 with Lincoln Gordon, Professor of Public Administration at Harvard, that summed up the situation. He told me that he had just been taking part in a summer school in business administration, and this had been a new and interesting experience. There was a man on the course who attracted his attention because he seemed to have little to learn, and after one session Linc drew him aside and asked, "Are you enjoying this?" "Yes, very much." "But don't you know it all already?" "Well, I suppose I do." "Then why do you think it worth your while to come on the course?" "It's like this," said the man. "I work for the Grace Line, down in Chile, thousands of miles away. When I meet a difficult problem. I've been in the habit of saying to myself, 'I wish I could ask some of these bright fellows up in New York what I should do.' Now I've heard them on this course, I've found they don't know any more than I do. When I go back to Chile, I'll be a different man."

From time to time I ask myself whether I have employed my talents as successfully as I should. I have made little impression on academic economics, partly, no doubt, because I have always been less interested in theoretical models than in action and have written little in the journals, partly because I have never tried to draw together the new ideas that surface here and there in my writing. I have had only limited success as a government servant, and was more at home as a member of a group than as its leader. Like many others, I fancied myself as a poet, but failed to excite much interest in the little I wrote. Above all, I leave behind no school, no disciples, no recognisable followers. My influence has been directed towards the immediate future and its problems, not the more lasting issues of modern life.

I abominate dogma, and yet recognise that the world is ruled by dogma. It is easy to see how that arises. One the one hand is the need for a purpose in life which many people find in a creed: either religious belief or political aims or a rigorous code of social behaviour. On the other hand is the ignorance and uncertainty in which nearly all decisions — and especially the major ones — have to be taken.

I am by temperament distrustful of creeds, most of all when commitment to them in a church or party is total and loyalty is demanded to the symbols as well as the substance of the creed without regard to the consequences of such blind loyalty for the lasting welfare of the human race. I am almost incapable of joining a political party (although I admit to having been a founder member of the Social Democrats) because I instinctively want to urge objections to the sort of policies parties devise. The natural piety of my youth and the fascination that the phenomena of mysticism once had for me have long since faded, and left me purged of any deep religious faith. As for a routine of submission to established convention, however much that may promote orderly social conditions, it could never impose itself as a principal aim in my life.

Yet I do not lack faith in a creed of another kind or loyalty to those who subscribe to it. My faith is in the power of human reason in the face of ignorance and uncertainty, and my intellectual convictions are tinged with a hue of doubt. Truth is provisional, to be deserted if it conflicts with experience. The touchstone of action is the lesser evil, rarely some unquestioned good. My consuming interest is in what works and what does not work. But the knowledge of what works is hard to come by and needs exact observation as well as logic. Sometimes we are misled by observation and sometimes we go wrong with confidence under the influence of theory. Nearly always we don't really know for sure or can't find out in time and yet have to decide. Sometimes it is the things we know least about that we are asked to decide, and the less we know, the hotter the argument. So dogma takes the place of investigation and may not only short-circuit but suppress it.

The world has changed in many ways since I was born. It is nearly a century since my parents married in 1900; and a century later I and my youngest sister alone survive from the eight children they reared. It is typical of the changes that have occurred over the century that where my parents had eight children, my wife and I have had five and they in turn have none of them had more than three. It is typical also that while I was born and sent to school in a village, none of us now lives in a village except on holiday. In other ways I have been carried along by the currents of the twentieth century, participating in the early stages of many of its developments, profiting from the opportunities it afforded, caught up in its struggles.

Of all the changes that have taken place since I was born, the most striking is what my daughter calls "the death of distance". She is thinking of the far greater ease and cheapness of communication between one part of the world and another, thanks to advances in telecommunications. But distance has shrunk in many other ways. Without stirring from one's home, thanks to radio and television, one can attend concerts, operatic performances, plays and debates; learn what is going on throughout the world; and be present at great events like the coronation of a Queen or the funeral of a Churchill. However frivolous what comes to us in such ways may be, we are brought far closer to events of which we were hardly conscious in my boyhood. Similarly with travel: distance can be overcome far more easily and cheaply than at the beginning of the century. The consequences include the astonishing growth in holidays abroad and have contributed to the equally astonishing growth in international trade.

When I was a boy, nobody I knew holidayed abroad. I had left school by the time I first went abroad, on a walking tour on the outskirts of Paris with my brother Andrew in 1930. My journeys to and from other continents began with ocean travel on a Cunard liner, the Carinthia, in 1936. Now even a student can think of travelling around the world, or going to New York for a day. Travel which the young take for granted was a much rarer event in those days. The sight of an aircraft in the sky or even cars in the street was extremely rare in my boyhood, when one could sledge down the streets of the village with no fear of any worse accident than an encounter with a horse-drawn milk cart. For many years, the only aircraft I had ever seen was a biplane that made a forced landing in about 1917 in a field nearby, to which I was carried on my elder brother's shoulders. I can still remember vaguely the crowd that formed around it, but not the accident that followed when the propeller was spun and ripped the stomach of a fat young bystander.

My father never owned a motor car, and nor did I until I bought a second-hand Jowett in Cambridge in 1933 or 1934: the first in the family to run a car. The only motor vehicles owned by any relatives of mine were a motor bicycle and side-car belonging to my cousin, George Winder, an electrician by trade; and a Jowett four-seater owned by his father. In my wife's family, things were different: we have a photograph of her father in full motoring kit, standing proudly beside his de Dion Bouton coupé round about 1906, long before she was born.

Travel has given me enormous pleasure, and there have been times, such as my first visit to the United States, when it was also a great source of education. It is now the tourist aspect, the entertainment and the novelty that predominate. One can, with imagination, learn almost as much by staying at home, reading and discussing, parasitical on the travel of others. Yet of all things that have changed the modern world, travel must rank high. When people move about they are forced to reconsider, to adjust to new ideas and ways of life.

Asked whether things have improved since I was born, I am in no doubt. I need only look at the figures of infant mortality. In the mid-19th century, at least one child in seven died, and even in the last three years of that century, infant mortality averaged 160 of every 1,000 live births in England and Wales and 134 in Scotland. Only after that did the real decline set in. By 1911, the year of my birth and a year of exceptionally high infant mortality because of the hot summer, the rate was down to 130 in England and Wales and in Scotland, where 1911 was a less exceptional year, it stood at 112. By 1938, the figures had dropped to 53 and 70 respectively; and by the 1990s, to under seven per 1,000 live births.

The fall in infant mortality contributed to a longer expectation of life at birth. By the mid-1980s, that had risen in Scotland to 70 years, compared with 50 in 1911. If one measures the improvement in terms of the further years of life expected after the age of 20, it remains striking. Men in Britain at the age of 20 in 1901 could expect to live for 42 more years; and for 56 more years if they reached that age in the 1990s. This is, of course, only one illustration of the improvement in health and well-being. There are plenty of others. Income per head, for example, is more than three times as high as in 1911; and, while spending on food accounted for 29% of all consumer spending in the year of my birth, it now accounts for 12%. Clothing and even drink have also become smaller shares of the family budget, while pleasures such as entertainment, holidays and dining out have become larger.

Of course, there have been changes for the worse, too: the rise in crime of all kinds, in drugs and in violence. The homicide rate is far higher than it was before the war and theft more common. Where once no one thought it necessary to lock the front door or put a chain on their bicycle, now it is almost universal. People give more thought to the dangers of everyday life than they used to do. Unemployment remains a constant threat.

But for the mass of population, life has changed enormously for the better. For the poor and those who fall on hard times, the social services, which hardly existed in 1911, have brought a remarkable change. For women in particular, life has changed enormously for the better. Women have far fewer children to care for and far less housework to do: they can go out to work for pay and supplement the family income. Indeed, women workers will soon outnumber men.

Greatest of all the changes has been the downfall of the totalitarian regimes that flourished in my lifetime throughout Europe: Communism, Fascism, National Socialism, each built on dogma and violence. In Europe especially, the outlook for humanity has been completely transformed since those days in the 1930s when the freedoms we took for granted were under threat, a second world war seemed inevitable, and the chances of surviving it were poor indeed. Of all the events in my life, the struggles of those years were the most terrible. It was hard to understand how entire nations could succumb to an ideological plague that turned them into willing followers of madmen in authority. It was even more difficult to see how the United Kingdom could stand alone — as for a year she did — against the warmongers.

It is with a sense of gratitude to those who took part in that stand, and allowed us to exchange the dreads of the first half of this century for the hopes of the second half that I end this sketch of a life shaped by the currents of both halves.

*Appendix*

The name of my younger brother John is much better known to the public than that of any other Cairncross down the ages, but his life and personality remain largely unknown. My account of John does not rest on what he told me (for at no time did he confide in me over his role as a Soviet agent); nor is it based on official disclosures, deliberate or accidental, apart from what I was told in the interview at the Treasury in 1964 described below. I will draw more on my own recollections of him in his early years and on my memory of intermittent contacts with him subsequently. Nearly everything that has been in the press about him, whether by British or Soviet writers, has been by people who did not know him and is unsupported by firm evidence.

John was the youngest and I the second youngest in our family. I was nearly two and a half years older than he was, so that he must have felt a little under my shadow. We were close to one another throughout our boyhood and later, attending the village school together, sharing a bedroom, and sharing interests, too, in what we studied. At an early stage, John gave evidence of his intellectual gifts. After two years at Hamilton Academy in 1928–30 (most of us needed three years), before going on to Glasgow University, he sat what was called the bursary competition on the basis of which university scholarships were awarded, and came fifth — an unprecedented achievement.

When he came up to Glasgow University in 1930, he joined me and a student of mathematics in the same digs, and spent the next two years with us, until the time came, since he was studying French and German, to spend a year abroad. For this, he was offered a teaching attachment to a school in Gueret, a small town in the middle of France, but decided instead to go to Paris and take his *license-ès-lettres* at the Sorbonne, eking out what little money he had with contributions from his parents.

At that stage in his life, of which I can speak at first hand, there could be no possible doubt as to his honesty and truthfulness. He was a prickly young man, who was difficult to argue with and resented things rather readily. However, there was nothing devious about him, no sense of being other than completely straightforward and sensible. I have no reason to think that life in Paris changed him in these respects.

During his studies at the Sorbonne in 1932–34, in the middle of the slump, he inevitably remained for most of the time on the Continent, with long bicycle tours in the summer in Germany and Austria. These journeys brought home to him the menace of National Socialism, and this remained a major preoccupation, as it did with many others in those days. He wrote me many letters (which I preserved) in the course of the journeys, and they give a vivid picture of the changes in progress in Germany.

Life in Paris gave him an appetite for French literature and philosophy, and he developed a lifelong interest in the French dramatists of the seventeenth century. Once he had completed his degree, he decided to follow me to Trinity College, Cambridge, and won a major scholarship at the college in the summer of 1934. So, in his first year in Cambridge (1934–35) , which was also my last, John again shared rooms with me. But we did not see as much of one another as this might be taken to imply. By this time, he had his own circle of friends, as I had mine, and was studying a very different subject (French and German), so that our conversations were rather intermittent.

It had been in his mind to pursue an academic career, and he had hoped that his tutors would find him something appropriate. But, when no offers of academic employment reached him after graduation in 1936, he decided to enter Government service, and sat the examinations for the Foreign Office and for the Home Civil Service. He came top in both examinations, which no one had ever done before.

That was, in some ways, the high point of his career. He spent two years in the Foreign Office, in 1936–38, mainly dealing with Spanish affairs in the middle of the Spanish civil war — an event that dominated undergraduate political interests in the 1930s. I recall one conversation with him, about the time of Munich. I expressed the view that, if we had made a stand against Germany, the Soviet Union would have joined us. He strongly disagreed. "Russia", he said with great emphasis, "would not have fought." I felt bound to accept what I took to be a Foreign Office view.

John did not take to the Foreign Office, nor the Foreign Office to him. After two years there, in 1938, he transferred to the Treasury. After a further two years there, towards the end of 1940, he was posted to the office of Lord Hankey, a former head of the Civil Service and a cabinet minister under Neville Chamberlain, who by now was Chancellor of the Duchy of Lancaster. It was while he was acting as private secretary to Hankey that the incident occurred that caused him to be denounced, 40 years later, as an atom spy who conveyed to the Russians the secret of the atomic bomb.

The possibility of constructing an atom bomb was under examination late in 1940 by the Maud Committee, a group of highly distinguished scientists, of which the secretary was Dennis Rickett (later an important figure in the Treasury). John's name appeared by mistake, along with Rickett's, on the minutes of a meeting he did not attend. To the best of my knowledge, it appears on no other minute of any meeting of the Maud Committee. Indeed, since he was never secretary or even assistant secretary of the committee (as these were Cabinet Office posts), he is most unlikely to have had any involvement with the committee, let alone to have attended a session. His duties were of a different kind, such as obtaining passages for members or advisers on overbooked transatlantic aeroplanes.

That the Russians were made aware of Britain's decision to build an atomic bomb is not in doubt. But there is no hard evidence that the information came from John. I am not alone in thinking that the most likely source was Donald Maclean.

In 1943, John was moved to the Government Code and Cipher School in Bletchley and it was in that year that he undoubtedly passed to the Russians information of the greatest military value. To judge by what he says in his book[1], anything he supplied before the War, or in the early stages of the War, was of limited importance. The work at Bletchley was exhausting and told on John's health. After a year he transferred to Section

[1] "The Enigma Spy", Random House, 1997.

Five of SIS (the Secret Intelligence Service), dealing with counter espionage abroad. He continued to pass information to the Russians, but apparently similar information reached them from other people.

At the end of the War, he remained in touch with the Russians, but my own experience in the Treasury convinces me that he is most unlikely to have supplied valuable information to them: he would not have had access to any in the junior Treasury job to which he had by now returned.

John's book, "The Enigma Spy", which he was writing before his death in October 1995, seems to me to be a truthful account of his contacts with the Russians. However, until 1964, I was completely ignorant of his activities as an agent. It was not until the last days of the Conservative government, in August 1964, that I had any idea that John had been a Soviet agent, and it was not until the end of 1979 that the story appeared in the press. The revelation came to me as perhaps the greatest shock I ever experienced.

The head of the Civil Service, Sir Laurence Helsby, told me at the beginning of August that "the security people wanted to have a word with me." There was a suggestion of urgency since the first available date was chosen for our meeting and a whole morning set aside for the interview. My expectation was that it might have to do with a prospective change of government; and in my reply, I told Helsby that I was perfectly prepared to give up my post as Economic Adviser to the Government if requested, but thought it wrong in principle that I should be asked to do so. Nothing of the kind occurred.

Instead, the security official who was my interrogator began by asking me, as I recorded in my diary at the time, "some general questions about Cambridge in 1932–35 and my attitude to Communism at that time". I told him what I took be the common attitude of Cambridge undergraduates and more particularly of the graduate economists, who were rarely very interested in Communist solutions, but not great admirers, either, of capitalism or of the existing government.

He then told me that MI5 now had information that John was a member of the Communist Party when he was at Cambridge. I said this came to me as a very great surprise. He had never mentioned it to me; nor had anyone else. Yet we shared rooms in Cambridge: was it really possible that I could be as ignorant of John's mind and thoughts? From what I have since learned, the evidence that John was ever a Communist is very flimsy. I have little doubt that, while he associated a good deal with Communists at Cambridge, he was never actually a member of the Party. In his autobiography, John says very emphatically that this was so.

The man from MI5 went on to say that John had been talent-spotted when at Cambridge by the Russian intelligence service while at Cambridge, and recruited to the service. I said at once that this was almost inconceivable. John was ill and must be mentally deranged. He assured me that the information came from John, of his own free will, within the past six months. There was no doubt at all of his involvement with Russian security. I said that if anyone else had told me, I would not have believed it, and found it very hard to reconcile with what I knew of him. I mentioned MacLean, Burgess and Philby, but was assured that they were not related to his case.

I asked my interrogator why John should have continued to act in this way. He said it had gone on until he left the Civil Service in 1952. Once on the hook, it was not easy to get off again. I said that John had no reason to fear exclusion from academic employment if he had quit. But the interrogator assured me that John only got out when he did because he suspected that the security forces were getting hot. Had he never mentioned to me that he had been interviewed by security on more than one occasion? I said that I had assumed that his failure to be promoted, after 16 years in the Civil Service, sufficiently explained why he had left.

I told my interrogator that I was likely to see John in Rome on my way to the annual meeting of the World Bank and IMF in Tokyo. He said that I should not raise the matter, unless John himself did, but he thought this unlikely. In fact, John did not raise it.

Some time after this interview, I wrote to John, indicating what I had been told. I received no reply. I was thus never able to check MI5's statements with him. John gave me no indication in later years of the part that he had played. He had been bound to silence by MI5 in 1964 and stuck to his undertaking — in spite of all that appeared uncontradicted in the press and in books on spying. Fortunately, before he died in September 1995, he wrote his own account of his activities. From it, it is clear that he believed that his outlook when he became a Soviet agent was essentially that of Churchill in 1941, and that if he took issue with the pre-war British government, he was no more at fault than de Gaulle when he took issue with the Vichy government. Since he remained an employee of the British Government, that seems to me to go too far, but in my opinion, it was never in his mind to harm the interests of his country.

John was very much alive to the importance of an understanding with the Soviet Union in face of the growing military power of Germany. Few people today appreciate how grim was the international outlook in the late 1930s, under a government that went to extraordinary lengths and persevered for an extraordinary time to appease a Germany arming for war. A young man alive to the danger felt doomed by the policies of his government. Not only did the Chamberlain Government do nothing to check the growing military power of Germany when it was still possible. It seemed content to let Hitler (if he so chose) attack Russia unimpeded, ignoring the obvious risk that, if Russia were subdued, it would not be long before Britain too was brought under the control of the Nazis. If Britain was to survive, with any semblance of independence, its best hope was to make common cause with Russia, the only power capable of withstanding a German assault. Helping the Soviet Union in those circumstances could be an act of patriotism, as it became in June 1941, when Britain allied itself to Russia after Russia had been attacked by Germany.

John was particularly upset by the accusation that he had been an atom spy — indeed, the first atom spy. He was also indignant to be labelled "The Fifth Man", or as one of the "Ring of Five". That he knew Blunt, Burgess, MacLean and Philby has never been in question. But that he knew that any of them was a Soviet agent until it was publicly disclosed, he strenuously denied in his book. The "Ring of Five" appears to have been a phrase used by the Russians in 1943 to bring under one heading the agents to whom they felt particularly indebted. It does not establish that there was any link between John Cairncross and other agents, any co-operation between them or knowledge of what the others were doing.

That his help to the Russians was very material is now recognised. The intercepts that he passed on from German radio communications, decoded at Bletchley, made a major contribution to the defeat of the German army at the decisive tank battle of Kursk in 1943. The information which he supplied of German plans had not been made available to the Russians by the British, presumably from fear that to do so might have revealed to the Germans that their code had been broken, but John was satisfied that the Russians would be at pains to preserve secrecy, as indeed they were.

In general, I find John's account of his motives and activities entirely convincing. It was not in his nature to invent the kind of details he gave of his dealings with Soviet agents. His book makes it clear that what he did was done deliberately, after satisfying himself that the decisions he took could be justified to himself. He was a truthful person, highly intelligent, but with strong views of his own. What I have said rests on personal impressions and on John's own writing, rather than firm evidence of another kind; but I have to say that nearly everything appearing in the press about him has been equally unsupported with firm evidence. Most of it has come from people who neither knew John nor had direct contact with him. Those who did, such as the writer Graham Greene, supported him to the end.

John may have been a Soviet agent, substantially for the duration and for intelligible reasons. He was also a distinguished man of letters, a scholar and a poet, rather than a man of affairs. For most of his life, after he left the Treasury in 1952, he was able to give himself to what he most excelled in and most enjoyed. In that time, he embarked on a new career, and built up an international reputation as an authority on French literature of the seventeenth century.

He wrote three books on Molière, translated into English verse the plays of Racine and Corneille and the Fables of La Fontaine, and produced poetry of his own. Among his other publications was an original and highly entertaining account of polygamy in the West from the 16th century onwards. What most fascinated him throughout his life was the emergence of modern ways of thinking in 17th century France, although he never produced the development of the perception that he contemplated. It is the work for which he would surely have most wished to be remembered.

# Index